Honoré de Balzac, Katharine Prescott Wormeley

Lost Illusions

The Two Poets, Eve and David

Honoré de Balzac, Katharine Prescott Wormeley

Lost Illusions
The Two Poets, Eve and David

ISBN/EAN: 9783337778446

Printed in Europe, USA, Canada, Australia, Japan

Cover: Foto ©Thomas Meinert / pixelio.de

More available books at **www.hansebooks.com**

HONORÉ DE BALZAC

TRANSLATED BY

KATHARINE PRESCOTT WORMELEY

·LOST ILLUSIONS·

THE TWO POETS
EVE AND DAVID

ROBERTS BROTHERS
3 SOMERSET STREET
ᵢ BOSTON
1893

NOTE.

" ILLUSIONS PERDUES " is in three parts, of which
the first and third (" Les Deux Poètes " and " Ève et
David ") belong consecutively together; while the
second part ("Un Grand Homme de Province à
Paris") is, comparatively, an independent history. For
the convenience and uniformity of this series of translations the first and third parts are here placed together; the second part will follow under the title:
" A Great Man of the Provinces in Paris."

.

CONTENTS.

Part First.

THE TWO POETS.

.

Part Second.

EVE AND DAVID.

LOST ILLUSIONS.

PART FIRST.

THE TWO POETS.

I.

A PRINTING-HOUSE IN THE PROVINCES.

At the period when this history begins, Stanhope's press and cylinders for the distribution of ink were unknown to provincial printing-houses. In spite of the specialty which brought Angoulême into close relations with Parisian typography, that town was still making use of wooden presses, — from which the term, now meaningless, a "groaning press," was derived. The antiquated leathern pads, daubed with ink, with which the pressmen stamped the type, were still in use. The movable frame where they now place the form, filled with letters on which the paper is applied, was then of stone, and justified its technical name of "marble." The ravenous mechanical presses of our day have made us forget so completely this old-time mechanism (to which, in spite of its imperfections, we owe the noble work of Elzevir, of Plantin, Aldini, Didot, and others) that it is necessary to mention these old tools for which

1

their owner, Jérôme-Nicolas Séchard, felt a superstitious affection; they have a part to play in this great little history.

Séchard was formerly a journeyman printer, of the kind which the workmen whose duty it was to collect the letters called, in typographic slang, a "bear." The incessant coming and going and turning, very like that of a bear in his cage, with which the pressmen moved from the ink to the press, and from the press to the ink, was no doubt the origin of the nickname. In return, the bears called the compositors "monkeys," on account of the agility with which those gentry were obliged to catch up the letters from the hundred and fifty little cases which contained them. At the disastrous period of the Revolution, Séchard, then about fifty years old, was lately married. His age and his marriage saved him from the great draft which swept nearly all the workmen of France into the army. The old pressman was left alone in the printing-office, the master of which (otherwise termed the "naïf") had just died, leaving a widow and two children. The establishment seemed threatened with immediate collapse. The solitary bear could not be transformed into a monkey for the reason that, in his capacity as a pressman, he had not known how to read or write. At this juncture a representative of the people, eager to distribute the noble decrees of the Convention, bestowed upon the pressman, without paying any heed to his incapacity, the license of a master-printer, and gave him the work to do.

Having accepted this perilous license, citizen Séchard bought out the widow of his master with the savings of his own wife, paying for the establishment about half its actual value. But that was nothing. He was now constrained to print, without error or delay, all the Republican decrees. At this difficult juncture Jérôme-Nicolas Séchard, luckily for him, met a Marseilles nobleman who was anxious to neither emigrate (and lose his property), nor be noticed (and lose his head), but who was forced to earn his living by some form of toil. Accordingly he, Monsieur le Comte de Maucombe, donned the humble jacket of a foreman of a provincial printing-office. He set up in type and corrected the proofs of the very decrees which condemned to death all citizens who harbored and hid the nobles ; the bear (now become a "naïf") struck them off and posted them ; and the pair, thus employed, remained safe and sound.

In 1795, when the whirlwind of the Terror was over, Nicolas Séchard was obliged to look out for another foreman. An abbé, afterwards bishop under the Restoration, who had refused the oath, took the place of the Comte de Maucombe until Napoleon restored the Catholic worship. The count and the bishop met later on the same bench in the Chamber of peers.

Though Jérôme-Nicolas Séchard knew no more about reading and writing in 1802 than he did in 1793, he had, nevertheless, accumulated enough of this world's goods to hire a foreman. The journeyman once so careless of his future had now become extremely terrifying to his monkeys and his bears. Avarice begins where poverty ends. The day on which the printer perceived that he might possibly make his fortune, self-interest developed in him a material intelligence, keen as to his trade, greedy, suspicious, and penetrating. His practice set theory at defiance. He learned to estimate at a single glance the cost of a page or a sheet, according to the type employed. He proved to ignorant customers that large letters cost more to handle than small ones, — unless it were a question of the small ones, for then they became the more difficult of the two to manage. *Composition* being a part of typography of which he knew nothing, he was so afraid of making mistakes that he never trusted himself on any but sure ground. If his compositors worked by the hour, his eye never left them. If a paper-dealer were in difficulties, he bought up his stock at a low price and stored the paper. By this time he owned the house in which the printing business had been carried on by his predecessors from time immemorial. He had all sorts of good luck. He became a widower, and had but one son ; whom he sent to the town lyceum, less for the sake of benefiting the youth than to get himself a successor. He treated his son sternly, to prolong the period of parental power ; he made him spend his holidays at the cases, telling him to learn how to make his living, and some day reward his poor father, who was using his life's blood to bring him up.

When the abbé left the office Séchard chose a foreman from among the four compositors whom the future bishop assured him were as honest as they were intelligent. In this way he managed to carry on his establishment until his son was old enough to direct it. David Séchard made brilliant progress at the Lyceum of Angoulême. Though old Séchard — as a bear who had made his way in life without knowledge or educa-

tion — despised learning, he sent his son to Paris to
study the best typography ; but he gave him such vehement orders to amass a good round sum in a city which
he called the "workman's paradise" (telling him not to
expect a penny from the parental purse) that he must
have seen a means to his secret ends in this sojourn of
the lad in the "land of knowledge."

While learning the trade David finished his education. The Didot's foreman became a man of science.
Toward the close of the year 1819 he returned from
Paris without having cost his father a single penny.
The old man had recalled him to put the helm of the
business into his hands. The printing-house of Nicolas
Séchard published the only journal of legal advertisements which existed in the department ; it had also the
custom of the prefecture, and that of the bishopric, —
three sources of prosperity which ought to bring fortune
to an active young man.

Just at this very time the Cointet Brothers, paper-
makers, bought up the second printing license in Angoulême, which Séchard had hitherto managed to reduce to inaction, thanks to the various military crises
which, under the Empire, repressed all industrial enterprise. For this reason he had neglected to buy it ;
and this parsimony was one cause of the ultimate
ruin of the old printing-house. When he heard of the
purchase old Séchard complacently reflected that the
struggle with the Cointets would now be carried on by
his son and not by himself. "I should have broken
down," thought he ; "but a young man trained by the
Didots will pull through it." The old man was longing for the time when he could live as he pleased. He

had, it is true, little acquaintance with the upper walks
of typography, but he was thought very able in the art
which workmen have called in jest *soûlographie*, an
art highly esteemed by the marvellous author of "Pan-
tagruel;" the culture of which, persecuted by what are
termed temperance societies, is now, we may almost
say, abandoned. Jérôme-Nicolas Séchard, true to the
destiny which his name bestowed, was gifted with an in-
extinguishable thirst. His wife had managed for a long
time to keep within due limits this passion for grape-juice,
— so natural to a bear that Monsieur de Chateaubriand
observed it among the real bears of America. But
philosophers have recorded that the habits of youth are
wont to return with added strength in old age. Séchard
was an example of this moral law; the older he grew,
the more he loved drink. This passion left upon his
ursine countenance certain marks which gave it origi-
nality; his nose had taken the form and development of
a capital A; his veiny cheeks, like vine-leaves covered
with purple gibbosities and streaked with various colors,
gave to his head the appearance of a monstrous truffle
clasped by the shoots of autumn. Hiding behind thick
eyebrows, which resembled bushes covered with snow, his
small gray eyes, glittering with the avarice which had
killed every other emotion within him, even that of
paternity, kept their intelligence when he himself was
drunk. His bald head, fringed with grizzly hair that
curled at the points, recalled to the imagination the
friars of La Fontaine. He was short and corpulent
like the old-fashioned church lamps which consume
more oil than wick; for excess in anything forces the
body in the direction of its own tendencies; drunken-

ness, like study, makes a fat man fatter and a thin man thinner.

For the last thirty years Jérôme-Nicolas Séchard had worn the famous three-cornered municipal hat, which in some of the provinces may still be seen on the head of the drum-majors of the neighborhood. His waist-coat and trousers were of greenish velveteen, and he wore an old brown coat, blue and white cotton stockings, and shoes with silver buckles. This costume, in which the workman and the tradesman were combined, was so well suited to his habits, it expressed his being so admirably, that he seemed to have been born ready dressed; you could no more imagine him without his clothes than you could see an onion without its layers of skin.

If the blind and besotted greed of the old printer were not already well known, his method of getting rid of his printing business would suffice to show his char-acter. In defiance of the better knowledge which his son was certain to bring back from the great house of the Didots, old Séchard intended to strike the hard bar-gain he had long meditated, — a bargain of which he was to make a good thing and his son a bad one. But to his mind there was no such thing as father or son in business matters. He may at first have considered David in the light of an only child, but he now saw him only as a purchaser, whose natural interests were op-posed to his own. He meant to sell dear ; David, of course, would wish to buy cheap ; his son became, therefore, an enemy to conquer. This transformation of feeling into selfish interest, which is ordinarily slow, tortuous, and hypocritical in educated persons, was

rapid and undisguised in the old bear, who lost no time
in showing how wary grogginess could get the better of
educated typography. When his son arrived he received him with the commercial tenderness which all
clever dealers show to their dupes ; he showed as much
solicitude as a lover for his mistress ; gave him his arm,
told him where to walk out of the mud, had his bed
warmed, a fire lighted, and a supper made ready. The
next day, after trying to intoxicate his son at a copious
dinner, Jérôme Séchard (himself very drunk) said suddenly, "Now we 'll talk business," — a proposal emitted
between two hiccoughs in so singular a manner that
David at once proposed to put off the matter till the
next morning. But the old bear knew too well how to
make use of his drunkenness to give up the battle he
had long been planning. Besides, having carried his
ball and chain for fifty years he was determined not to
bear it an hour longer ; his son should be its victim on
the morrow.

Here we must say a word about the printing-office.
It stood at the corner of the rue de Beaulieu and the
place du Mûrier, in a house it had occupied since
the close of the reign of Louis XIV. All parts of
the building had long been arranged for the different
departments of a printer's trade. The ground-floor
made one enormous room, lighted towards the street
by an old casement, and by a very large window opening on an inner court. The master's private office
could be reached by a small alley-way ; but the various
processes of typography are the objects of such lively
curiosity in the provinces that the clients and customers preferred to enter by a glass door which opened on

the street, although they were obliged to go down some
steps, the floor of the printing-room being below the
level of the roadway. Inquisitive visitors, who were always bewildered by the scene, paid little or no attention to the intricacies of the place. While they gazed
at the vault of paper, stretched on ropes, hanging from
the ceiling, they stumbled against the rows of cases, or
had their hats knocked off by the iron bars which held
up the presses. If they watched the active motions of
a compositor, picking his letters from the hundred and
fifty-two compartments of his case, reading his copy,
rereading his composed line, then slipping in the lead,
they would blunder into reams of damp paper, pressed
by weights, or catch their hips against the angles of a
form, to the great delight of bear and monkeys. No
one had ever reached, without some such accident, the
two large cages at the farther end of this cavern, which
formed two dismal pavilions looking on the courtyard,
in one of which the foreman had his desk, while the
other was the master's office.

The walls of the courtyard were agreeably decorated
with trellises covered with vines, which, in keeping with
the reputation of the owner, had an appetizing local
color. At the farther end, backing on the division wall,
was a shed where the paper was damped and cut.
There, too, was the sink in which they washed the forms,
or, to use the common term, the type-boards ; a decoc-
tion of ink flowed from this sink and mingled with the
household drainage, making the peasants who came to
town on the market days imagine that the devil had
been cleaning himself in that house. This shed was
flanked on one side by the kitchen, on the other by the

wood-pile. The first floor of the house, above which there were only two attic chambers, contained three rooms. The first, lighted towards the street by a small oblong window and on the courtyard by a circular one, served as antechamber and dining-room in one. The cynical simplicity of commercial stinginess was shown by the whitewashed walls; the tiles of the floor were never washed; the furniture consisted of three rickety chairs, a round table, a sideboard placed between two doors, which opened, one into a bedroom, the other into the salon. Doors and windows were dingy with dirt. White or printed paper usually choked up this room, and Nicolas Séchard's bottles and dinner dishes might often be seen on the bales and reams.

The bedroom, the window of which, with its leaded panes, looked on the courtyard, was hung with old tapestry, such as we often see draping the walls of provincial houses on the occasion of the Fête-Dieu. In it was a four-post bedstead with curtains, valance, and coverlet of red serge, two worm-eaten armchairs, two other chairs covered with tapestry, an old desk, and a clock on the chimney-piece. The salon, modernized by the late Madame Séchard, presented a horrible combination of woodwork, painted a vivid blue; panels, papered with Oriental landscapes, and colored with sepia on a white ground; and six chairs, covered with sheep-skin, dyed blue, the backs of which represented lyres. The two windows were clumsily arched and looked out, curtainless, on the place du Mûrier. The chimney-piece had no ornament, neither clock, candlesticks, nor mirror. Madame Séchard died in the midst of her projects of embellishment, and the bear, seeing no use in adornments which brought him nothing, discontinued his wife's plans.

It was to this room that Jérôme-Nicolas Séchard, *pede titubante*, brought his son to show him, on a round table, the inventory of the establishment, made out under his directions by the foreman.

" Read that, my lad," said he, rolling his tipsy eyes from the paper to his son, and from his son to the paper. " You 'll see what a jewel of a business I 'm going to let you have."

David began to read : —

" ' Three wooden presses held together by iron bars, with beds of marble in iron frames — ' "

" That 's an improvement of mine," said old Séchard, interrupting his son.

" ' With all their utensils, — ink-pots, balls, banks, etc., sixteen hundred francs ' — But, father," said David, letting fall the inventory, " your presses are old-fashioned things, not worth three hundred — in fact, they are only fit for firewood."

" Old-fashioned ! " cried his father. " Old-fashioned ! Take the inventory, and let 's go down and look at them. You shall see that your trumpery mechanical inventions can't work like these long-tried tools. When you 've seen them, you won't have the heart to villify honest presses which roll like mail-coaches, and can go a lifetime without repairs. Old-fashioned, indeed ! Yes, old fashions, which will give you porridge ; old fashions, which your father has handled these twenty years, and which served him to make you what you are now."

So saying he shambled down the rickety, trembling

staircase without tripping, rushed at the first press, which had just been craftily oiled and cleaned, and pointed to its strong oaken sides freshly polished by an apprentice.

" Is n't that a love of a press?" he cried.

A marriage invitation happened to be on it. The old bear lowered the frisket on the tympan, and the tympan on the slab, which he rolled beneath the press ; then he pulled the bar, unrolled the rope to draw back the slab, and raised the frisket and the tympan with the agility which a young bear might have given to it. The press thus handled emitted a cry like that of a bird which strikes against a window-pane and flies away. " Where 's there a single English press able to work as fast as that?" he said to his amazed son.

The old fellow hurried to the second press, then to the third, on both of which he performed the same ma-nœuvre with the same agility. The last betrayed to his vinous eye a spot neglected by his apprentice, and the old drunkard with edifying oaths took the tail of his coat and rubbed it clean, as a jockey polishes the hide of a horse he wants to sell.

" With those three presses you can earn nine thou-sand francs a year without a foreman, David. As your future partner, I oppose your replacing them with those cursed cast-iron things which wear out the type. You all cried miracle in Paris over the invention of that damned Englishman, the enemy of France, whose only object was to make the fortune of foundries. Ha! you wanted stanhopes, did you? a fig for your stanhopes, which cost two thousand five hundred francs apiece, nearly twice what those three jewels of mine are worth,

—machines which crack the type in two for want of elasticity. I'm not a learned man like you, but just remember this that I tell you ; the life of stanhopes is the death of type. These three presses will do you good service, the work will be properly done, and what more do you want? Whether you print with iron or wood or with gold or silver, you won't earn a farthing the more by it."

" ' Item,' " continued David : " ' five million pounds of type from the foundry of M. Vaflard —' "

The pupil of the Didots could not repress a smile at the name.

" Laugh ! oh, yes, you may laugh ! After twelve years' use that type is as good as new. M. Vaflard is what I call a good founder ; he 's an honest man, who supplies lasting stuff. To my thinking the best founder is the one to whom you seldom go."

" ' appraised at ten thousand francs ' " said David, reading on. " Ten thousand francs, father ! why, that is forty sous a pound, and Messrs. Didot ask only thirty-six for their pica when new. Your nail-heads are worth nothing more than the weight of the iron, ten sous a pound."

" Do you call such letters as those nail-heads ? why, they were made by Gillé, formerly printer to the Emperor ! type which was worth six francs a pound ; masterpieces of the art, bought five years ago, and still as bright as the day they were cast. See here ! " and old Séchard caught up several scoopsful of " sorts " which had never been used, and showed them to his son.

" I 'm not learned," he said, " I can't read or write, but I know enough to make a guess that the type of the firm of Gillé were the patterns used by your Didots and your Englishmen. Here's a *ronde*," pointing to a case, and taking out an M, — "a *ronde* of pica which has never yet been undone."

David saw that there was no way of discussing the matter with his father. He must either agree to all or refuse all. He was held to a yes or a no. The old bear had put everything into the inventory, even to the ropes in the drying-room. The smallest job-case, wetting-board, water-jug, even the scrubbing-brushes, were reckoned into the account with the minuteness of a miser. The total was thirty thousand francs including the license of the master and the good-will of the business. David asked himself whether or not the matter were feasible.

Seeing that his son was silent after hearing the amount demanded, old Séchard became uneasy; for he much preferred a violent discussion to a silent acceptance. In such dealings as these a discussion is the test of a business man who is able to hold his own. "He who demurs to everything," old Séchard was wont to say, "pays nothing." While watching the mind of his son, he ran over the list of his wretched utensils, and showed David a press for glazing, and another for trimming edges, boasting of their long usage and solidity.

"Old tools are always the best," he said. "In the printing business they ought to bring more than new ones, just as they do in the gold-beater's trade."

Horrible vignettes representing Hymen, or Cupid, or the dead raising the stones of their sepulchres and forming huge V's and M's, and enormous masked frames for

·theatrical posters became, under the vinous eloquence of Jérôme-Nicolas, items of immense value. He told his son that the habits of provincials were so deeply rooted that he might try in vain to give his clients better things. He, Jérôme-Nicolas Séchard, had endeavored to sell better almanacs than the " Double Liégeois," which was printed on the commonest paper! Well, that old Li 'geois was preferred, actually preferred, to his magnificent almanacs! David, he knew, would soon find out the importance of old things, which would always sell for more than new-fangled ones.

" Remember this, my lad, the provinces are the prov· inces, and Paris is Paris. If a man from l'Houmeau were to come to you for his marriage notice, and you printed it without a Cupid and garlands, he would n't think himself married; I tell you, he 'd send it back if you printed him the sort of thing they do at your Didots, who may be an honor to typography, but whose inventions won't be adopted in the provinces for the next hundred years, so there now ! "

Generous souls are defective in business faculty. David had one of those modest, tender natures which dread argument and yield to their opponent the moment he touches their heart. His own noble feelings, and the sway the old drunkard had always held over him, made him still more unfit to hold his own in a money discussion with his father, more especially as he thought him actuated by good intentions : for he honestly attributed the old printer's voracity of self-interest to a genuine love of his tools. However, as Jérôme Séchard had bought the whole establishment originally for ten thousand francs in assignats, and the price he now asked

was exorbitant, David did exclaim with some vehe-
mence, " Father, you will ruin me ! "

" I, who gave you life ! " said the old drunkard, with
a wave of his hand to the drying lines. " Why, David,
you don't consider the value of the business. Do you
know what the Journal brings in for advertisements at
ten sous a line? five hundred francs for the last month !
Open those books, my lad, and see for yourself what
the advertisements and police notes and the custom we
get from the mayor's office and the bishopric bring
in. You 're a soft one who can't see your way to fortune ; you want to cheapen the horse that is going to
take you there."

A deed of partnership was annexed to the inventory.
By it the worthy father leased his house to the buyer
for twelve hundred francs a year (though he had only
paid five thousand for it), reserving to himself the use
of a chamber in the attic. Until the time when David
should have paid the thirty thousand francs in full, the
profits were to be divided; but after the said payment
to his father he was to be sole proprietor of the establishment. David took into consideration the license,
the good-will of the business, and the custom of the
Journal, disregarding the apparatus. He thought he
could clear himself, and so thinking accepted his
father's proposal. The old man, used to the crafty
dealings of the peasantry, and ignorant of the broader
business views of the Parisians, was amazed at such
prompt decision.

" Can my son have made money? " he thought ; " or
has he some scheme for not paying me ? "

With that suspicion in his head he questioned David

.to find out if he had money with him, in order to take
it on account. The father's inquisitiveness roused the
son's distrust. David bottled up his thoughts.

The next day old Séchard made an apprentice move
all the furniture of the house to a room in the attic,
from which he intended to remove it to his country
place on the first opportunity of a wagon returning
empty. He gave up the three rooms on the first floor
(left bare of everything) to his son, and put him in
possession of the printing-office without advancing him
one penny with which to pay the workmen. When
David begged his father as a partner in the concern to
pay his share towards carrying on their mutual enterprise, the old man turned a deaf ear. He was not
obliged, he said, to give money as well as property ;
besides, all he had was invested. Urged by his son, he
declared that when he bought the establishment originally he had not a sou to carry it on ; if he, a poor
workman without friends, had succeeded, surely a pupil
of the Didots could do as well. Besides, David had
earned money through his education which the sweat of
his father's brow had given him, and he ought to use
that money now.

" What have you done with your earnings?" he
asked, returning to the charge. determined to clear up
the problem which his son's silence had left in doubt
the night before.

" I had to support myself, and I had to buy books,"
replied David, indignantly.

" Buy books, indeed ! Ha ! you 'll never do well.
People who buy books are not fit to be printers," cried
the old bear.

2

David endured the worst of all humiliations — that of a father's degradation. He was forced to listen to a flux of reasons, villanous, whining, meanly commercial, and cowardly, with which the old miser supported his refusal. The poor lad smothered his pain, conscious that he was alone, without resource, in presence of a schemer instead of a father, whom he now determined, partly out of philosophical curiosity, to understand thoroughly. He pointed out to the old man that he had never yet asked him to account for his mother's fortune. If that fortune were not to enter as part compensation for the price of the printing-office, it ought at least to be used in carrying on the partnership.

" Your mother's fortune ! " cried old Séchard ; " why, she had nothing but her beauty and her cleverness."

That answer revealed him to his son without disguise. David saw plainly that to obtain his rights he would have to enter upon an interminable, costly, and discreditable lawsuit. His noble heart accepted the burden laid upon him, conscious in advance of the struggle involved in fulfilling the engagements he had made with his father.

" I will work," he thought. " After all, if it is hard for me, it was once hard for him. It will be working for myself, anyway."

" I shall leave you a treasure," remarked the father, uneasy at his son's silence.

David asked what it was.

" Marion," replied the old man.

Marion was a stout peasant-woman, who was quite indispensable to the working of the printing-office. She damped the paper and trimmed it, did the errands and the cooking, washed the linen, unloaded the bales of paper from the wagons, collected the bills, and cleaned the pads. If Marion had known how to read, old Séchard would have made her work as a compositor.

The old man started on foot for his country home. Though pleased with the sale (disguised under the name of partnership), he felt uneasy about the payment. After the agonies of a sale come those of securing payment. All passions are essentially jesuitical. This old man, who considered education useless, endeavored to believe in the influence of education. He relied for the payment of his thirty thousand francs on the ideas of honor which education ought to have developed in his son. Well trained as he was, David would surely sweat blood and water to pay his debts; the knowledge he had acquired would give him resources; he seemed to show fine feelings — yes, he would pay! Many fathers, acting as old Séchard did, would have felt they had done their fatherly duty; and by the time the old man reached his vineyard at Marsac, a little village twelve miles from Angoulême, he was persuaded he had done his. This domain, on which the preceding owner had built a pretty house, had increased in size since the old bear purchased it in 1809.

During the first year of his life in the country old Séchard's face looked anxious among his vine-poles; for he was always in his vineyard, as he had formerly been always in his press-room. The thirty thousand expected francs excited him even more than the September harvest; he dreamed of fingering them. The less the money was really due, the more he longed to get it safely in his strong-box. His uneasiness on the subject often took him to Angoulême; he climbed the steep slopes of the rocky ground on which the town is built, to reach the printing-house, and watch how his son was managing the business. After dining with David, he would make his way back to Marsac, ruminating over his fears.

Avarice, like love, has the gift of second sight for future contingencies; it scents them, it surmises them. The old man fancied he saw in his son disquieting symptoms of lethargy. The name of "Cointet Bros." alarmed him; he foresaw it rising above that of "Séchard and Son." He felt the wind of ill-fortune. And he was right; trouble was, indeed, hovering over the firm of Séchard. But misers have a god of their own; and this god, by a combination of unforeseen circumstances, was destined to slip into the drunkard's pouch the price of his usurious sale.

The reasons why the Séchard printing-house was about to fall were as follows: David was indifferent to the religious reaction which the Restoration produced in the government of the country, and he was also indifferent to liberalism; consequently, he maintained a neutrality most injurious to his interests in all matters political or religious. He entered business at a time when provincial business men were forced to have opinions in order to win customers, and it was necessary to choose between the liberal custom and the royalist custom. In David's case, a love which had entered his heart, his scientific proclivities, and his noble nature kept him from that eagerness after gain which characterizes the true business man, and which might otherwise have led him to study the difference between provincial industries and those of Paris. The clear-cut lines of the departments disappear in the whirl of the great city.

The brothers Cointet had chosen the monarchical side ; they kept all fasts ostentatiously ; lingered in the cathedral ; cultivated the priests ; and brought out new editions of pious books the moment the want of them was felt. Thus they caught the lucrative trade on this line from the first, while David was unjustly accused of liberalism and atheism. " Why employ," they said, " a man whose father was a revolutionist, a drunkard, a Bonapartist, and above all an old miser, who will leave behind him heaps of gold? They were poor and had families to support, while David was a bachelor and certain to be rich." Influenced by such arguments, the prefecture and the bishopric gave their printing to the Cointets. Before long these eager competitors, emboldened by David's indifference, set up an advertising journal of their own. The Séchard profits were reduced to less than one half. Before long the Cointets, who were making money, proposed to buy out the other journal, and thus obtain control of all advertisements and legal notices. When David transmitted this proposal to his father, the old man, already frightened by the success of the Cointets, hurried from Marsac to the printing-office with the haste of a buzzard scenting bodies on a battle-field.

" Let me manage those Cointets. Don't you meddle in this business," he said to his son.

The old man began by asking the Cointets sixty thousand francs to protect his son ; he loved his son

and meant to defend him. The old fellow used his son
as the peasants use their wives ; he declared him to be
willing or unwilling to agree to the proposals which he
wrung, little by little, from the Cointets. Finally, he
led them, not without difficulty, to pay a sum of twenty-
two thousand francs for the old journal, but this was
coupled with the condition that David must engage
never to print any other journal under a penalty of
thirty thousand francs damages. This sale and agreement was the suicide of the Séchard printing-house ;
but the old bear was indifferent to that. After theft
comes murder. He took the sum thus gained in part
payment of his sale to David ; to finger that money he
would have thrown David himself into the bargain, —
all the more because his irksome son had a right to half
this indemnity. To make things right, as he said, the
generous father gave up all claims on the printing-office,
but demanded the rent of the building at the old price
of twelve hundred francs.

The indifference of David Séchard had certain under-
lying causes which will help us to exhibit the nature of
this young man. A few days after his installation at the
printing-office he met a college friend who was then in
the depths of poverty. This was a youth about twenty-
one years of age, named Lucien Chardon, the son of a
former surgeon in the Republican army. Nature had
made a chemist of the father, and fate had settled him
as apothecary at Angoulême. Death overtook him in
the midst of preparations to put to use a lucrative discovery on which he had spent years of scientific research. He wished to cure all kinds of gout. Gout is
a malady of the rich, and the rich will pay dear for

health when they lose it; for which reason the chemist had chosen this problem from among the many his meditations had led him to consider. Forced to choose between science and quackery, the late Chardon had seen plainly that science only would make his fortune. He therefore studied the malady and based his remedy on a certain régime regulated to each patient's temperament. He died in Paris while soliciting the approval of the Academy of Sciences, and the fruit of his toil was lost. He not only left his family in poverty, but he had, unfortunately, brought them up to expect a brilliant future, which ended with his life. The mainspring of his ambition was his passionate love for his wife, a last scion of the noble family of de Rubempré, whom he had, almost miraculously, saved from the scaffold in 1793. Without her consent, he had postponed her execution by declaring her *enceinte.* Having thus as it were created a sort of right to make her his wife, he married her in spite of their mutual poverty. Their children, like all the children of true love, inherited the marvellous beauty of their mother, a gift that is often fatal when poverty accompanies it. The poor widow sold the business, the price of which brought her in three hundred francs a year, a sum insufficient to support herself and her children. But she and her daughter accepted their position without a blush, and did such work as they could find. The mother nursed women in childbirth, and her careful method soon took her into families where she was able to earn a franc a day besides her food. To avoid mortifying her son by letting it be known that his mother was employed in such menial work, she had taken the name of Madame Char-

lotte, and persons who needed her left their orders with
Monsieur Postel, her husband's successor.

Lucien's sister, Eve Chardon, worked for a very
worthy woman, Madame Prieur, a getter-up of fine
linen, where the girl earned fifteen sous a day. She
managed the washerwomen and held a superior position
among them, which raised her a little from the level of
a grisette. The slender profits of their labor, added to
Madame Chardon's little income, amounted to eight
hundred francs a year, on which these three persons
had to feed and lodge and clothe themselves ; and yet
the greater part of this sum was absorbed by Lucien.
Madame Chardon and Eve believed in Lucien as the
wife of Mohammed believed in her husband ; their devotion to his future was boundless. This poor family
lived in the suburb of l'Houmeau, in the house of Monsieur Postel, Lucien occupying a garret room. Stimulated by his father, who had a passion for the natural
sciences, Lucien was one of the most brilliant scholars
in the college at Angoulême, where he happened to
be in the third class during the last year of David
Séchard's course.

When fate again brought these comrades together,
Lucien, weary of the vulgar cup of poverty, was on the
point of taking one of those desperate steps which a
youth of twenty sometimes resolves upon. Forty francs
a month generously offered by David who proposed to
take him as foreman and teach him his duties (though
a foreman was quite unneeded by him) saved Lucien
from despair. The ties of this college friendship thus
renewed were soon drawn closer by the similarity of
their fate and the difference of their natures. Both of

them, trained by vicissitudes, possessed that superior
intelligence which puts a man on the level of all heights,
and yet they were each flung by fate to the lower depths
of society. This injustice in their destiny was a powerful bond. Moreover they had both attained to the
poetic spirit, though by different ascents. Lucien had
been destined by his father to the speculations of natural science, but he himself longed ardently for literary
fame ; whereas David, whose reflective nature predis-
posed him to poesy, inclined by taste to the exact
sciences. This interchange of parts led to a sort of
spiritual brotherhood. Lucien communicated to David
the grand ideas he had derived from his father as to
the application of science to industry, and David taught
Lucien to understand the new ways in which to enter
literature and make both fame and fortune. The friendship of these young men became before long one of
those passions which come to men only as they issue
from adolescence.

Soon after their meeting David saw Eve and loved
her, as melancholy and meditative souls do love a
woman. The *et nunc et semper et in secula seculorum*
of the liturgy is the motto of the sublime but unfamed
poets whose works are glorious epics, born and buried
within two hearts. When this lover had perceived the
secret hopes which mother and sister placed upon the
beautiful brow of their idol, when their blind devotion
became known to him, he took delight in drawing
nearer to his mistress by sharing her hopes and sacrifices. Lucien was to David the chosen brother of his
heart. Like the ultras who desire to be more royalist
than royalty itself, David exaggerated the faith which

the mother and sister felt in Lucien's genius ; he spoilt
him as a mother spoils a child. During one of the conversations, in which, harassed by the want of money,
which tied their hands, they discussed, like all young
men, the chances of making their fortune quickly by
shaking the trees already despoiled of fruit by the first-
comers, Lucien bethought himself of two ideas which
emanated from his father. Monsieur Chardon had on
one occasion spoken of reducing the cost of sugar by
the use of some novel chemical agent, and also of di-
minishing the price of paper by importing certain vegetable products from America analagous to those used
in China, the cost of which would be very small. David,
who knew the importance of the latter question, which
had been much discussed at the Didots, seized upon the
idea, believing he saw a fortune in it. and he henceforth
regarded Lucien as a benefactor for whom he could
never do enough.

It is easy to see how such inner lives and leading
ideas unfitted these young men to manage a printing-
oflice. Far from bringing in from fifteen to twenty
thousand francs, like that of the Cointets, the establishment of Séchard Son yielded a profit of scarcely three
hundred francs a month, out of which the salary of the
foreman, the wages of Marion and the workmen, taxes,
and rent were all to be paid, leaving David less than a
hundred francs a month on which to live. Active and
industrious men would have bought new type, and
changed their wooden presses for iron ones ; but master
and foreman, lost in absorbing mental occupations,
contented themselves with printing the work their few
remaining customers brought to them. The Cointets

had fathomed David's character and habits and no longer attacked him; on the contrary, a wise policy led them to encourage the feeble existence of the establishment and help its honest mediocrity, lest it might fall into the hands of some formidable antagonist; they even sent it some local work.

Thus, without being aware of it, David Séchard only existed, commercially speaking, by the shrewd calculation of his competitors. Delighted with what they considered his idiocy, the Cointets treated him, to all appearance, honestly and loyally; in reality they were acting like the Messageries Royales when they set up a sham rival coach to avoid a real one.

II.

MADAME DE BARGETON.

THE exterior of the Séchard establishment was in
keeping with the crass meanness of its interior, where
the old bear made no repairs. Rain and sun and the
inclemency of all the seasons had furrowed the door
on the alley with uneven cracks till it looked like the
trunk of an old tree. The front of the building, badly
constructed of stone and brick, put together without
symmetry, seemed to bend beneath the weight of a
mouldy roof covered with those hollow tiles which are
used for all the roofs of Southern France. To the
rotten window-casings were fastened the enormous
shutters, held by transverse bars, which the heat of
that climate requires. It would have been hard to find
in all Angoulême as cracked a building; it was held
together solely by cement. Imagine the press-room,
lighted at both ends and dark in the middle, the walls
(covered with posters) blackened at the bottom by the
rubbing of many workmen for the last thirty years; an
apparatus of ropes overhead, piles of paper, the old
presses, heaps of cobblestones to weight the dampened
sheets, lines of cases, and, at the farther end, the cages
or offices in which the master and foreman sat; imagine
all this and you will get an idea of the daily life of the
two friends.

Early in May, 1821, David and Lucien were near the window looking on the courtyard about two in the afternoon, just as their four or five workmen left the pressroom to go to dinner. When the master saw the apprentice close the door which opened on the street he carried Lucien off into the courtyard, as if the very smell of the papers, inkpots, presses, and old wood was intolerable to him. They both sat down under an arbor from which they could see if any one entered the pressroom. The sunlight, which was dancing among the vine-shoots, played on their heads and circled them as it were with a halo. The contrast of the two natures and the two faces was so vigorously brought out that a painter would have yielded to the seduction. David had the frame that Nature gives to those who are destined for great struggles, whether secret or illustrious. His stalwart chest was flanked with strong shoulders in keeping with the amplitude of his whole figure. His face, bronzed in tone, high-colored, fat, borne on a stout neck and topped with a thicket of black hair, seemed at first sight like those of Boileau's friars; but a closer examination would have shown you in the curves of the thick lips, in the dimple of the chin, in the cut of the square nose cleft at the point, but above-all in the eyes, the undying fire of a single love, the sagacity of a thinker, the ardent melan-choly of a soul which could see both extremities of the horizon and penetrate all labyrinths, — a soul that soon palled of ideal enjoyments, bringing the lights of analy-sis to bear upon them. If the flashes of aspiring genius were to be seen in that face, the ashes of a volcano were there also; hope was submerged beneath a deep consciousness of the social nothingness to which a lowly birth and want of means condemn so many superior natures.

Beside the poor printer, whose trade, although so closely allied to intellect, was nauseating to him, beside this Silenus, heavily withdrawn within himself and drinking long draughts of science and poesy in order to forget in such intoxication the miseries of his narrow sphere, Lucien was sitting in the graceful attitude which sculptors bestow upon their Indian Bacchus. His face had the clear-cut lines of antique beauty ; the forehead and ₍nose were Greek, the skin of a dewy whiteness like a woman's ; his eyes were so deep a blue that they seemed black, — eyes full of love, the balls of which were pure and fresh as those of childhood. These beautiful eyes were surmounted by brows that were surely traced by a Chinese pencil and fringed with lashes that were long and dark. On his cheeks lay a silken down which matched in color the fair hair curling naturally. A divine suavity was on that brow of a golden white. Inborn nobility was depicted by a chin that was short and raised, but without assumption. The smile of a saddened angel flickered on his coral lips and showed the contrast of his beautiful teeth. He had the hands of a man of birth, — elegant hands, which men obey and women love to kiss. Lucien was slender and of middle height. On seeing his feet a man might have thought him a girl in disguise, all the more because like many subtle, not to say tricky men, his hips were formed like those of a woman. That indication, which is seldom misleading, was verified in Lucien ; the tendency of whose restless mind often led him, when analyzing the actual condition of society, to the immoral ground of diplomatists who believe that all means, however shameful, are justified by success. One of the trials to which great intellects are subjected is to be forced to know all things, evil as well as good, vice as well as virtue.

These two young men judged society the more loftily because their own position was so low; for those who are neglected and unknown counterbalance their humiliation by the height of their stand-point. But their despair was all the more bitter because they felt themselves going rapidly in the direction of their actual destiny. Lucien had read much and compared much; David had thought much and meditated deeply. Notwithstanding his appearance of robust health, the bent of the printer's nature was melancholy and even morbid; he doubted himself. Whereas Lucien, gifted with an enterprising, restless spirit, had an audacity which was out of keeping with his soft, almost feeble physique and tender feminine graces. Lucien's nature was in the highest degree gascon, — bold, brave, and adventurous; a nature which magnifies good and glosses evil; which recoils from no wrong-doing if there is profit in it, and laughs at vice while making it a stepping-stone. Such ambitious tendencies were at the present time repressed in Lucien by the beautiful illusions of youth, by the ardent impulses which led him to noble means, such as all ambitious men amorous of fame, seek first. He was, as yet, only grappling with his desires, and not with the difficulties of life; with his own forces, not with the baseness of other men — which sets a fatal example to impulsive spirits.

David, keenly fascinated by the brilliancy of Lucien's
mind, admired him, and at the same time corrected some
of the errors into which the *furie française* flung him.
Upright as he was, Séchard's character was timid and
out of keeping with his powerful frame. He was not,
however, devoid of the steady persistence of a Northern
man. If he foresaw all difficulties he at least resolved
on mastering them without giving way; and though in
this respect his virtue had a firmness that was truly
apostolic, he tempered it with the mercy of inexhaustible indulgence. In this friendship, which seemed already old, David was the one who loved with idolatry;
Lucien ruled him like a woman who feels herself beloved. David obeyed with delight. The physical
beauty of his friend carried with it to his mind a superiority which he accepted, recognizing his own per-
sonality to be heavy and common.

"Farming for the patient ox, a life of airy freedom
for the bird," thought he. "I will be the ox, Lucien
shall be the eagle."

For the last three years these friends had mingled
their existence. They read the great works which had
appeared on the literary and scientific horizon since the
Peace, — the works of Schiller, Goethe, Byron, Walter
Scott, Jean-Paul, Berzelius, Davy, Cuvier, etc. They
heated themselves at those great fires, attempting works,
which they pursued, abandoned, and again took up with
equal ardor. They worked continually without fatiguing
the inexhaustible powers of youth. Equally poor, yet
passionately in love with art and science, they forgot
their present misery in laying the foundations for their
future fame.

" Lucien, what do you think I have just received from Paris?" said David, pulling from his pocket a little 18mo volume. " Listen ! "

And David read, as only poets read, the idyl of André Chénier, entitled " Néère ; " next " La Jeune Malade," and then the elegy on suicide, and the last two iambics.

" So that's André Chénier ! " Lucien kept exclaiming. " It is enough to make one despair," he said for the third time, when David, too agitated to read on, let him take the volume. " A poet rediscovered by a poet ! " said Lucien, noticing the signature to the preface — that of Henri de la Touche.

" After producing what that volume contains," said David, " Chénier thought he had written nothing worthy of publication."

Lucien read aloud the epic fragment of the " Aveugle " and several elegies. When he chanced upon the line —

" If *they* have no joy, is there joy upon earth?"

he laid down the book, and they both wept, for each loved to idolatry. The vine-leaves glowed, the fissures of the old stone walls, cracked, battered, and split, took to their eyes the semblance of carvings and mouldings and bas-reliefs of some unknown or fairy architecture. Fancy scattered her roses and her rubies into the dark little court. André Chénier's Camille was to David his adored Eve, and to Lucien a great lady with whom he was in love. Poesy had swept the majestic folds of her starry robe through the empty press-room, whither the monkeys and the bears were about returning. Five

o'clock struck; but neither Lucien nor David was
hungry. The golden dream was their life; the treasures of earth were at their feet. They saw the glittering spot on the horizon to which Hope points, as her
siren voice says to those whose life is troublous, " Fly
thither! you shall escape your misery through that
little space of gold, of silver, or of azure." Just then
a young apprentice, a Paris gamin whom David had
brought to Angoulême, opened the glass door which
led from the press-room to the courtyard, and pointed
out the two friends to a stranger who advanced to meet
them, bowing.

" Monsieur," he said to David, pulling an enormous
manuscript from his pocket, "here is a pamphlet which
I am anxious to have printed; will you please estimate
the cost?"

" Monsieur, we do not print such voluminous manuscripts," replied David, without examining the package.
"You had better go to the Messrs. Cointet."

" But we have a very pretty type which would
just suit it," remarked Lucien, taking the manuscript.
" Will you have the kindness to leave us your work
for an estimate, and return to-morrow?"

" Have I the honor of speaking to Monsieur Lucien
Chardon?"

"Yes, monsieur."

" Then I am fortunate," said the author, " in meeting
a young poet with a noble destiny before him. I am
sent here by Madame de Bargeton."

Lucien colored at the name and stammered a few
words expressive of his gratitude for the interest Madame de Bargeton had shown in him. David noticed

the embarrassment of his friend, and he left him alone with the country-gentleman, whose manuscript was a monograph on the culture of silk-worms, which vanity had prompted the writer to print that it might be read by his colleagues in the Agricultural Society.

"Lucien," said David, when the gentleman had departed, "are you in love with Madame de Bargeton?"

"Deeply."

"But you are more separated from her by the prejudices of social life than if she were at Pekin and you in Greenland."

"The will of lovers can triumph over everything," said Lucien, dropping his eyes.

"You will forget us," said Eve's timid lover.

"On the contrary, I may have sacrificed my mistress to my friendship for you, David," cried Lucien.

"What do you mean?"

"In spite of my love, and all the divers interests which urge me to become of consequence in her house, I have told her that I cannot return there if a man whose talents are superior to mine, whose future ought to be glorious, if David Séchard, my friend and brother, is not received by her. I shall find her answer when I go home. But though she has invited all the aristocrats in town to hear me read my verses to-night, I am resolved never to set foot in Madame de Bargeton's house again if the answer is in the negative."

David pressed his friend's hand violently and wiped his eyes. Six o'clock struck.

"Eve will be uneasy; good-by," said Lucien, hastily.

He rushed off, leaving David in the grasp of one of those emotions which are felt in all their completeness

at his age, and more particularly in the position of
these young swans whose wings were as yet not clipped
by the experiences of their provincial life.

"Heart of gold!" cried David, following Lucien with
his eye as he crossed the press-room.

Lucien made his way down to l'Houmeau by the
beautiful promenade of Beaulieu and the Porte Saint-
Pierre. If he took the longest road you may be quite
sure that Madame de Bargeton's house was on the
way. He felt such pleasure in merely passing her windows, even without her knowing it, that for the last
two months he had daily taken that circuitous route.

When he reached the trees of the Avenue Beaulieu
he stopped and contemplated the distance between Angoulême and l'Houmeau. The manners and customs
of the region had set up moral barriers between the
inhabitants of the two places which were far harder to
cross than the flights of steps which Lucien was about
to descend. The ambitious young fellow, who had
lately succeeded in entering the hotel de Bargeton on
the strength of a poetic fame which he cast like a draw-
bridge between the town and its suburb, was, in truth,
very uneasy about his mistress's decision, — like a courtier who fears disgrace for having attempted to extend
his power.

Cut It is not difficult to explain why the spirit of caste
should have great influence on the feelings which divide
Angoulême from the suburb of l'Houmeau. The business community is rich; the nobility is mostly poor.
One revenges itself upon the other by a contempt which
is equal on both sides. The bourgeoisie of Angoulême
espouse the quarrel. The merchant of the town re-

marks of the shop-keeper of the suburb : "Oh! he is
a l'Houmeau man." The Restoration increased the
moral distance between the suburb and the town by
holding out hopes to the nobility of France which could
be realized only by a general overthrow. The aristocratic society, once more united with the government,
became even more exclusive in Angoulême than in other
parts of France. The dwellers in l'Houmeau were made
to resemble pariahs. Thence those deep and secret hatreds which gave such terrible unanimity to the insurrec-
tion of 1830, and destroyed the elements of a lasting
social order in France. The haughty pride of the court
nobility alienated the loyalty of the provincial nobility,
just as the latter alienated the bourgeoisie by affronting
all its vanities.

That a man from l'Houmeau, the son of an apothecary, should be admitted to Madame de Bargeton's house
constituted a small revolution. Who were the authors of
it? None other than Lamartine and Victor Hugo, Casimir Delavigne and Jouy, Béranger and Chateaubriand,
Villemain and M. Aignan, Soumet and Tissot, Étienne
and Davrigny, Benjamin Constant and Lamennais,
Cousin and Michaud; in short, all the old as well as
the new glories of literature, — liberals and royalists
both. Madame de Bargeton liked art and letters, — an
extravagant taste, a mania much deplored in Angoulême, but one which it is necessary to remember in
sketching the life of a woman born to be distinguished,
yet condemned to obscurity by fatal circumstances ;
a woman whose influence determined the fate of Lucien
Chardon.

Monsieur de Bargeton was the great grandson of an

alderman of Bordeaux, named Mirault, ennobled by
Louis XIII. for his long civic services. Under Louis
XIV. his son, then Mirault of Bargeton, was an officer
of the Household Guard, and made so great a marriage
that, under Louis XV. his son was called Monsieur de
Bargeton. This descendant of the alderman was so bent
on behaving like a perfect gentleman that he wasted the
substance of the family and cut short its career. Two of
his brothers, great-uncles of the present Bargeton, returned to business, and as the estate of Bargeton as well
as the house in Angoulême, called the hôtel de Bargeton,
was entailed, the grandson of Bargeton the spendthrift
inherited them. In 1789 he lost his territorial rights,
retaining only the rental of the property, which amounted
to six thousand francs a year. If his grandfather had
followed the example of his progenitors the present
Bargeton (surnamed " the Mute ") might have made
a great marriage and ended as duke and peer of
France ; as it was, he was extremely flattered to be
able to marry, in 1805, Mademoiselle Marie-Louise-
Anaïs de Nègrepelisse, daughter of a gentleman of
rank long forgotten in his country home, though he
belonged to the younger branch of one of the oldest
families in the south of France. There was a Nègrepelisse among the hostages of Louis XI. ; but the head
of the eldest branch bore the illustrious name of
d'Espard, acquired under Henry IV., through a marriage with the heiress of that family.

Circumstances that were somewhat rare in the depths
of the provinces had inspired Madame de Bargeton with
a taste for music and literature. During the Revolution
a certain Abbé Niollant, the best pupil of the Abbé

Roze, hid himself away in the neighboring little castle
of Escarbas, belonging to her father. He repaid the
hospitality shown to him by the old gentleman by edu-
cating his daughter Anaïs (abbreviated to Naïs) who,
but for this accident, would have been left to herself, or
worse still, to some ignorant chamber-maid. Not only
was the abbé a musician, but he possessed a wide knowledge of literature and also knew Italian and German.
He taught those languages and counterpoint to Mademoi-,
selle de Nègrepelisse ; explained the great literary works
of France, Italy, and Germany, and practised with her the
music of the chief composers. Besides this, he taught
her Greek and Latin, as a resource against the weary
inoccupation of solitude to which political events condemned him, and he gave her a fair inkling of natural
science. A mother's presence was not there to modify
the masculine tendencies of such an education on a
young girl who was already too inclined to independence
by the freedom of her country life. The Abbé Niollant,
with a poetic soul full of enthusiasm, was remarkable
for the sort of mind peculiar to artists, which, while
possessing many other precious qualities, rises above
the bourgeois and philistine ideas by the breadth of its
perceptions and its freedom of judgment. Though the
world may pardon the temerity of such minds in virtue
of their original profundity, it is often harmful in private life by the unconventionalities of thought and conduct which it inspires. The abbé was brimful of
ardor ; his ideas were therefore contagious to a girl in
whom the natural enthusiasm of her youth and sex was
greatly increased by the solitude of her country life.
Monsieur Niollant inoculated his pupil with his own

boldness of discussion and facility of judgment, without reflecting that those qualities so necessary to a man become defects in a woman whose destiny is that of a mother to her family. Though the abbé was constantly recommending his pupil to be all the more modest and and graceful because her knowledge was extensive, Mademoiselle de Nègrepelisse acquired a very good opinion of herself, and a very robust contempt for humanity. Seeing no one about her but inferiors and persons who hastened to obey her will, she assumed the haughtiness of a great lady without the soothing craft of a great lady's politeness. Flattered in every fibre of her vanity by a poor abbé, who admired himself in her as an author is proud of his work, she was unfortunate enough to meet with no point of comparison by which to judge herself. The lack of companionship is one of the greatest drawbacks to country life. For want of practising the little sacrifices of dress and behavior due to others, we lose the habit of constraining ourselves in their service. Habits and thoughts become vitiated. The boldness of the young girl's thoughts gradually passed into her manners and into her eyes; she acquired the cavalier air which seems at first sight original, but which really belongs only to women of loose lives. Thus her education, the sharp points of which might have been rubbed off in higher social regions, was likely to make her simply ridiculous in Angoulême whenever her admirers should cease to deify peculiarities which were charming and graceful only so long as her youth lasted.

As for Monsieur de Nègrepelisse, he would have given away all his daughter's books to save the life of

a sick cow ; he was so niggardly that under no circumstances would he have allowed her two farthings above
her actual rights, not even for the purchase of some
trifle for her education. The abbé died in 1802, three
years before the marriage of his dear child, — a
marriage he would doubtless have opposed. The old
gentleman felt himself hampered by his daughter after
the abbé's death. He was too feeble for the struggle
he knew must break forth between his avarice and her
independent will. Like other young women who have
turned out of the beaten track on which women are
expected to walk, Naïs had judged of marriage and felt
little desire for it. It was repugnant to her to submit
her mind and her person to the men of small worth and
no personal dignity with whom she was acquainted.
She wished to rule, and marriage would force her to
obey. Between obeying the coarse caprices of minds
which had no understanding of her tastes, and flight
with a lover who pleased her, she would not have hesitated. Monsieur de Nègrepelisse was enough of a
gentleman to dread a mésalliance. Like many other
fathers, he resolved to marry his daughter for his own
comfort. What he wished to find was a man of rank
without much sense ; one who would not haggle over
the guardianship account of his daughter's fortune from
her mother ; a man sufficiently wanting in mind and
will to enable Naïs to rule him as she pleased, yet disinterested enough to marry her without a dowry. But
how find such a man, who would please both father and
daughter? a son-in-law with those qualities would be a
phœnix. With this idea in his mind, the old gentleman
studied all the marriageable men in the province, and

Monsieur de Bargeton seemed to him the only one who answered his requirements.

Monsieur de Bargeton, a man in the forties, much dilapidated by the amorous dissipations of his youth, was held to be remarkably inferior in mind ; but he had enough sense to manage his property and sufficiently good manners to maintain his position in the society of Angoulême without committing either follies or solecisms. Monsieur de Nègrepelisse bluntly explained to his daughter the negative value of the model husband he proposed to her, and made her see the manner in which he might be made to conduce to her individual happiness. He reminded her that she would marry arms that were two centuries old ; — for the Bargetons bear : quarterly, or, three deer's-heads erased gules ; per chevron gules, three bull's-heads caboched sable ; third and second party per fesse of six pieces, azure and argent, the azure charged with six cockles or. Introduced to the world by some woman of distinction, she might, he told her, manage her fortune as she pleased, and obtain a social rank in Paris through the intimacies which her mind and her beauty would be certain to obtain for her. Naïs was taken by this perspective of future liberty. Monsieur de Bargeton felt he was making a brilliant marriage, believing that his father-in-law would soon depart this life and leave him the estate, though the old gentleman was unwilling to charge it with a dowry ; the real fact being, however, that at that moment, Monsieur de Nègrepelisse was more likely to write the epitaph of his son-in-law.

At the time of which we speak Madame de Bargeton was about thirty-six, and her husband fifty-eight. This disparity was the more unpleasant because Monsieur de Bargeton seemed at least seventy, whereas his wife could very well pass as a girl, dress in pink, and wear her hair down her back. Though their income was not much more than twelve thousand francs a year, it was classed among the six largest fortunes in Angoulême, — those of the merchants and municipal officers excepted. The necessity of conciliating their father, on whose inheritance Madame de Bargeton's future career in Paris depended, obliged them to live for the present in Angoulême, where the brilliant qualities of mind and the unused riches of Naïs's heart were wasting fruitlessly, and even, as time went on, drifting into absurdity. The truth is, our absurdities are often, in a great measure, caused by some noble feeling or virtue or faculty carried to extremes. For instance, pride, if it is not modified by the usages of good society, becomes stiff and starched, and is occupied with little things instead of ennobling itself by great ones. Enthusiasm, that virtue within a virtue, which inspires secret devotions and dazzling or poetic deeds, turns to exaggeration when expended on the nothings of provincial life. Far from the centre where great minds light the horizon, where the atmosphere is charged with thought, where all things renew their life and make progress, education grows stale and taste corrupt, like stagnant water. For want of exercise the passions are belittled by the very fact of their magnifying petty things. In that lies the secret of the avarice and the slander which poison provincial life. It is not long before the most distinguished minds are led to share the narrow ideas and imitate the mean social customs of country places.

Men born to greatness, and women who might be
charming if trained to a better life by superior minds,
perish in this way. Madame de Bargeton seized the
lyre on all occasions, without knowing how to distinguish between the poetry which ought to be sacred to
her own heart and that which could be offered publicly.
There are various sensations, incomprehensible to
many, which should be kept to ourselves. A sunset is
certainly a grand poem, but a woman who depicts it in
grand words to material minds is absurd. There are
delights which can be really felt only when two souls
meet, poet to poet, heart to heart. She made the mistake of using long sentences larded with magniloquent
words, and was prodigal of superlatives, which over-
weighted her conversation so that trifling things assumed gigantic proportions. At about this period of
her life she began to analyze, synthesize, individualize,
poetize, dramatize, angelicize, and tragicize, — for we
must for a moment violate language to express the
extravagance of which some women are capable. Her
mind was fully as excitable as her language. Dithy-
rambics were in her heart as well as on her lips. She
palpitated, turned faint, or grew wildly enthusiastic
over all events, — over the devotion of a sister of
charity, or the execution of the Faucher brothers :
over the "Ipsiboé" of Monsieur d'Arlincourt, or Lewis's
"Anaconda ;" over the escape of La Valette, as ardently
as over the bravery of a friend who had put burglars
to flight by pretending to be a man. For Madame de
Bargeton all things were sublime, extraordinary, amaz-
ing, divine, marvellous. She was animated, angered,
or depressed; taking a fresh spring, she would fall

back upon herself, gazing at earth and heaven with eyes full of tears. She spent her life in perpetual admiration, and wasted her strength in curious dislikes. She envied Lady Hester Stanhope, the blue-stocking of the desert. She longed to be a sister of Sainte-Camille, and die of yellow fever in Barcelona, while nursing the sick; that indeed was a noble, a grand fate! In short, she thirsted for all that was not the clear water of life flowing in hidden ways. She adored Lord Byron, Jean-Jacques Rousseau, and other poetic and dramatic beings. She had tears for all misfortunes, and trumpets for all victories. She sympathized with Napoleon vanquished, and she sympathized with Mehemet Ali massacring the tyrants of Egypt. She encircled genius with a halo and believed that those who were gifted with it lived on light and perfume. Some persons thought her harmlessly crazy, but a true observer would have seen in these things the fragments of a great emotion destroyed as soon as it existed, the ruins of a celestial Jerusalem, — in short, a love without a lover. This was, indeed, the truth.

The first eighteen years of Madame de Bargeton's married life can be told in few words. For a time she lived on her own nature and her distant hopes. Then, after recognizing that the Parisian life for which she longed was beyond her limited means, she took to examining the persons among whom she had to live, and she trembled at her solitude. There was no man within the circle of her knowledge who could inspire her with one of those devotions to which women are prone when driven to despair by a life without object, events, or interest. She could look to nothing, not

even to chance, — for there are lives to which chance
never comes. At the time when the Empire shone in all
its glory after Napoleon's passage into Spain, whither
the flower of his army went, Madame de Bargeton's
hopes revived. Natural curiosity led her to regard
with interest the heroes who were conquering Europe
on the inspiration of a few imperial words added to
the orders of the day; renewing, to her mind, the fabu-
lous exploits of chivalry. All the towns on the route
of the army, niggardly or refractory as they might be,
were compelled to entertain the Imperial Guard; the
mayor and prefects were required to meet them at the
gates with an harangue on their lips as if for royalty.
Madame de Bargeton was present at a fête given by a
passing regiment to the town of Angoulême and there
she saw and admired a young nobleman, a sub-lieu-
tenant to whom the bâton of a marshal of France was
a hope in perspective. This restrained passion, noble
and grand in itself and contrasting strongly with the
facile passions of the time, so quickly bound and un-
bound, was consecrated by death. The only portrait
which existed of Madame de Bargeton was shivered by
a shot through the heart of the Marquis de Cante-Croix
at Wagram. She long mourned the fine young man,
who, eager for fame and love, had become a colonel,
and regarded a letter from Naïs as far above all imperial distinctions.

Grief henceforth cast its veil of sadness on her
face, which was never lifted until the terrible day when
a woman begins to perceive that her best years are
gone without enjoyment, that her roses are faded, while
the yearning for love revives in a passionate desire to

prolong the last memories of youth. All her superior qualities made, as it were, wounds in her heart when the cold chill of this condition seized her. Like the ermine, she would have died of·grief had she stained herself by contact with men whose only thought was their whist and a good dinner. Her pride preserved her from such miserable provincial loves. Between the nonentity of the men who surrounded her and absolute nothingness of life, so superior a woman would naturally choose the latter. Marriage and society were therefore to her like a nunnery. She lived in their midst by poetry, as a Carmelite lives by religion. The works of distinguished foreigners, till then untranslated and unknown, which were published from 1815 to 1821, the great essays of Monsieur de Bonald and Monsieur de Maistre, those eagles of thought, and the lighter works of French literature which were beginning to put forth vigorously, occupied and embellished her solitude, but they did not give pliancy to either her mind or her person. She remained erect as a tree which has been struck by lightning and survived the shock. Her dignity grew rigid, and it made her affected and over-critical.

Such was Madame de Bargeton's past life, — a chilling history, which it is necessary to know in order to understand her relations with Lucien, who was rather singularly introduced into her house. During the preceding winter a gentleman had come to live in Angoulême as revenue director, whose adventurous career brought the interest of curiosity into the monotonous life of Madame de Bargeton.

Monsieur du Châtelet, born plain Sixte Châtelet, though after 1806 he had the sense to give himself a title, was one of those agreeable men who, under Napoleon, contrived to escape conscriptions by keeping in the light of the imperial sun. He began his career as secretary to the caprices of an imperial princess. Monsieur du Châtelet possessed all the incapacities required for that position. Well-made, handsome, a good dancer, clever billiard-player, an adept at all bodily exercises, a rather poor amateur actor, a singer of ballads, applauder of other people's witticisms, ready for anything, wily and envious, he knew and was ignorant of most things. Ignorant of music, he accompanied on the piano, after a fashion, any woman who was pressed to sing impromptu a song practised for a month. Incapable of a feeling for poetry, he would boldly ask permission to retire for ten minutes while he composed a couplet or a quatrain, flat as a pancake, in which rhyme was made to stand for ideas. Monsieur du Châtelet was further gifted with a talent for filling up in worsted work the flowers which his princess had begun ; he held her skeins of silk with infinite grace, while she wound them, and told her gossip of which the smuttiness could be seen through rents in the veiling. Ignorant of art, he could copy a landscape, sketch a profile or a costume, and even color it. In short he had all those little talents which proved such vehicles to fortune in the days of the Empire, when women had more influence than we admit in public affairs. He claimed to be clever in diplomacy, the science of those who have no other, and whose depth seems the greater because they are empty, — a science extremely convenient because, while professing to be discreet, it allows an ignorant man to say nothing, to confine himself to mysterious becks and nods ; in fact the ablest man in the science of diplomacy is he who swims with his head well up above the current of events which he thus appears to lead, — a question of specific levity. Here, as in the arts, we find a thousand commonplace talents for one man of genius.

Notwithstanding his regular and his irregular service to the imperial princess, the influence of his protectress was insufficient to place him in the Council of State. But he was made a baron and sent to Cassel as envoy extraordinary, where the effect he produced was truly extraordinary. At the moment of the fall of the Empire Baron du Châtelet was expecting the appointment of minister to Westphalia, Jerome's court. Losing what he called his family post, despair seized upon him. He made a journey to Egypt with General Armand de Montriveau. There he became separated from his companion by singular events, and wandered for two years from desert to desert and tribe to tribe, a captive among the Arabs, who sold and resold him to one another. Fate at last brought him to the coast about the time that Montriveau was at Tangier, and he was lucky enough to get on board an English brig, and so return to Paris, one year before the general. These misfortunes and a few services rendered in earlier days to persons now in power, brought him to the notice of Monsieur de Barante, who gave him his present post in Angoulême. The position he had held towards the imperial princess, his reputation for gallantry, the singular adventures of his journey, and the tale of his sufferings, excited the curiosity of the women of Angoulême. After studying the manners and customs of

4

that provincial high life, Monsieur le Baron Sixte du Châtelet conducted himself accordingly. He pretended ill-health, and played the part of a blasé man of the world.

He was fond of seizing his head as if his sufferings gave him no respite, a little performance which reminded others of his travels and made him interesting. He visited among the chief authorities of the place, the general, the prefect, the receiver-general, and the bishop; but he was everywhere cold, polite, and slightly disdainful, as a man out of place and awaiting the time when the government should bestow its favors. He allowed the society of Angoulême to guess at his talents, which gained rather than lost by this reticence; then, after making himself an object of interest without wearying or satisfying curiosity, and having himself recognized the commonplaceness of the men, and knowingly examined the beauty of the women for several Sundays in the cathedral, he came to the conclusion that Madame de Bargeton was the person with whom an intimacy would be most profitable to him. The old beau (for he was forty-five years old) saw in this woman a youth that might be revived, treasures to put to use; possibly the chance of a rich widowhood, which would enable him to marry into a family connected with the Marquis d'Espard, whose influence would open to him a political career in Paris. In spite of the gloom and solitude of this fine tree he resolved to take hold of it, prune it, cultivate it, and obtain fine fruits. The aristocracy of Angoulême cried out at first against the introduction of a Giaour into the Kasba, for Madame de Bargeton's salon was a centre of society kept pure of alloy. The bishop alone went there habitually; the prefect was received only two or three times a year; the receiver-general had never been invited there at all. Madame de Bargeton went to his public parties and concerts but never dined at his house. Not to receive an official of his rank, and then to admit a mere director of taxes was an upsetting of the hierarchy which seemed incomprehensible to the affronted authorities.

Those who can bring their mind to imagine such pettiness, which may be found, by the bye, in all social spheres, will understand how imposing the hôtel de Bargeton was to the bourgeoisie of Angoulême. As for the dwellers in the suburb of l'Houmeau, the grandeurs of this little Louvre, the fame of this Hôtel de Rambouillet shone like a distant galaxy. Those who there assembled were, in truth, a pitiable company of inferior minds, the poorest intellects to be found in a circumference of sixty miles. Politics were discussed with wordy and virulent commonplaces, the "Quotidienne" was thought lukewarm. Louis XVIII. a Jacobin. As for the women, the greater part of them were awkward, silly, and ill-dressed; all had some defect which detracted from their merit; nothing was complete or perfect about them; neither their dress nor their conversation, their flesh nor their spirit. Châtelet would never have endured this society were it not for his designs on the mistress of the house. And yet the manners and tone of caste, the atmosphere of breeding, the haughtiness of a small nobility, and a thorough practice of the rules of politeness covered this void as with a veil. The sentiment of nobility was also more genuine than it is in the sphere of Parisian grandeur:

and at times a true attachment to the Bourbons *quand
même* showed itself. This society can be compared (if
we may use the simile) to a silver service of antique
form, tarnished, but solid and weighty. The immova-
bleness of its political opinions had a character of
fidelity. The distance maintained between itself and
the bourgeoisie, the difficulty of entering its borders,
gave it an appearance of elevation and a certain conventional value.

Du Châtelet began his siege of Madame de Bargeton
by lending her all the new books, and reading to her
the poems of the day. Together they went into ecsta-
cies over the new school of poets, she in good faith, he
with inward weariness, though patiently enduring the
romanticists, who, as a man of the Empire, he was
wholly unable to comprehend. Madame de Bargeton,
enthusiastic over the renaissance which the Restoration
had brought about, loved Monsieur de Chateaubriand
because he had called Victor Hugo " a sublime youth."
Saddened at the thought that she should only know
genius from afar, she longed for Paris, the centre of
great minds. Du Châtelet, initiated into these feelings,
thought he did a marvellous stroke of policy by telling
her that another " sublime youth " was buried in Angoulême, — a young poet who, without knowing it, sur-
passed in brilliancy the Parisian galaxy. This future
great man was born and lived in the suburb of l'Houmeau ! He, du Châtelet, had been shown a few of his
poems by the head of the college. Poor and modest,
the lad was another Chatterton, but without political
baseness, without the ferocious hatred against social
grandeur which drove the Englishman into writing pam-

phlets to insult his benefactors. Nothing could describe
Madame de Bargeton's joy at the news. She must see
this poet, this angel; she went distracted about him,
and talked for hours enthusiastically. Two days later
du Châtelet arranged, through the principal of the college, to meet Lucien the following evening and present
him in Madame de Bargeton's salon.

None but the poor provincial helots to whom social
distances are so vast, and to whom the iron railings
through which the different classes anathematize and
call each other Raca seem so forbidding, can fully understand the upheaval of brain and soul in Lucien
Chardon when his late imposing head-master informed
him that the doors of the hôtel de Bargeton were about
to open to him! his fame had swung their hinges! he
was welcomed to a great house, the ancient gables of
which attracted his gaze when he walked with David in
the evenings towards Beaulieu, each telling the other
that their names would never reach the ears that were
deaf to talent when it came from below. He told no
one but his sister of this great event. In her capacity
as good housewife, a divine diviner, Eve produced several louis from a secret hoard to furnish Lucien with
the handsomest shoes made by the best bootmaker in
Angoulême, and a dress suit from a celebrated tailor.
She trimmed his best shirt with a ruffle which she
washed and pleated herself. What joy to see him thus
attired! how proud she was of him! what advice she
gave him! She foresaw little ignorant absurdities;
for instance, Lucien had a habit of leaning on his
elbows whenever he sat down; he would even draw a
table to his side for that purpose. Eve forbade him to

give way to such actions in the sacred aristocratic pre-
cincts he was about to enter. She accompanied him to
the Porte de Saint-Pierre almost in front of the cathedral, and thence she watched him following the rue de
Beaulieu to the avenue on which Monsieur du Châtelet
was to meet him. The poor girl was as much overcome with emotion as if some great event were taking
place. Lucien in Madame de Bargeton's salon seemed
to Eve in the dawn of his future fame. The pure
young creature was unaware that when ambition begins
single-hearted feelings end.

When he reached the house in the rue de Minage,
Lucien found nothing astonishing in its exterior. The
palace so magnified by his expectations was only a
house built of a freestone peculiar to the region and
gilded by time. The front on the street was gloomy,
that on the courtyard was very simple, — cold and neat
like all provincial houses, plain, almost monastic, archi-
tecturally, and well preserved. Lucien passed up an
old-fashioned staircase, with chestnut balusters, the
steps of which ceased to be of stone after the first
flight. Crossing a mean little antechamber and a large,
ill-lighted salon, he found the sovereign of Angoulême
in a little room panelled with carved woodwork, in the
style of the last century, and painted gray. The designs
above the doorways were in imitation of cameo. An
old red damask, scantily trimmed, filled the spaces
between the panels. Furniture of antique shape was
rather pitifully hidden by loose covers of a red-and-
white check. The poet beheld Madame de Bargeton
seated on a sort of sofa covered with a thin mattress,
before a round table with a green cloth, on which

stood a candelabrum of ancient shape, holding two
candles, that were covered with a shade. The sovereign did not rise, but twisted herself gracefully on her
seat, smiling at the poet, who was much moved by the
serpentine motion, which he thought extremely distinguished. Lucien's beauty, the timidity of his manner,
his voice, everything about him, instantly attracted
Madame de Bargeton. The poet proved to be poetic.
The young man, on his part, ventured to examine, with
discreet glances, the woman who seemed to him to
justify her renown; she suited all his ideas of what a
great lady might be.

Madame de Bargeton wore, as the fashion then was,
a head-dress of black velvet which suggested recollections of the middle-ages, and to Lucien's eyes gave a
certain stateliness to her head. From beneath it fell a
wealth of hair of a reddish auburn, gold in the sunshine, ruddy in the curve of its waves. Her skin was
of that dazzling purity which consoles a woman under
the mistaken prejudice against red hair. Her gray
eyes sparkled; her brow, which was beginning to show
wrinkles, surmounted them finely with its white mass
boldly modelled; the eyes themselves were circled by a
pearly margin, in which, on either side of the nose, two
blue veins brought out vividly the whiteness of this
delicate complexion. The nose had a Bourbon curve
which increased the fire of the rather long face. The
hair did not altogether hide the neck. Her gown,
negligently crossed, revealed a white throat and allowed
the eye to trace a well-formed bust that was rightly
placed. With her tapered and delicately kept fingers
(which were a little too thin), Madame de Bargeton

made a friendly sign to the young poet, bidding him
take a chair that was placed beside her. Monsieur du
Châtelet took another. Lucien then noticed that no
one else was present. Madame de Bargeton's conversation completely intoxicated him. The three hours
passed beside her were to him one of those dreams
which we would fain make eternal. He thought her
slender rather than thin, loving without passion, delicate in spite of her vigor. Her defects, which her
manners exaggerated, pleased him ; for young men
begin by liking exaggeration, — the falsehood of fine
souls. He did not notice that the slightly blotched
cheeks, to which ennui and some physical sufferings
had given a brick-dust tone, were withering. His
imagination seized upon those eyes of fire, those graceful curls rippling with light, that dazzling whiteness, —
luminous spots to which he flew like a moth to candles.
Besides, her soul spoke to his too urgently to let him
judge her as a woman. The warmth of her feminine
enthusiasm, the ardor of the speeches (somewhat hack-
neyed) which she was in the habit of uttering (though
they were new to Lucien), fascinated him all the more
because he wished to be charmed. He had brought no
poetry with him, but there was no mention of it ; he
had purposely forgotten his verses that he might be
asked to bring them later ; Madame de Bargeton, on
her part, avoided asking for them, that she might invite
him to read them on another occasion. Surely this
was a first understanding between the two ! Monsieur
du Châtelet was not over-pleased by this reception. He
saw too late a possible rival in the handsome young
man, whom he accompanied part of the way home for

the purpose of subjecting him to his diplomacy. Lucien was not a little astonished to hear this Mentor lay claim to the credit of presenting him, and offer him advice on the strength of this service.

"It was to be hoped Monsieur Chardon would be better treated than himself," said Monsieur du Châtelet. "The king's court was less pretentious than this society of blockheads. There was nothing but scorn and mortification to be got in it. The revolution of 1789 would have to be done over again if such persons were ever to be reformed. As for himself, if he continued to go into society at all, it was only for the sake of Madame de Bargeton, the one woman in Angoulême who had any real merit; he had paid court to her out of mere idleness, but now he was desperately in love. She would soon be his; she loved him. The conquest of this haughty lady was the revenge he meant to take on the fools of her wretched society."

Châtelet expressed himself in terms which implied that he would kill a rival if he ever had one. The old imperial flutterer fell with his whole weight upon the luckless poet, trying to crush him with his, du Châtelet's, importance, and so frighten him away. He did succeed in impressing the imagination of the poet, but he could not check the lover.

Since that evening, and in spite of du Châtelet's threats and glances, Lucien had frequently visited Madame de Bargeton; at first with the modesty of a man from the suburbs; but after he became accustomed to what at first he had thought a great favor, he went oftener and oftener. The son of an apothecary was held by the persons of her society to be of no ac-

count. If some of them at the beginning of the intimacy chanced to meet him when they visited Naïs, they
treated him with the overwhelming politeness which persons of quality employ toward their inferiors. Lucien
at first thought them gracious and charming, but later
he perceived the sentiment that lay at the bottom of
their specious courtesy. He detected a tone of superiority, which stirred his bile and confirmed him in the
republican hatred with which many future patricians
begin their intercourse with the upper classes. But by
this time he was willing to endure that, and all other
sufferings, for Naïs, as he heard her called; for
among the intimates of this clan, as among the Spanish grandees and the cream of Viennese society, men
and women are known by their Christian names, — a de-
vice invented to procure exclusiveness, and the practice of which gave distinction to the inner circles of
the Angoulême aristocracy.

Naïs was loved as all young men love the first woman
who flatters them ; and she did this by prophesying a
great future and vast fame for his talents. Madame de
Bargeton put all her natural cleverness to use in giving
her young poet a foothold in her house. Not only did
she place him intellectually very high, but she represented him as a youth without fortune whose future she
desired to secure. She made him her reader and secretary, but she loved him more than she had thought herself
capable of loving after the great catastrophe of her life.
She arraigned herself mentally ; declaring in her own
mind that it was folly to love a boy of twenty, whose
social position was far beneath her. Their familiar relations were often capriciously hampered by the haughti-

ness which her scruples prompted. She was proud or protecting, tender or distant, as the feeling took her. Lucien, who was intimidated by her rank, went through all the terrors, hopes, and despairs which torture a first love, and give it such power over the heart by alternate blows of pain and pleasure. For two months he regarded her as a benefactress who took a motherly interest in his concerns. Then confidences began. Madame de Bargeton called her poet " dear Lucien ; " then "dear" alone. The poet, thus emboldened, called the great lady " Naïs." Hearing this, she was angry, with the anger so bewitching to youth ; she reproached him for employing a name which all the world used, and she offered her handsome genius the name by which no one called her ; to him she would be Louise, — Louise de Négrepelisse. Lucien was in the third heaven.

One evening he entered the room unexpectedly while Louise was gazing at a portrait, which she hastily put away. He asked to see it. To calm this first attack of jealousy, Louise showed him the portrait of young Cante-Croix, and told him, not without tears, the mournful history of her love, so pure and so cruelly extinguished. Was she considering an infidelity to her departed lover, or merely proposing to give Lucien a rival in his picture ? Lucien was too young to analyze his mistress ; he fell naïvely into despair at this opening of a campaign in which women defend their scruples at the breach. Their discussions on duty, on conventions, on religion, are redoubts which they like their lovers to take by assault. But the innocent Lucien did not need such coquetries ; he would have fought the battle of love quite naturally.

"I will not die, *I* will live for you," said Lucien, audaciously, resolving one evening to make an end of Monsieur de Cante-Croix, and casting a look at Louise which proved to her that his passion had reached its height. Frightened at the progress the new love had made, not only in her poet but in herself, she asked him for the verses he had promised for the first page of her album, and tried to make a quarrel of his delay in writing them, declaring that it proved she was incapable of inspiring him.

This doubt, prompted by the coquetry of a woman who took pleasure in thus playing with fire, brought tears to Lucien's eyes; she calmed him and kissed his forehead for the first time. Lucien was a great man, whom it was her mission to train ; she would teach him German and Italian, and improve his manners. All these, of course, were pretexts to keep him constantly by her side, under the noses of her wearisome admirers. What an interest in her dull life ! She took up her music to reveal a world of harmony to her poet, whom she ravished with Beethoven. Happy in his delight she said one day, hypocritically, seeing him as it were transported, " Is not this happiness enough for us ? " To which the poor poet had the stupidity to answer, " Yes."

At last matters reached a point when Louise invited Lucien to dine with her alone with Monsieur de Barge-ton. In spite of this latter precaution the whole town heard of the event, and thought it so extraordinary that every one asked everybody else if it could be true. The uproar was immense. Some thought society was on the eve of disruption. Others cried out, " See the

fruit of radical opinions!" At this crisis du Châtelet
learned that Madame Charlotte, the monthly nurse,
was no other than Madame Chardon, mother of the
suburban Chateaubriand. Thus worded, the information passed for wit. Madame de Chandour rushed in
haste to Madame de Bargeton.

"Do you know, my dear Naïs, what all Angoulême
is saying?" she cried. "That little rhymester is the son
of Madame Charlotte who took care of my sister-in-law
in her last confinement."

"My dear," replied Madame de Bargeton, with a
regal air, "what is there in that? she is the widow of
an apothecary, a hard fate for a Demoiselle de Rubempré.
Suppose you and I had n't a penny in the world, what
could we do to make a living? how would you feed
your children?"

Madame de Bargeton's coolness nipped in the bud
the lamentations of her friends; they made a virtue out
of the misfortune; in fact they presently saw only good
in a thing they had begun by incriminating; they even
found invincible attractions in it — innocence does
sometimes have the piquancy of vice. At first Madame
de Bargeton's salon was filled with friends who intended
to remonstrate; but she met them with caustic rejoin-
ders; she said that if noblemen were unable to become
Molières, Racines, Rousseaus, Voltaires, Massillons, or
Diderots, the least they could do was to welcome among
them the sons of tradesmen after they had proved themselves great men. She declared that genius was
nobility. She sneered at the country squires for not
perceiving their true interests. In short, she talked a
great deal of nonsense which might have enlightened a

set of people who were not ninnies ; her friends, however, set them all down to the score of her great origi-
nality. In short, she averted the storm by firing
cannon. When Lucien, on her invitation, first entered
the faded old salon where the company were playing
whist at four tables, she welcomed him graciously, and
presented him to her friends, like a queen who expects
to be obeyed. She called du Châtelet "Monsieur
Châtelet," and petrified that personage by making him
understand she was aware of his illegal assumption of
the particle.

But in spite of this triumph Naïs did lose her su-
premacy ; certain disaffected persons proposed to emigrate. By du Châtelet's advice Amélie (who was
Madame de Chandour) determined to raise altar
against altar and receive every Wednesday. But
Madame de Bargeton's salon was open every evening,
and the guests who frequented it were such creatures
of routine, so used to looking at the same carpets, playing with the same chequers, seeing the same servants,
the same torches, putting on their cloaks, overshoes,
and hats in the same antechamber, that they loved the
very steps of the stairway as much as they did the mistress of the house. Consequently they resigned themselves to endure the goldfinch thus thrust upon them.
The sedition was finally quelled by an authoritative
remark of the president of the Society of Agriculture.

"Before the Revolution," he said, " the highest personages received Duclos, Grimm, Crébillon, all men of
no consequence like this little poet of the suburbs ; but
they never admitted a tax-collector, and that, after all,
is what Châtelet is."

Du Châtelet was made the scape-goat for Chardon; every one gave him the cold shoulder. Finding himself thus attacked, du Châtelet, who, from the day Madame de Bargeton called him Châtelet, had vowed to bring her under his thumb, acquiesced in all the views of the mistress of the house. He openly declared himself a friend of the young poet. This great diplomatist, whom the Emperor had foolishly neglected, began by introducing Lucien. He gave a dinner for the poet, at which were present the prefect, the receiver-general, the colonel of the regiment in garrison, the director of the naval school, the chief-justice, and other distinguished men. They flattered the poor poet to such a pitch that any one but a youth of twenty-two would have suspected that some hoax was being played upon him. At dessert he was made to recite his ode on the "Dying Sardanapalus," his latest masterpiece. The head-master of the college, a phlegmatic individual, clapped his hands and said that Jean-Jacques Rousseau could not have done better. Baron Sixte du Châtelet flattered himself that the little rhymester would sooner or later wilt in this hot-house of praise, or else, intoxicated with the idea of coming fame, he would be guilty of some impertinence which would send him back to his original obscurity. While thus awaiting the fall of genius he seemed to be immolating his own desires to those of Madame de Bargeton; but, with the cleverness of all scamps, he had formed a plan and was following with strategic attention the conduct of the two lovers, watching for an occasion to exterminate Lucien.

From this time forth there was heard in Angoulême and its environs a murmured rumor of a great man in

their midst. Madame de Bargeton was praised for her
discernment and the attentions she lavished on the
young eagle. Finding her conduct approved by many,
she went further to obtain a universal sanction. She
announced throughout the department a soirée with
ices, cakes, and tea, — an immense innovation in a
town where tea was sold at the apothecaries' as a drug
for indigestion. The flower of the aristocracy was
invited to hear a great work which Lucien was to read
aloud. Louise concealed her conquered difficulties from
her poet; but she gave him a few hints as to the
cabal formed against him by society; for, she said,
she did not wish him to be ignorant of the dangers
which beset the career of all men of genius, and the
obstacles which are insurmountable to inferior minds.
She made her victory the text of a lesson. She talked
of the pyre of martyrdom and the glory won by continual suffering; she larded her sermon with pompous
expressions, emulating those fine improvisations which
disfigure the novel of "Corinne." Louise felt so glorious
in her eloquence that she loved the Benjamin who
inspired it all the more. She now advised him to
boldly repudiate his father, and take his mother's noble
name of de Rubempré, and pay no attention to the
outcry excited by a change which the king would
certainly legalize. Being related to the Marquise d'Espard, a demoiselle de Beaumont-Chauvry who was held
in great esteem at court, she promised to obtain this
regal favor for him. The very words, "king," "Marquise d'Espard," "court," dazzled Lucien like a display of fireworks, and proved to him the necessity of
another baptism.

" Dear one," said Louise, in a tenderly persuasive voice, " the sooner it is done, the sooner it will be sanctioned."

She showed him, one after the other, the successive strata of the social world, and made her poet count how many steps of the ladder he would mount at once through this brilliant determination. Under this influence Lucien abjured in an instant his democratic ideas of the delusive equality of 1793. Louise awoke in his soul a thirst for distinctions, which David's cool reasoning had quieted ; she pointed out to him that the highest society in the land was the only stage on which he could display his gifts. The bitter radical now became monarchical *in petto ;* Lucien ate of the apple of aristocratic luxury and fame. He swore to lay a crown, were it even of thorns, at his lady's feet ; he would win it at any price, *quibuscumque viis.* To prove his courage, he revealed to Louise the real sufferings he had hitherto hidden from her with the instinctive reserve attached to our first sentiments, — a reserve which is based on a longing to have our souls appreciated while yet incognito. He described to her the pinchings of poverty proudly endured, his work in David's printing-house, his nights employed in study. This youthful ardor reminded Madame de Bargeton of her late colonel, and softened still further the expression of her eyes. Seeing that his proud mistress was visibly relaxing, Lucien clasped the hand he was allowed to take, and kissed it with the fervor of a poet, a young man, and a lover. Louise even went so far as to allow the son of the apothecary to touch her forehead and apply his palpitating lips to it.

5

" Child ! child ! " she exclaimed, awaking from an ec-
static torpor, "if any one were to see us, how ridiculous
I should seem."

During this evening Madame de Bargeton's wit made
great inroads into what she was pleased to call Lucien's
prejudices. To hear her, one would suppose that men
of genius had never had either fathers or mothers or
brothers or sisters ; the great works they were supposed
to put forth imposed an apparent egotism upon them
which demanded the sacrifice of all things to their
intrinsic grandeur. If their family suffered at first from
the all-absorbing exactions of their gigantic brains,
later it would receive back a hundred-fold the cost of
the sacrifices made in the first struggles of thwarted
royalty by sharing in the fruits of the regal victory.
Genius could rise only in and through itself; it alone
was the judge of its own methods, for it alone could
judge of its ends. It was therefore right in placing itself
above all laws, appointed as it was to reform them.
Besides, whosoever grasps his own period, must seize
all, hold all, risk all, for all is his. She cited the
opening lives of Bernard Palissy, Louis XI., Fox, Bonaparte, Christopher Columbus, Cæsar, and other illustrious gamblers in fortune, — men, in the first instance,
crippled with debt or poverty-stricken, misunderstood,
considered fools, madmen, bad sons, bad fathers, bad
brothers, but who afterwards turned out the pride of
their family, their country, and the world. Such arguments found their abettors in Lucien's inward vices ;
they promoted the corruption of his heart; for, in the
ardor of his desires, he admitted all means *à priori*.
Not to succeed is a crime of social lèse-majesté. A

beaten man has throttled to no purpose all the commonplace virtues on which society rests, repudiating with
horror the Marius who sits before his ruins. Lucien,
unaware that he was placed between the infamy of the
galleys and the laurel crown of genius, hovered above
the Sinai of the Prophets without perceiving the Dead
Sea below him and the shroud of his Gomorrha.

Louise loosened the mind and heart of her poet
from their provincial swaddling-clothes so completely
that Lucien determined to put her to the proof and
discover, without the shame of a refusal, whether this
fine prize were actually his. The projected party was
to give him his opportunity. Ambition mingled with
his love. He did love, but he wished to raise himself;
a double desire natural to young men who have a heart
to satisfy and indigence to escape. Society, which in
these days bids all her children to the same table,
awakens all ambitions in the dawn of life. It deprives
youth of its graces, it vitiates generous sentiments,
mingling selfish calculation with all things. Poesy
would fain have it otherwise ; but the fact remains, and
denies so often the fiction we desire to believe that the
historian cannot represent the young man of the nineteenth century other than what he is. Lucien's selfish
calculation, however, seemed to him tributary to a fine
sentiment, — his friendship for David.

He wrote a long letter to his Louise, for he was
bolder with a pen in his hand than by word of mouth.
In twelve pages, thrice copied, he told her of his
father's genius, his thwarted hopes, and the horrible
poverty to which he was a victim. He pictured his
beloved sister as an angel, and David as a future Cuvier,

who was father, brother, friend to him. He should be, he said, unworthy of the love of his own Louise if he did not ask her to do for David what she was ready to do for him; nay, he would renounce all rather than desert David, — David must be a sharer in his success. In short, he wrote one of those absurd letters in which young men point a pistol at refusal; juvenile in their casuistry and filled with the inconsequent logic of noble souls; delightful verbiage dashed with ingenuous declarations of love escaping unconsciously from the heart of the writer, and precious to that of the woman who receives them.

Having delivered this letter to Madame de Bargeton's maid, Lucien went to the printing-office and spent the day in correcting proof, directing certain work and putting in order various small matters of the business, saying nothing of his own affairs to David. While the heart is still childlike young men preserve this reticence. Besides, Lucien had begun to dread Phocion's axe, which David knew well how to wield; perhaps, too, he feared the clearness of an eye which could look to the depths of his soul. But reading with David those poems of Chénier, his secret passed from his heart to his lips, stung by a reproach which he felt as a patient feels the finger a surgeon lays upon his wound.

III.

IMAGINE now the thoughts which assailed Lucien as he went from the office to his suburban home. Would the great lady be angry with him? Would she receive David? Had he not doomed himself forever to obscurity by that letter? Though Lucien, before reaching the point of kissing Louise on the forehead, had had full opportunity to judge of the distance between a queen and her favorite, it did not occur to him that David could not jump in a moment over a social distance it had taken him five months to cross. Ignorant of the ostracism enforced against persons of no account, he did not see that a second attempt to introduce such persons would end in the loss to Madame de Bargeton of her own position. Accused and convicted of preferring low company, Louise would have to leave the town, where her caste would avoid her as in the middle-ages men fled from a leper. The clan of aristocracy, and the clergy themselves would protect Naïs from and against all attack were she guilty of conjugal infidelity, but the crime of receiving her social inferiors would never be forgiven: for it is a maxim that if the faults of one in power may be excused, they are punished in case of abdication. Now to receive David was virtually to abdicate.

Although Lucien did not see this side of the question, his aristocratic instinct made him conscious of certain other difficulties which alarmed him. Nobility of soul does not always carry with it nobility of manners. If Racine had the air of a finished courtier, Corneille was more like a cattle-dealer. Descartes' appearance was that of a stolid Dutch merchant, and visitors to Breda, meeting Montesquieu with a rake on his shoulder, often took him for a gardener. The manners of good society, when they are not a gift of birth, an acquisition sucked in with the milk, or transmitted in the blood, are the result of education, which accident often seconds by native elegance of form, distinction of feature, or tones of the voice. Such great little accessories were lacking in David, while nature had endowed Lucien with all of them. Born a gentleman through his mother, he had the signs of breeding, even to the arched instep of a Frank; whereas David Séchard was flat-footed as a Gaul, and clumsy as his father the pressman. Lucien foresaw the ridicule that would rain upon David; he even fancied he could see the smile which Madame de Bargeton would repress. Without being actually ashamed of his friend he resolved not to let this first impulse defeat him, but to leave it for future discussion. Thus, after an hour of poetry and devotion, after reading André Chénier and beholding with his friend new fields of literary possibilities lighted by a new sun, Lucien dropped back into social policy and calculation. As he walked back to l'Houmeau he repented his letter and wished he could recover it; the pitiless laws of society came in a flash before his mind. Remembering how acquired fortune would promote even a poet's ambition,

he could not endure to take his foot from the first rung
of the ladder by which he was to mount to greatness.
But soon the recollections of a simple, tranquil life, made
beautiful with the flowers of feeling ; of David, that
soul of genius, who had nobly succored him and would,
if need be, give him his very life ; of his mother, a true
great lady in her humble condition, who thought him
as good as he was brilliant ; of his sister, so graceful
in her sacrifice ; of his own pure childhood, his spotless
conscience, his hopes that no keen wind had yet de-
flowered, — all these things blossomed in his memory.
Then, indeed, he told himself it was finer to break the
serried ranks of the social herd by the force of his own
success than owe his entrance to a woman. The light
of his genius would shine, sooner or later, like that of
other men, his predecessors in the path of fame, who
had conquered society. Women would love him then !
The example of Napoleon, fatal in the early part of the
nineteenth century to commonplace minds by inspiring
them with pretensions they could not fulfil, appeared in
all its glory to Lucien, who flung his calculations to
the wind and blamed himself for making them. Such
was Lucien, going from evil to good and from good to
evil with equal facility.

For the last month he had felt a sort of shame in
reading over the door of the shop above which he lived :
" Postel, apothecary, successor to Chardon," painted
in yellow letters on a green ground. The name of his
father thus exposed in a thoroughfare traversed by all
the carriages of Angoulême distressed him. On the
evening when he left the door of his house (ornamented
with an iron grating in the worst taste), to appear at

Beaulieu among the elegant young men of the town with Madame de Bargeton on his arm, he was particularly annoyed by the obvious discrepancy between his dwelling and his new prospects.

" To love Madame de Bargeton, to win her love, and live in such a rat-hole ! " he thought, issuing from the alley into a little yard where scraps of vegetables were scattered about, where the office-boy was cleaning the laboratory utensils, where Monsieur Postel, girt with his working apron, retort in hand, was examining some chemical product, keeping watch meanwhile upon the shop ; for if his eyes were fixed upon the drugs, his ears were attentive to the bell. The odor of camomile, peppermint, and other distilled herbs filled the court-yard and penetrated to the modest apartment above the shop, which was reached by one of those straight, narrow stairways called millers' stairs, without other balusters than a couple of ropes. Above this apartment was a single attic room, where Lucien slept.

" Good-morning, my lad," said Monsieur Postel, the true type of a country shopkeeper ; " how are you feeling ? As for me, I have been making experiments with treacle ; but it would take your father to find what I've been looking for. He was a wonderful man, he was ! If I had known his secret against gout, we might both be rolling in our carriages now."

There was never a week that the apothecary, as stupid as he was kind, did not stab Lucien to the heart with some remark about the fatal discretion with which his father had kept the secret of his discovery.

" Yes, it is a great misfortune," replied Lucien, curtly, for he was beginning to think his father's pupil extremely vulgar, after many a time blessing him; for the worthy Postel had succored more than once the widow and children of his late master.

" What's the matter? " asked Monsieur Postel, laying his gauge on the laboratory table.

" Has any letter come for me? "

" Yes, and it smells like balm. It is there on the counter, near my desk."

Madame de Bargeton's letter to be lying in a chemical mess! Lucien sprang into the shop.

" Make haste, Lucien, your dinner has been ready some time; it is getting cold," cried a sweet voice, which Lucien did not heed, through a half-opened window.

" Your brother is a bit crazed, mademoiselle," said Postel, looking up at the window.

This bachelor, who closely resembled a small keg of brandy above which an artist had painted a large face pitted with the small-pox and very crimson, gazed at Eve with a polite and ceremonious air, which showed that he thought of marrying the daughter of his predecessor, though a struggle of love and self-interest was still going on within him. He often remarked to Lucien, with a smile, and he now repeated the observation as Lucien passed him with his letter: " Your sister is mighty pretty! you are not bad-looking yourself; your father did things well."

Eve was a tall, dark girl, with black hair and blue eyes. Although she showed several signs of a virile character she was personally gentle, tender, and devoted. Her frankness, her naïveté, her tranquil resignation to a hard-working life, the propriety of her conduct, which

no gossip ever slandered, had won the heart of David
Séchard. From their very first interview a secret
natural passion had stirred their souls, as it does
among Germans, without manifestation or importunate
declaration. Each thought secretly of the other, as
though they were separated by the existence of a husband whom such sentiments might offend. Both hid
their feelings from Lucien ; and it is not unlikely that
they thought their regard for each other was a wrong
done to him.

David was afraid of not pleasing Eve, who, on her
side, had many of the timidities of poverty. A born
working-woman, a grisette, would have been bolder,
but a girl brought up in other circumstances and now
deprived of them had taught herself to conform to her
fate. Humble apparently, proud in reality, Eve would
not allow herself to attract the son of a rich man. Those
who were knowing in the rise of values estimated old
Séchard's domain of Marsac at eighty thousand francs,
not counting other property which the old man, rich
by saving, lucky in acquiring, and clever at buying,
added from time to time as occasion offered. David
was, perhaps, the only man who knew nothing about
his father's wealth. To him, Marsac was a poor place,
bought in 1810 for fifteen thousand francs, where he
went once a year during the harvest, on which occasions his father marched him up and down among the
vines and boasted of their profits, which the printer
did not see and as to which he never concerned himself.

The love of a man accustomed to solitude and withdrawn into habits of study needs encouragement, for
such a life only deepens sentiment and exaggerates

difficulty. To David, Eve was a far more imposing woman than the greatest lady to a simple clerk. Awkward and uneasy in her presence, as eager to get away as he had been to come there, the printer was repressing his passion instead of expressing it. Often, after inventing some pretext of consulting Lucien, he would go down to l'Houmeau in the evening; but no sooner had he reached the house with the green door than he turned and fled away, fearing to have come too late, or to seem to importune his love, who was, perhaps, already in bed. Although this great love was shown in small ways only, Eve had fully understood it. She was gratified, but not exalted, by feeling herself the object of the deep respect conveyed in the looks, the words, the manners of her lover; but David's strongest attraction was his fanaticism for Lucien; instinctively, he had guessed the means of pleasing Eve. If we must say in what the mute delights of their love differed from the tumultuous joys of passion, we must compare them to the flowers of the field contrasted with the dazzling beds of a garden. Soft, shy glances, like the blue lotos floating on a lake; expressions murmured, like the fitful fragrance of the eglantine; tender sadness, soft as the velvet of the mosses; the native flowers of two fine souls born in rich soil, fruitful, perennial, — such were their joys of love. Eve had so often felt the power beneath this seeming weakness, she knew so well the hopes that David dared not as yet express, that the slightest incident might now produce a closer union of their hearts.

Lucien found the door opened for him by Eve, and he sat down, without a word to her, at a little table where his knife and fork were laid. There was no tablecloth, and the poor little household owned but three silver forks. Eve employed them all in the service of this dear brother.

" What are you reading? " she said, after setting on the table a dish she had taken from a heater and putting out the flame with an extinguisher.

Lucien did not answer. Eve brought a little plate daintily arranged with vine-leaves and placed it on the table with a jug of cream.

" See, Lucien, I have got you some strawberries."

Lucien was so absorbed in his letter that he did not hear her. Eve then sat down beside him without a murmur; for in the feeling of a sister for her brother there is a powerful element of pleasure in being treated without consideration.

" But what troubles you? " she cried suddenly, as the tears glittered in his eyes.

" Nothing, nothing, Eve," he said, taking her round the waist and drawing her close to him as he kissed her forehead and hair and then her neck with surprising effusion.

" You are hiding something from me."

" Well, then, she loves me ! "

" I knew you were not kissing me," she said, in a pouting tone, and coloring.

" We shall all be happy," cried Lucien, swallowing his soup in great gulps.

" We? " queried Eve. Then inspired by the same presentiment which had seized upon David, she added, " You will love us less."

" How can you think so — you who know me? "

Eve stretched out her hand and pressed Lucien's. Then she removed his empty plate and the earthenware tureen, and put before him the dish she had cooked for his dinner. Instead of eating it Lucien reread Madame de Bargeton's letter, which the discreet Eve did not ask to see, so great was her deference to her brother ; if he wished her to see it she could wait ; if he did not wish it, why should she require it? So she waited. Here is the letter : —

My FRIEND, — How can I deny to your brother in science the assistance that I have given to you? In my eyes, all talents have equal rights. But you are not aware of the prejudices of those who form my society. We cannot make nobility of mind acceptable to those who are the aristocracy of ignorance. But if I am not powerful enough to force them to receive Monsieur David Séchard I will gladly make you the sacrifice of their acquaintance. It shall be like a hecatomb of antiquity.

But, dear friend, you will not, of course, require me to accept the acquaintance of a man whose mind and manners may not please me personally. Your flatteries have long taught me that your friendship may be blind. You will not, I am sure, be angry if I add a condition to my consent. I wish to see your friend, to judge him, and know for myself, in the interests of your future, whether or not you can rely upon him. This is one of those maternal precautions which ought to be taken for you, my dear poet, by

LOUISE DE NÈGREPELISSE.

Lucien was utterly ignorant of the art with which the great world uses " yes " when it means " no " and *vice versa.* He regarded this letter as a triumph. David would go to Madame de Bargeton's salon, and shine in all the majesty of genius. In the intoxication of a victory which made him believe in the power of his ascendency over others, he took, unconsciously, so proud an attitude, his face reflected so many hopes with so dazzling a radiance that his sister could not help exclaiming that he was beautiful.

"If she has any mind at all, — that woman, — she must love you ; and to-night she will be made unhappy enough, for I am sure all the other women will court you. How handsome you will look when you read them your 'Saint John at Patmos.' I wish I were a mouse and could slip in after you. Come, I have your evening clothes all ready in mother's room."

This room was one of decent poverty. It contained a walnut bedstead with white curtains, and a strip of green carpet beside it. On the bureau was a mirror ; and a few chairs, also of walnut, completed the furniture. On the mantelshelf was a clock which recalled the days of departed comfort. The window had white curtains. The walls were hung with a gray paper, gray-flowered. The floor tiles, colored and rubbed by Eve, shone with cleanliness. In the middle of the room stood a round table, where, on a red tray with gilt rosettes, were three cups and saucers and a sugar basin of Limoges ware. Eve slept in a small adjoining room or closet, which contained a narrow bed, an old sofa, and a work-table near the window. The narrowness of this ship's cabin, as it might be called, required that the door should stand open in order to give it air. Though poverty was visible in everything, the modesty of a studious life was in the atmosphere. To those who knew the mother and her two children, the scene was full of tender harmonies.

Lucien was putting on his cravat when David's step
was heard in the little courtyard, and the printer presently appeared with the manner of a man who had come
in haste.

" Well, David," cried Lucien, " we have triumphed ;
she loves me ; you are to go."

" No," said the printer, with an embarrassed air ; " I
have come to thank you for that proof of friendship,
about which I have reflected seriously. My life, Lucien is settled. I am David Séchard, printer to the
king in Angoulême ; the name is read on the walls and
posters and advertisements. To persons of Madame
de Bargeton's caste I am an artisan, a merchant if you
prefer it, but at any rate, a working-man, with a shop,
rue de Beaulieu, at the corner of the place du Mûrier.
I have n't the fortune of a Keller, nor the fame of a
Desplein, — two sorts of powers which the nobles still
endeavor to ignore and which (I agree with the nobles
here) are of no account without the manners and knowledge of life of a gentleman. What would justify me
in stepping up in this way? I should simply be laughed
at, by the bourgeois as well as by the nobles. Your
position is different. As a clerk you are committed to
nothing. You can make acquaintances and choose
some other way of life to-morrow ; you can study law,
or diplomacy, or enter a government office. Profit by
your social virginity, walk alone and lay your grip upon
honors. Enjoy all pleasures joyously, even those of
gratified vanity. Be happy, and I shall be happy in
your success, — you will be to me a second self. Yes,
my thought will make me live in your career. To you
the banquets of life, the glory of this world, and the rapid

results of its strategy ; to me the sober, laborious life of
a tradesman, and the slow occupations of science. You
shall be our aristocracy," he added, with a smile, looking
at Eve. " When you totter my arm shall be ready to
support you. If you meet with treachery take refuge
in our hearts ; their love is unchangeable. Should you
try to divide between yourself and me the protection,
favor, and good-will of these great persons, you may
weary them, and we shall simply have injured each
other. No, go your way, — it is before you ; we will
not be a drag upon you. Far from envying your career, I devote myself to it. What you have just done
for me — I mean in risking the favor of your benefactress rather than leave me or seem to turn your back
upon me — just that simple thing, Lucien, is so grand
that it would bind me to you for life if we were not already brothers. Have no remorse or doubt in taking
the higher place. Even if you cause me anxiety, perhaps I shall still be your debtor." As he said these
words he glanced timidly at Eve, whose eyes were full
of tears, for she guessed all. " Besides," he added to
Lucien, who was much surprised, " you are handsome
and well made, your figure is fine, you wear your
clothes with an air, you look like a gentleman in that
blue coat with brass buttons and those nankeen
trousers. As for me, I should look like a workman
among all those fine people. I should be awkward,
embarrassed, and say either foolish things or nothing
at all. If you choose to yield to the prejudice of names
and take that of your mother you can call yourself Lucien de Rubempré ; but I am and ever shall be David
Séchard. Everything will serve you and everything

would injure me in the world where you are going. You are born to succeed in it. For one thing, the women will adore that angelic face of yours — won't they, Eve?"

Lucien fell on David's neck and kissed him. His friend's modesty solved all doubts, all difficulties. How could he help showing a redoubled love for the man who made, out of friendship, the same reflections he had just made out of ambition. The ambitious lover felt that the road was levelled for him, and his heart glowed. It was one of those rare moments in life when the cords of being are gently stretched, and rich sounds come from their vibration. But the loyal wisdom of this noble soul increased in Lucien a tendency that exists, more or less, in all men to centre everything upon himself. We all feel as Louis XIV. said: "The State, it is I." The exclusive tenderness of his mother and sister, David's devotion, the habit of seeing himself the one object of these three persons, gave him the vices of an elder son and produced in him the selfish egotism which ruins a young noble, and which Madame de Bargeton fostered by inciting him to resign his name and his obligations towards his mother, sister, and David. This point, was not yet reached, however; but it was to be feared that the widening of the circle of his ambition, promoted by his friends, soon would constrain him to think only of himself.

When their emotion had passed off, David remarked to Lucien that his poem of "Saint John at Patmos" was rather too Biblical to be read before a company who probably knew little of apocalyptic poetry. Lucien, who feared his audience, grew uneasy. David ad-

vised him to take the volume of André Chénier with
him and change a doubtful pleasure into a certain one ;
Lucien read admirably ; he could not help delighting an
audience, and his modesty in choosing another poet
would be put to his credit. Like most young men he
believed in the intelligence and virtue of persons of
rank. If youth which has never sinned is without
mercy for the known sins of others it also attributes to
others its own magnificent faiths. We must experience
life before we recognize that, as Raffaelle finely said,
comprehension alone makes us equal to it. As a general thing, the sense of poesy required for a full understanding of the art is rare in France, where wit and
intellect dry up the sacred sources of the tears of
ecstasy, where none will take the pains of deciphering
the sublime, of sounding sublimity in search of the
infinite. Lucien was about to meet his first experience
of the ignorance and coldness of social life. He took
the volume of André Chénier with him.

When Eve and David were alone together the lover
became more embarrassed than at any previous moment of his life. Oppressed by many fears, he desired
and dreaded approval ; he longed to get away, for shyness has a coquetry of its own. The poor lover dared
not say a word which might seem to ask for thanks ;
all words appeared to him compromising, and therefore
he kept silence with the air of a criminal. Eve, who
instinctively understood the tortures of his shyness,
found pleasure in this silence ; but when David twisted
his hat as if to go, she smiled.

" Monsieur David," she said ; " as you are not going
to pass the evening at Madame de Bargeton's, we might

spend it together. It is so fine, suppose we take a walk along the Charente ; we could talk of Lucien."

David had a momentary idea of prostrating himself before that enchanting girl, who had put into her voice certain tones of hope rewarded. By the tenderness of those ·tones she meant to solve the difficulties of the situation. Her proposal was more than a flattery, it was love's first favor.

" But," she said, seeing David's gesture, " give me time to dress."

David, who never in his life had known what it was to turn a tune, went out into the courtyard singing, which greatly surprised the worthy Postel and gave him dark suspicions as to the relations between Eve and the printer.

The slightest circumstances of this momentous evening acted powerfully upon Lucien, whose character was greatly influenced by first impressions. Like all inexperienced lovers he arrived so early that Louise was not yet in the salon. Monsieur de Bargeton was there alone. Lucien had already begun his apprenticeship in the petty meannesses by which the lover of a married woman buys his happiness (which give a woman the measure of those she may exact) but he had never yet been alone with Monsieur de Bargeton.

That gentleman had one of those small minds that are mildly interposed between an offensive nullity which understands to some extent, and an arrogant stupidity which receives nothing and returns nothing. Full of his duties to society, and striving to make himself agreeable in it, he had adopted the smile of a dancer

before the footlights as his only language. Pleased or
displeased, he smiled, — smiled at disastrous news as
he smiled at good news. That smile answered all purposes through the expressions that Monsieur de Bargeton gave to it. If direct approbation was absolutely
required he added a complacent laugh, using language
only in the last extremity. A tête-à-tête was the only
situation of his vegetable life which caused him embarrassment, for he was then obliged to search in the im-
mensity of his inward vacuum for something to say.
Generally he escaped this difficulty by having recourse
to the naïve ways of his childhood ; he thought aloud ;
he revealed every detail of his life, and expressed all
his wants and sensations, which, to him, took the place
of ideas. He never talked of the weather, or the usual
commonplaces of conversation in which fools take
refuge, he went straight to the most private affairs of
life. "To please Madame de Bargeton," he would say,
" I ate veal this morning for breakfast ; she likes it,
but my stomach aches in consequence. I knew how it
would be, I am always taken so ; can you explain it?"
Or he would remark, " I shall ring for a glass of *eau
sucrée*, will you have one?" or, "I shall ride out on
horseback to-morrow ; I want to see my father-in-law."

These little remarks, which involved no discussion,
required only a yes or no, and the conversation dropped.
Monsieur de Bargeton would then implore assistance,
turning his nose to you like a wheezy pug, and gazing
in your face with his prominent bleary eyes in a way
that seem to query, " What did you say?" He cherished the bores who talked of themselves, and listened
to them with a loyal, delicate attention which made him

so dear to the gabblers of Angoulême that they vaunted his intellect and declared it was underrated. When they could find no other listeners these folk would fall back on Monsieur de Bargeton and tell him their tales or pursue their arguments, sure of receiving his approving smile. His wife's salon being always full, he liked to be there, and was usually at his ease. He busied himself in the smallest details; watched who came in, bowed, smiled, and presented all strangers to his wife. He met those who were leaving, conducted them to the door, and received their parting words with the same eternal smile. When the party was gay and he saw every one well employed, he would stand mutely, planted on his two long legs like a stork, apparently listening to a political conversation (of which he heard not a word), or studying the cards of a player without understanding the game (for he knew none), or else he walked about snuffing tobacco, and trying to work off his indigestion. Anais was the one happiness of his life; she gave him infinite enjoyment. When she played her part as mistress of the house he lay back in his easy chair and admired her — she was talking for him. He took pleasure in searching out the meaning of her sentences, and as it frequently came to him long after they were uttered, his smiles would often explode unexpectedly, like torpedoes that have been buried in the ground. His respect for his wife amounted to adoration ; and, we may ask, is not adoration, of whatever kind it be, sufficient to make the happiness of a life? Anaïs, who was generous and intelligent, had not abused her power, recognizing in her husband the facile nature of a child, which asks nothing better than to be governed. She had taken care of him as she would of a mantle; she had brushed him, kept him clean, wrapped him up, and used him carefully. Finding himself thus looked after and brushed and cared for, Monsieur de Bargeton had acquired an almost canine affection for his wife; it is so easy to give one's self a happiness that costs nothing! Madame de Bargeton, knowing that her husband's greatest pleasure was good living, provided him with excellent dinners. She pitied him, and never did she complain of him; so that some persons, misunderstanding her proud silence, supposed Monsieur de Bargeton to be possessed of hidden merits. His wife had long brought him under military rule, and he obeyed her passively. She would say, " Pay a visit to Monsieur or Madame Such-a-one," and he went like a soldier to his post. In her presence he stood as it were at attention, motionless. At this particular time there was some question of nominating this mute being as deputy. Lucien had been an intimate of the house too short a time to have lifted the veil which hid this unimaginable character. Monsieur de Bargeton, buried in his armchair, apparently seeing all and understanding everything, and making a dignity of his silence, seemed to Lucien a most imposing personage. Instead of taking him for a granite post, he regarded him as a formidable sphinx, after the manner of imaginative men whose tendency it is to magnify and give a soul to forms. He thought it necessary to court his host.

" I am the first to arrive," he said, bowing to the master of the house with more deference than was usually accorded to him.

" That is natural," replied Monsieur de Bargeton.

Lucien took the remark as the sarcasm of a jealous husband ; he turned red and looked in a mirror, trying to recover himself.

" You live in the suburbs," said Monsieur de Bargeton ; "people who live far off always come earlier than those near by."

" Why is that?" asked Lucien, with an ingratiating air.

" I don't know," replied Monsieur de Bargeton, relapsing into his usual immobility.

" You don't seek to know," said Lucien. "A man who could make that observation can certainly find the cause of it."

" Yes," said Monsieur de Bargeton, " the final cause, hey, hey ! "

Lucien cracked his brains to continue the conversation, which had now dropped.

" Madame de Bargeton is dressing, I suppose?" he said, shuddering at the silliness of his question.

" Yes, she is dressing," responded the husband, naturally.

Lucien, unable to invent a single sentence, raised his eyes to the two great beams of the ceiling, painted gray, the space between them being plastered, and he then noticed with dismay that the glass chandelier with its numerous pendants was freed from its usual gauze and filled with wax candles. The covers of the furniture had been taken off, and the faded patterns of the red damask exhibited. These preparations announced an unusual festivity. The poet doubted the propriety of his dress, for he was wearing boots. He walked to a Japanese vase which was placed on a console of the

Louis XV. period, and looked at it in a stupor of fear;
then he was alarmed lest he should displease the husband by ceasing to court him, and he returned to the
charge, determined to discover some hobby on which
he could flatter him.

" You seldom leave town, monsieur? " he began.

" Seldom."

Silence fell again. Monsieur de Bargeton watched
Lucien's movements, which disturbed him, like a suspicious cat. Each was afraid of the other.

" Can he suspect my attentions to his wife? " thought
Lucien ; " he is certainly hostile."

Happily for Lucien, who was much embarrassed by
the uneasy glances which Monsieur de Bargeton cast at
him as he moved about the room, the old servant, who
had donned a livery, announced du Châtelet. The
baron entered with much ease of manner, greeted his
friend Bargeton, and gave Lucien the little nod which
was then the fashion, but which the poet, ignorant of
this fact, considered financially impertinent. Sixte du
Châtelet wore trousers of dazzling whiteness, with
straps which held their plaits in place, thin shoes, and
stockings of Scotch thread. Over his white waistcoat
floated the black ribbon of an eyeglass. The cut of his
coat was Parisian. He was quite the buck which his
antecedents proclaimed him, but years had supplied
him with a little round stomach which he found somewhat difficult to restrain within the lines of elegance.
He dyed his hair and his whiskers, whitened by the
sufferings of his exile, and it gave him a hard look.
His complexion, which had once been delicate, now
showed the copper tinge of those who return from east-

ern climes; nevertheless, his whole bearing, though rather ridiculous on account of its pretensions, did undoubtedly recall the fascinating secretary of her Imperial Highness.

The baron took up his eyeglass and surveyed Lucien's nankeen trousers, waistcoat, boots, and blue coat, made in Angoulême, — in short, the whole of his rival from top to toe. Then he returned the eyeglass to his waistcoat pocket, as if he would say, "I am satisfied." Crushed at first by the baron's elegance, Lucien soon reflected that his turn would come when he showed his face, instinct with poetry, to the company; but none the less he felt a keen annoyance, added to the inward discomfort which Monsieur de Bargeton's imaginary hostility had caused him. The baron seemed to Lucien to bear with all the weight of his prosperity upon him to humiliate his poverty. Monsieur de Bargeton, having nothing to say, was in consternation at the silence maintained by the rivals, who were eyeing each other; but when he found himself in a crisis of this kind, he had one question which he reserved, like a pear for a thirsty moment, and he now thought the time had come to launch it with a businesslike air.

"Well, monsieur," he said to du Châtelet, "what is the news? what do people say?"

"The news?" replied the baron, mischievously, "Why the news is, Monsieur Chardon. Ask him. Have you brought us a charming poem?" added the sparkling baron, correcting a curl which was a little out of place.

"I ought to consult you as to that," replied Lucien. "You practised poetry long before me."

" Pooh ! a few vaudevilles ; well enough for an occasion, ballads to which the music gave charm, a lyric to
a sister of Bonaparte (ungrateful fellow!) — they are
no claim to posterity."

At this moment Madame de Bargeton entered in all
the brilliancy of a studied toilet. She wore a turban
fastened with an oriental buckle. A gauze scarf, beneath which could be seen a cameo necklace, was gracefully twined about her throat. The short sleeves of
her painted muslin gown enabled her to wear several
tiers of bracelets on her beautiful white arms. This
theatrical attire enchanted Lucien. Monsieur du Châtelet gallantly addressed a number of fulsome compliments to the queen, which made her smile with pleasure,
so delighted was she to be praised before Lucien. She
exchanged but one look with her dear poet, and replied
to the baron with a politeness which mortified him by
excluding him from her intimacy.

The invited guests began to arrive. The first to
enter were the bishop and his grand-vicar, two solemn
and dignified figures, forming, however, a violent contrast to each other. Monseigneur was tall and thin ;
his acolyte was fat and short. Both had brilliant eyes,
but the bishop was pale, while the vicar was crimson
with abounding health. In each — and here there was
no difference between them — gesture and movement
were extremely rare. Both seemed prudence itself;
their reserve and their silence intimidated others, and
they passed for being very intellectual.

The priests were followed by Madame de Chandour
and her husband, two extraordinary personages whom
those who are ignorant of the provinces will declare to

be imaginary. The husband of Amélie (the woman who was posing as Madame de Bargeton's antagonist), Monsieur de Chandour, called Stanislas, was a would-be young man, still slender at forty-five years of age, with a face like a sieve. His cravat was always tied in a way that presented two threatening points; one at the level of his right ear, the other lower down towards the red ribbon of his cross. The sides of his coat were flung back; a wide-open waistcoat disclosed a swelling shirt, fastened and weighted with pins of elaborate jewelry. His whole apparel had an exaggerated air, which gave him so great a likeness to caricatures that even strangers laughed when they saw him. Stanislas viewed himself with continual satisfaction; he looked himself over from head to foot and verified the buttons on his waistcoat, smoothed the undulating line of his tight trousers, and caressed his legs with a loving glance which ended at the toes of his boots. When he ceased to thus gaze upon himself he looked for a mirror, in which to see if his hair were still in curl; he challenged the notice of women with a contented eye, sticking his thumbs into the pockets of his waistcoat, and leaning backward to throw himself into a three-quarter position, — allurements of a cock, which had brought him much success in the aristocratic circles of which he was the beau. His talk was for the most part in the smutty style of the eighteenth century. This odious form of conversation gave him some success with women; he made them laugh. He was beginning to get uneasy about Monsieur du Châtelet. In fact, the women in society, puzzled by the implied contempt of that dandy, stimulated by his affectation, and piqued by his tone of a

satiated sultan, had begun to pay him much more attention since Madame de Bargeton had taken up the Byron
of Angoulême than they did on his first arrival.

Amélie was a little woman, clumsily comic, fat, white,
with black hair; overdoing everything, talking loud and
twirling her head, which was laden with feathers in
summer and flowers in winter, — a lively talker, but
quite unable to finish a sentence without the accom-
paniment of an asthmatic whistle.

Monsieur de Saintot, called Astolphe, president of the
Agricultural Society, was a tall, stout man with a high
color, who seemed to be led by his wife, called Lili
(an abbreviation of Eliza), a sort of figure not unlike
a withered fern. Her name, which implies something
childlike in its owner, contrasted absurdly with the
character and manners of Madame de Saintot, a solemn
woman, extremely pious, very quarrelsome and exacting at cards. Astolphe was held to be a scholar of the
first water. Ignorant as a carp, he had nevertheless
written the articles on sugar and brandy in the "Agricultural Dictionary;" two works for which he had pil-
fered his facts here and there from newspapers and old
manuals relating to those productions. The department believed he was now occupied in writing a treatise on modern culture. Though he shut himself up in
his study all the morning he had not written a page for
the last twelve years. If any one called to see him they
found him sorting papers, searching for a missing note,
or mending a pen; his whole time when alone in his
study was spent in idling. He read the papers slowly,
carved corks with his penknife, drew fantastic figures
in his blotting-book, turned over Cicero in search of a

sentence or passage applicable to some event of the
day, so that he might lead the conversation in the evening to a topic which enabled him to say : " There is a
passage in Cicero which seems actually to have been
written for these days." Then he would recite it to the
great edification of his hearers, who remarked to each
other : " Astolphe is really a wellspring of knowledge."
This interesting fact would then be told all over town,
and it maintained the faith which society bestowed on
Monsieur de Saintot's acquirements.

After this couple, came Monsieur de Bartas, called
Adrien, a man who sang bass and had immense pretensions to be musical. Self-conceit had set him astride
of the solfeggio. He began by admiring himself as he
sang ; then he talked music, till at last he ended in
being musical exclusively. The art of music became to
him a monomania ; he never brightened unless the subject were talked of ; he was miserable the whole evening until asked to sing. But as soon as he had bellowed
a tune, life began for him ; his chest swelled, he rose
from his heels to receive compliments ; he pretended
modesty though he went from group to group to gather
flattery ; then, when there was no more to be had, he
would open a discussion on the piece he had just sung
and praise the composer.

Monsieur Alexandre de Brebian, a sepia hero, a
sketcher who infested the houses of his friends with ridiculous drawings and spoiled all the albums of the
department, came with Monsieur de Bartas. Each
gave his arm to the wife of the other. Gossip said that
the exchange was permanent. These women, Lolotte
(Madame Charlotte de Brebian) and Fifine (Madame

Josephine de Bartas), both equally interested in chiffons, trimmings, and the matching of heterogeneous colors, were eaten up with a desire to appear Parisian. They neglected their households, where matters went ill. But if the two women were squeezed like dolls into gowns that were scantily constructed and presented on their own persons an assortment of excruciating colors, the husbands, in their capacity as artists, allowed themselves a provincial freedom of apparel which made them wonderful to behold. Their creased coats gave them the look of supernumeraries who figure as guests at a wedding on the boards of a petty theatre.

Among the personages whom fate landed in the salon the most original was undoubtedly Monsieur le Comte de Sénonches, aristocratically called Jacques, — a great huntsman, haughty, lean, sunburnt, amiable as a wild boar, distrustful as a Venetian, jealous as a Moor, and living on very good terms with Monsieur du Hautoy, otherwise called Francis, the friend of the household.

Madame de Sénonches (Zéphirine) was tall and handsome, but unfortunately blotched in complexion owing to an affection of the liver which made people take her for a fretful woman. Her slender waist and delicate proportions allowed her to assume a languor of manner which seemed affectation, but was really expressive of the emotions and constantly gratified caprices of a woman beloved.

Francis was a man of some distinction, who had abandoned a consulate at Valence and all his hopes in diplomacy to come to Angoulême and live near Zéphirine, — called also Zizine. The former consul took charge of the household and the education of the children, taught the latter foreign languages, and managed the property of Monsieur and Madame de Sénonches with absolute devotion. Angoulême, noble, administrative, and bourgeois, had long gossiped over the perfect unity of this household of three persons ; but in the long run, this mystery of conjugal trinity had seemed so rare and so charming that Monsieur du Hautoy would have been regarded as outrageously immoral had he thought of marrying. Besides, the community was beginning to suspect in the attachment of Madame de Sénonches to a goddaughter named Mademoiselle de la Haye, who lived with her as companion, another and more disquieting mystery ; and in spite of certain absolute impossibilities of date a strong likeness was said to exist between Françoise de la Haye and Francis du Hautoy. When Jacques hunted the country, persons would ask him news of Francis, to which he would reply with information about the latter's health, apparently considering his welfare before that of his wife. This blindness seemed so remarkable in a jealous man that his best friends would sometimes play upon it. Monsieur du Hautoy was a scrupulous dandy, whose personal solicitudes had turned to the finical and fussy. He was always thinking of his cough, or his want of sleep, of his digestion, and of what he ate. Zéphirine had coddled her factotum into thinking himself a man in poor health ; she wadded and muffled and physicked him ; she stuffed him with tidbits like the pug of a countess ; she ordered or forbade him to take such and such food ; she embroidered his waistcoats, the ends of his cravats, and his handkerchiefs, and ended by making

him wear so many of her pretty constructions that he
looked like a Japanese idol. Their understanding of
each other was flawless. Zizine looked to Francis for
everything and Francis seemed to take his ideas from
Zizine's eyes. They smiled and thought and blamed
as one being; they even seemed to consult each other
as to saying the simplest good-day.

The richest landowner of the neighborhood, a man
envied by all, the Marquis de Pimentel and his wife,
who together possessed forty thousand francs a year,
and passed the winters in Paris, came in from the
country in their calèche, bringing with them their
neighbors, the Baron and Baroness de Rastignac and
their daughters, two charming young women, well
brought up, poor, but dressed with the simplicity
which enhances natural beauty. These persons, who
were certainly the *élite* of the company, were received
in cold silence, with a respect full of jealousy, especially
when those present saw the distinguished greeting
which Madame de Bargeton gave to them. The two
families belonged to the small number of those who, in
the provinces, hold themselves above local gossip and
mix in no general society; they lived quietly in retreat
and maintained an imposing dignity. Monsieur de
Pimentel and Monsieur de Rastignac were called by
their titles; no familiarities connected their wives and
daughters with the upper clique of Angoulême; they
were too nearly allied to the court nobility to share the
pettiness of provincial high-life.

The prefect and the general were the last to arrive,
accompanied by the country gentleman who had carried
his treatise on silk-worms to David's printing-office in

the morning. He was no doubt the mayor of some district, chosen for his landed property; but his behavior and clothes betrayed rustiness in society; he never knew where to put his hands, turned around the person who spoke to him, rose or sat down to reply to whoever addressed him, was obsequious, uneasy, and solemn by turns, hastened to laugh at a joke, listened with servile attention, and wore at times a surly look when he thought others were laughing at him. Several times during the evening, feeling oppressed by his treatise, he tried to talk silk-worms, but the unfortunate man (his name was de Séverac) fell into the hands of Monsieur de Bartas, who answered music, and Monsieur de Saintot, who quoted Cicero. Towards the middle of the evening the luckless mayor managed to find auditors in a widow and her daughter, Madame and Mademoiselle de Brossard, who were not the least interesting of the personages of this society. One word will tell all : they were as poor as they were noble. Their dress showed the effort at adornment which betrays secret penury. Madame de Brossard was continually praising, in season and out of season, her tall, stout daughter, twenty-seven years of age, who was supposed to be proficient on the piano. In her desire to marry her dear Camille she proclaimed her as sharing the tastes of all marriageable men, and had been known to declare in the course of a single evening that Camille loved the wandering life of garrisons, and the tranquil life of country gentlemen cultivating their own lands. Both women had the pinched, sour dignity of persons whom others are delighted to pity and in whom they take an interest through egotism; they

7

had sounded the hollowness of the consolatory words which society finds pleasure in bestowing on the unfortunate. Monsieur de Séverac was fifty-nine years of age, a widower without children ; mother and daughter listened with admiring devotion to the details which he gave them about his mulberries.

" My daughter has always been fond of animals," said the mother, " and as the silk these little creatures make is particularly interesting to women, I shall ask permission to go to Séverac and show Camille how you manage them. Camille has so much intelligence that she will seize your ideas in a moment. On one occasion she learned the inverse ratio of the square of distances."

This phrase was the glorious termination of a long conversation between Monsieur de Séverac and Madame de Brossard after Lucien had finished his reading.

A few habitués slipped familiarly into the salon ; also two or three young men, scions of nobility, shy, silent, faultlessly dressed, pleased at being invited to this literary solemnity, though only one was daring enough to emancipate himself to the extent of speaking to Mademoiselle de la Haye. All the women ranged themselves solemnly in a circle, behind which stood the men. This assemblage of queer personages, anomalous garments, and wrinkled faces, was extremely imposing to Lucien, whose heart began to palpitate as he felt himself the object of all those eyes. Bold as he tried to be, he could not endure this first social trial, though encouraged by his mistress, who made a great display of curtseys and all her most finished graces in receiving the illustrious personages of Angoulême society. The discomfort to which Lucien now fell a prey was increased by a circumstance easy to have foreseen, but which frightened a youth who was still unused to the tactics of the world. Being all eyes and ears, he heard himself called Monsieur de Rubempré by Louise, by Monsieur de Bargeton, by the bishop, and by several flatterers of the mistress of the house, and Monsieur Chardon by the majority of the formidable company. Intimidated by the inquisitive glances of those about him, he knew they were saying his bourgeois name by the mere motion of their lips; he anticipated the judgments they would form about him, with the provincial frankness that is often akin to brutality. These continual pin-pricks put him out of sorts with himself. He waited impatiently for the moment when he should be asked to read, and could take an attitude which would put an end to his inward torture. But Jacques was relating his last hunting feat to Madame de Pimentel; Adrien was talking of the new musical star, Rossini, to Laure de Rastignac; Astolphe, who had committed to memory the description given in a newspaper of a novel kind of plough, was describing it to the baron. Lucien, poor poet, was not aware that none of these minds, except that of Madame de Bargeton, could understand poetry. All these persons, hungering for emotions, had eagerly accepted the invitation, deceiving themselves completely as to the nature of the show that awaited them. There are words which always attract the public as trumpets, the clash of cymbals, or the booth of acrobats attract them. The words " beauty," " glory," " poesy," have a witchcraft about them which fascinates the commonest mind.

When the company had all assembled, and conversation was hushed, — not without many hints given to the interrupters by Monsieur de Bargeton, who was sent about by his wife like a beadle in a church who taps his staff on the pavement, — Lucien placed himself at a round table beside Madame de Bargeton, violently shaken up in soul. He announced, in an agitated voice, that, in order not to disappoint the expectations of his audience, he was about to read to them the masterpieces, lately rediscovered, of a great but unknown poet, André Chénier. Though Chénier's poems were first published in 1819 no one in Angoulême had ever heard of him. The audience, therefore, imagined that Lucien's announcement was an evasion suggested by Madame de Bargeton to save the modesty of her poet and put his hearers at their ease.

Lucien then read "Le Jeune Malade," which was received with flattering murmurs; then "L'Aveugle," a poem which these empty minds thought long. While he read, Lucien was a victim to those infernal sufferings which cannot be understood by any but great artists, or those whose enthusiasm and lofty intellect put them on that level. To render poetry by the voice and seize it by the ear, exacts an almost sacred attention. There must exist between the reader and his hearers the closest bond, without which the electric communication of feelings cannot take place. If this cohesion of souls is lacking, the poet is like an angel trying to sing the hymns of heaven amid the sneers of hell. Now, in circumstances which develop their faculties, persons of intellect have the circumferential sight of snails, the nose of dogs, the ear of moles; they see

scent, and hear everything about them... The musician
and the poet know as quickly whether they are admired
or misunderstood as a plant wilts or freshens in a suitable or unsuitable atmosphere. The muttering of the
men who had only come there to bring their wives and
were whispering among themselves echoed in Lucien's
ear by the laws of these special acoustics ; his eye
caught the sympathetic hiatus of jaws parted by a
yawn, and the teeth thus exposed seemed to mock him.
When, like Noah's dove, he looked for a spot on which
to rest, he encountered the impatient eyes of those who
were waiting an opportunity to recommence their talk.
With the exception of Laure de Rastignac and two or
three young men, and the bishop, all present were
bored. Those who understand poetry try to develop
in their own souls that which the poet has put in its
germ into his verse. But these icy hearers, far from
aspiring to share the poet's soul, could not even listen
to his accents. Lucien was so deeply discouraged that
a cold sweat moistened his shirt ; but a burning glance
from Louise, to whom he turned, gave him courage to
read on, though his poet's heart was bleeding at every
pore.

" Do you call that amusing, Fifine ? " said the gaunt
Lili to her neighbor.

" Don't ask me, my dear ; I go to sleep as soon as
any one reads aloud."

" I hope Naïs won't give us verses every night," said
Francis. " If I listen to anything after dinner, the
attention I am forced to pay hinders my digestion."

" Poor dear ! " said Zéphirine, in a low voice, " take
some *eau sucrée.*"

"It was very well declaimed," said Alexandre; "but I prefer whist."

Hearing this remark, which passed for witty because an English word was used, a few devoted card-players suggested that the reader ought to rest. Under this pretext a few couples escaped into the boudoir. Lucien, entreated by Louise, by the charming Laure de Rastignac, and by the bishop, roused fresh attention by rendering the anti-revolutionary fire of the "Iambes," which several persons, carried away by the roll of the language, applauded without comprehending. Such persons are excited by vociferation, as vulgar palates are by strong drink. During an interval, when ices were served, Zéphirine sent Francis to examine the volume, and reported to her neighbor Amélie that Lucien was really reading printed poems.

"Well," said Amélie, contentedly, "that's natural enough; Monsieur de Rubempré works for a printer. It is just as if a pretty woman," with a malicious glance at Lolotte, "should make her own clothes."

"He has printed his poems himself," said all the women.

"Then why does he call himself de Rubempré?" asked Jacques. "When a noble works with his hands, he ought to relinquish his name."

"He has done so," said Zizine; "his real name is bourgeois, and he has taken that of his mother, which is noble."

"If his verses are printed, we can read them for ourselves," said Astolphe.

This stupid mistake complicated matters until Sixte du Châtelet deigned to inform the ignorant company that the announcement was not an oratorical precaution, but that these beautiful poems were actually written by a royalist brother of the revolutionist Marie-Joseph Chénier. The audience, with the exception of the bishop and Madame de Rastignac and her daughters, chose to be affronted at this announcement, and to consider they had been cheated through their own mistake. A low murmur of opposition arose ; but Lucien did not hear it. Isolated for the moment from this odious company by the intoxication of inward melody, he continued his reading, and saw his audience, as it were, through a mist. He read the solemn elegy on Suicide, written in the antique vein, and full of a sublime melancholy ; and next the poem in which occurs the line, —

"Thy poems are sweet; I love to repeat them."

Then he ended his recitation with that beautiful idyl entitled "Néère."

Plunged in a delightful revery, one hand in her curls which had broken loose, the other hanging down, her eyes wandering, her mind solitary in the midst of her salon, Madame de Bargeton felt, for the first time, that her life had entered its proper sphere. She was unpleasantly aroused by Amélie, who had taken upon herself to inform the mistress of the house of the general opinion.

"Naïs, we came here to listen to Monsieur Chardon's poems, and you have given us printed verses. They may be very pretty, but these ladies would prefer, for the credit of Angoulême, the poetry of our own vintage."

"Don't you think that the French language is very unsuitable for poetry?" said Astolphe to Sixte du Châtelet. "For my part, I think Cicero's prose far more poetic."

"The true French poetry is lyric," replied du Châtelet, "songs —"

"Ah, yes, songs prove how musical our language is," said Adrien.

"I should like to hear some of the verses which made a conquest of Naïs," said Zéphirine; "but I judge from the way she received Amélie's remark that she won't give us a specimen of them."

"She owes it to herself to let us hear them," remarked Francis; "for the genius of her little poet was the reason of her inviting us here to-night."

"You have been a diplomat," said Amélie, addressing du Châtelet. "Can't you manage it for us?"

"Nothing easier," said the baron.

The former secretary of her Imperial Highness being used to such little manœuvres, went to find the bishop, and persuaded him to come forward. Requested by Monseigneur himself, Naïs was forced to ask Lucien to repeat something of his own which he knew by heart. Du Châtelet's prompt success in the negotiation won him a smile from Amélie.

"The baron is certainly very clever," she whispered to Lolotte.

Lolotte, bearing in mind Amélie's slur on women who made their own gowns, replied with a smile : "Since when have you recognized the barons of the Empire?"

Lucien had deified his mistress in an ode to which he

had given a title invented by every young man on leaving college. This ode, complacently cherished and beautified with all the love his heart contained, seemed to him the only one of his poems that was fit to compete with those of Chénier. Giving Madame de Bargeton a look that was not a little conceited, he said : " To HER!" Then he proudly assumed an attitude in which to deliver his masterpiece, for his vanity as an author felt at ease behind Madame de Bargeton's petticoat. This was the moment when Naïs unguardedly let all the women present into her secret. Notwithstanding her habit of ruling the social world around her by the strength of her intellect, she could not help trembling for Lucien. Her face was troubled, her eyes seemed to ask some forbearance ; then she lowered them, and hid her feelings as best she could while the following stanzas were recited : —

TO HER.

Within that radiance of light and glory,
Where listening angels tune their golden lyres,
Repeating at the feet of great Jehovah
    The prayer of plaintive stars,

Behold, a cherubin with golden hair,
Veiling her brow from God's effulgent light,
Leaves in the courts of heaven her silvery wings,
    And comes to us on earth.

With her she brings God's merciful compassion,
Quiets the anguish of a soul at bay,
Wreathes girlhood's beauty, cradles wintry age,
    With flowers of purity.

Inspires repentance to the sinning soul,
Whispers to anxious mothers, " Hope!"
Counts with glad heart the sighs of those
    Who pity misery.

One of these messengers is here among us;
A loving earth arrests her course;
And yet she weeps and looks up, longing,
    Toward the Father's bliss.

'T is not the dazzling whiteness of that brow,
Which tells the secret of a noble birth,
Nor that the fruitful ardor of that soul
    Reveals divinest worth.

It is that when my awe-struck love
Strives to unite with that pure nature,
It finds the impenetrable shield opposed
    Of God's archangel.

Ah! keep her, keep her, let her not revisit
The skies to which she longs to rise;
Soon she may learn the magic language
    Of human love and sighs.

Then shall we see two souls rending the veils
Of night, rising like dawn, attaining heaven
    In one fraternal flight.
The watching mariner, expecting signs,
Shall see the track of their illumined feet,
    Eternal beacon-light!

" Can you make anything out of that? " said Amélie
to Monsieur du Châtelet, with a coquettish glance.

" They are verses such as we all make when we leave
college," replied the baron with a bored air, carrying

out his rôle of critic who must naught admire. " In my day we all went in for Ossianic mists — Malvinas, Fingals, cloudy apparitions, warriors issuing from their tombs with stars above their heads. To-day, these poetic fripperies are replaced by Jehovah, lyres, angels, wings of seraphim, the whole wardrobe of Paradise made over new with the words ' immense,' ' intellectual,' ' solitary,' ' infinite ; ' it is all a species of Christianized pantheism, enriched with a few chance rhymes found with difficulty and seldom correct. In short, poetry has changed latitudes ; instead of being in the North, as it once was, it is now in the East ; but the clouds and darkness are as thick as ever."

" If the ode is obscure," said Zéphirine, " the declaration seems clear enough."

" The shield of the archangel is evidently a thin muslin gown," remarked Francis.

Though politeness required that the audience should ostensibly consider an ode to Madame de Bargeton admirable, the women, furious at not having a poet of their own to call them seraphs, rose as if bored to death, murmuring in icy tones : " Very good indeed," " Very pretty," " Perfect."

" If you love me, you will not compliment either the the poet or his angel," said Lolotte to her dear Adrien, with the despotic air he was wont to obey.

" After all, they are only phrases," said Zéphirine to Francis ; " love is poetry in action."

" There, Zizine, you have said a thing I have often thought, but I could never have expressed it so delicately," remarked Stanislas, looking himself over from head to foot with a loving air.

"I don't know what I would n't give," said Amélie to du Châtelet, "if I could see Naïs' pride brought low ; the idea of allowing herself to be called an archangel, as if she were better than the rest of us, when really and truly she is dragging us down to the level of the son of an apothecary and a monthly nurse, with a grisette for a sister, and himself a journeyman printer."

Everybody seeemed to have agreed to mortify Lucien. Lili, the pious, said it would be charitable to warn Naïs, who was evidently very near committing a false step. Francis, the diplomatist, undertook the management of this foolish conspiracy, in which all these petty minds became eagerly interested as if it were the conclusion of a drama, and in which they foresaw many a tale to be gossiped over on the morrow. Francis, not at all desirous of fighting the young poet, who, under the eyes of his mistress, would surely resent an insulting word, saw plainly that he must murder Lucien with some weapon against which vengeance was impossible. He imitated the example of du Châtelet when it was a question of making Lucien recite his own poetry ; he went to the bishop, pretending to share his enthusiasm for the ode ; then he told him that Lucien's mother was a most superior woman, of extreme modesty, who inspired her son with all his compositions. Lucien's greatest pleasure, he said, was to see justice done to his mother whom he adored. This idea once inserted into the prelate's mind, Francis left the rest to accident and the chances of conversation. When he returned, followed by the bishop, to the circle surrounding Lucien, they found him still being compelled to drink the hemlock in little sips. The poor poet, who was totally ignorant of the ways of society, could only look at Madame de Bargeton and answer awkwardly the stupid questions which were put to him. He was ignorant of both the names and the qualities of the persons present; he did not know how to reply to women whose silly remarks gave him a sense of shame ; he could only feel himself a thousand miles away from those social divinities, who addressed him sometimes as Monsieur Chardon, and sometimes as Monsieur de Rubempré, while they called each other Lolotte, Adrien, Astolphe, Lili, Fifine. His confusion was extreme when, having mistaken Lili for a man's name, he called the brutal Monsieur de Sénonches, Monsieur Lili.

" Naïs must be blinded indeed to bring that little fellow here and introduce him to *us*," said Fifine, in a whisper.

"Madame la marquise," said Zéphirine, addressing Madame de Pimentel in a low voice, but contriving that others should hear her, " don't you see a strong likeness between Monsieur Chardon and Monsieur de Cante-Croix ? "

"The resemblance is ideal," replied Madame de Pimentel, smiling.

" Genius has seductions which we can openly acknowledge," remarked Madame de Bargeton to the marquise. " Some women fall in love with grandeur of soul as others do with pettiness," she added, letting her eyes rest on Francis.

Zéphirine did not understand the malice of this speech, for she thought her hero a great man, but the marquise ranged herself on Naïs' side by laughing at it.

"You are fortunate, monsieur — " said the Marquis de Pimentel to Lucien, catching himself up after saying Chardon, and substituting de Rubempré, " fortunate in never being bored."

" Do you work quickly ? " asked Lolotte, as if she had asked a cabinet-maker, " Does it take you long to make a box ? "

Lucien was completely dumfounded by this crushing question ; but he raised his head when he heard Madame de Bargeton answer, with a laugh : " My dear, poetry does not grow in Monsieur de Rubempré's head like the grass in the courtyard."

" Madame," said the bishop to Lolotte, " we can hardly feel too much respect for the noble spirits into which God casts his rays. Yes, poesy is a holy thing. To speak of poesy is to speak of suffering. How many wakeful nights were the cost of those stanzas you have just admired ! Let us bow in love before a poet who leads, I may say, always, a troubled life, but for whom God has reserved a place in heaven among his prophets. This young man is a poet," he added, laying his hand on Lucien's head ; " can you not see his fate upon that noble brow ? "

Happy in being thus gloriously upheld, Lucien bowed to the bishop with his sweetest smile, little thinking that the worthy prelate was about to strike him a fatal blow. Madame de Bargeton glanced round the hostile circle with triumphant looks, which burned themselves like arrows into the hearts of her rivals.

" Ah, monseigneur," replied the poet, hoping to smite those imbecile heads with his golden sceptre, "the vulgar herd has not your mind nor yet your charity.

Our pains are ignored ; no one comprehends our labor. The miner, extracting gold from the bowels of the earth, does not toil as we do, to tear our images from the most refractory of languages. If the end of poesy be to bring ideas to the precise point where all the world can see them and can feel them, the poet must incessantly run the gamut of all human intellects, so that he may meet and satisfy them all ; he must cover with glowing colors both sentiment and logic, — two powers antagonistic to each other ; he must inclose a world of thoughts in a line, sum up philosophies in a picture ; his poems are seeds which must fructify in hearts, finding their soil in personal experience. Must he not have felt all, to give all? and to feel all, is not that to suffer everything? Poems are born after painful journeys through vast regions of thought and solitude. Surely those works are immortal which have created beings whose life is more living than that of other beings who have lived and died, — Richardson's Clarissa, Chénier's Camille, the Delia of Tibullus, the Angelica of Ariosto, the Francesca of Dante, Molière's Alceste, Beaumarchais's Figaro, the Rebecca of Walter Scott, the Don Quixote of Cervantes."

" And what will you create for us?" asked Monsieur du Châtelet.

" Were I to lay claim to such conceptions I should give myself a brevet rank of genius," replied Lucien. " Such glorious travail needs long gestation, much experience of the world, the study of passions and human interests which I cannot yet have made. But I am beginning," he added bitterly, with a revengeful look around the circle. " The brain gives birth —"

"I fear your travail will be laborious," said Francis, interrupting him.

"Your excellent mother will assist you," said the bishop.

This unexpected turn of vengeance brought flashes of joy into the eyes of all present. Smiles of aristocratic satisfaction ran from mouth to mouth, increased by the imbecility of Monsieur de Bargeton, who laughed aloud.

"Monseigneur, you are too witty ; these ladies cannot understand you," interposed Madame de Bargeton, who stopped the laughing by that remark, and drew all eyes upon herself. "A poet who finds his inspiration in the Bible must regard the Church as his mother. Monsieur de Rubempré, repeat to us your 'Saint John at Patmos,' or 'Belshazzar's feast,' to show Monseigneur that Rome is, as ever, the *Magna parens* of Virgil."

The women exchanged smiles when they heard Naïs speaking Latin.

At the opening of life the bravest hearts are not exempt from discouragement. The blow sent Lucien to the bottom of the sea, but he struck on his feet and returned to the surface, swearing to dominate this clique. Like a bull pierced with darts, he sprang up furious, and was about to obey Louise by declaiming his "Saint John at Patmos, " when he saw that the card-tables had drawn away his audience, who fell back into their usual ruts, finding a pleasure there which poetry could not give them. The vengeance of so many mortified self-loves would not have been complete without the exhibition of negative contempt for indigenous poetry shown in this desertion of Lucien and Madame de Bargeton. They all put on a preoccupied air; one talked to the prefect of a new district road; another proposed to vary the amusement of the evening with music. The highest society in Angoulême, feeling itself a poor judge in the matter of poetry, was particularly anxious to obtain the opinions of the Pimentels and Rastignacs on Lucien's merits, and several put questions to them. The influence which the two families exercised in the department was always recognized on great occasions; they were envied, but they were also courted, for every one foresaw the possibility of needing their protection.

"What do you think of our poet and his poetry?" said Jacques to the Marquise de Pimentel, to whom he was paying attentions.

"Well, for provincial verses they are not so bad," she replied, smiling; "besides, such a handsome poet can do nothing ill."

Every one thought the verdict admirable, and went about repeating it with an infusion of more malice than the marquise had put into it. Du Châtelet was called upon to accompany Monsieur de Bartas, who murdered Figaro's grand air. The way once opened for music, the company was obliged to listen to a chivalric song, written under the Empire by Chateaubriand, and sung by du Châtelet. Then came duets on the piano, played by young girls, suggested by Madame de Brossard, who wished to put the talent of her dear Camille in a shining light before the eyes of Monsieur de Séverac.

Madame de Bargeton, wounded by the indifference shown to her poet, returned disdain for disdain by retiring to her boudoir while the music went on. She

was followed by the bishop, to whom the grand vicar
had explained the unintentional sarcasm of his speech,
and who was now very anxious to recall it. Mademoiselle de Rastignac, who had been really charmed
with the poetry, slipped in after them without her mother's knowledge. As Louise seated herself on the sofa,
to which she drew Lucien, she was able to whisper in
his ear, without being overheard : " Dear angel, they
have not understood you, but 'Thy verses are sweet;
I love to repeat them.' "

Lucien, comforted by this flattery, forgot his troubles
for the time being.

"There is no glory to be had without cost," said
Madame de Bargeton, taking his hand and pressing it.
"Suffer, yes, you must suffer, my friend, to be great,
and sufferings will be the price of your immortality.
Would that I too had a struggle to endure ! God keep
you from an enervated, sterile life without contests,
where the wings of the eagle find no space to spread.
I envy your trials, for at least you live ! you exercise
your strength ! you aspire to victory ! Your struggle
will end in fame. When you reach the imperial sphere
where great minds sit enthroned, remember those poor
souls whom fate has disinherited, whose intellect is
annihilated, suffocated, by moral nitrogen ; who have
to die knowing what life is, but never having lived it ;
whose eyes are keen, and yet see nothing ; whose sense
of smell is delicate, and knows no fragrance but that of
poisoned flowers. When you are famous, my friend,
sing of the plant that is wilting in the depths of a
forest, choked by.lichen, by rank vegetations, never
loved by the sun, dying without having flowered ! Ah !

it will be a poem full of dreadful melancholy, a subject for all imaginations. What a sublime conception would be the picture of a girl born beneath the skies of Asia, or, better still, a girl of the desert, transferred to a cold Western land, calling to her beloved sun, dying of incommunicable anguish, oppressed alike by cold and love! That would be the type of many an existence."

"It is the type of a soul that remembers heaven," said the bishop; "a poem that exists for ages; I find a fragment of it in the Song of Songs."

"Undertake it," said Laure de Rastignac, with artless belief in Lucien's genius.

"France is in need of a great sacred poem," said the bishop. "Believe me, fame and fortune are waiting for the man of talent who shall give his labor to religion."

"He will undertake it, monseigneur," said Madame de Bargeton, emphatically. "Do you not see the idea of that poem already dawning with auroral flashes in his eye?"

"Naïs is very rude to us," Fifine remarked; "what is she doing in there?"

"Can't you hear her?" replied Stanislas; "she is astride of her big words which have neither head nor tail to them."

Amélie, Fifine, Adrien, and Francis appeared at the door of the boudoir accompanied by Madame de Rastignac, who was searching for her daughter to take leave.

"Naïs," said the two women, delighted to break up the little conclave, "do please be so kind as to come and play us something."

"My dear child," replied Madame de Bargeton, " Monsieur de Rubempré is going to read us his ' Saint John at Patmos,' a magnificent Biblical poem."

" Biblical ! " repeated Fifine, amazed.

Amélie and Fifine returned to the salon bearing the word as food for sarcasm. Lucien, however, excused himself from repeating the poem on the ground of want of memory. When he re-entered the salon no one showed the slightest interest in him. The company were talking or playing cards. The poet was shorn of all his rays ; the landowners saw nothing to be made of him ; the men of pretensions feared him as a power hostile to their ignorance ; the women, jealous of Madame de Bargeton, the Beatrice of this new Dante (as the vicar-general called him), gave him cold, disdainful glances.

" So that is society ! " thought Lucien, as he returned to his suburban abode, circuitously, by the steps of Beaulieu ; for there are moments in life when we choose to take a roundabout way and encourage by motion a rush of ideas on the current of which we desire to float. Far from feeling discouraged, the anger of his rejected ambition gave Lucien fresh strength. Like all persons led by their instincts into a higher sphere which they reach before they know how to sustain themselves in it, he resolved to sacrifice everything to secure his footing in society. As he walked along he pulled out one by one the poisoned darts which had stabbed him ; he talked to himself aloud ; he abused the ninnies with whom he had to do ; he invented clever answers to the foolish speeches which had been made to him, and was furious with himself for having thought of them too late. When he reached the Bordeaux road which winds around the base of the mountain and follows the bank of the Charente, he thought he saw by the moonlight Eve and David sitting on a log beside the river, and he ran down a side path towards them.

IV.

AN EVENING BY THE RIVERSIDE.

WHILE Lucien was making his way to his torture at
Madame de Bargeton's, his sister was putting on her
pink cambric dress and her white straw hat and little
silk shawl, a simple apparel which made her seem
charmingly dressed — as often happens to persons in
whom natural dignity adds value to the slightest acces-
sory. So it happened that whenever she changed from
her working-dress to these simple clothes, she greatly
intimidated David. Though the printer was resolved
to speak to her of himself and his wishes, he found
nothing to say to his beautiful Eve as he gave her his
arm through the suburb of l'Houmeau. The two lovers
walked silently to the bridge of Sainte-Anne, in order
to reach the left bank of the river. Eve, who felt the
silence to be awkward, stopped at the middle of the
bridge to look at the river, which from that point to
where the powder-mills stand forms a long broad sheet
of water, on which the setting sun was just then casting a joyous trail of light.

"It is a beautiful evening!" she said, seeking a subject of conversation; "the air is so warm and yet so
fresh; the flowers smell so sweet, and what a sky!"

"It speaks to the heart," replied David, trying to
arrive at his love by analogy. "There is infinite pleas-

ure for hearts that love when the accidents of a landscape, the transparency of the atmosphere, the perfumes
of the earth echo the poetry in their souls. Nature
speaks for them."

"And loosens their tongues," said Eve, laughing.
"You were very silent as we crossed l'Houmeau; you
embarrassed me."

"I thought you so beautiful I could find no words,"
said David, naively.

"Am I less beautiful now?" she asked.

"No; but I am so happy in being allowed to walk
alone with you that —"

He stopped, quite confounded, and looked at the hills
beyond them.

"If you find pleasure in this walk I am very glad,"
said Eve. "I felt bound to give you a pleasure in exchange for the one you have sacrificed for me. In
refusing to go to Madame de Bargeton's you were as
generous as Lucien, when he risked the loss of her
favor by his request."

"I was not generous," said David, "I was only
wise. As we are alone under the skies, with none to
hear us but the reeds and rushes, let me tell you, dear
Eve, a few of the anxieties I feel as to Lucien's career.
After what I have just said to him my fears may strike
you, and I hope they will, as an excess of friendly solicitude. You and your mother have done your best to
raise him above his position; but in exciting his ambition have you not imprudently involved him in great
suffering? How can he maintain himself in the great
world for which you have encouraged his tastes? I
know him; his is a nature that loves the harvests with-

out the toil. The duties of society will take up his
time, and time is the capital of men who have no fortune but their intellect. He loves to shine ; the world
will excite desires which he will find it hard to satisfy ;
he will spend money, and earn none. You have taught
him to think himself a great man, but before society
admits any man's greatness he must attain to some
marked success. Now literary success cannot be won
except in solitude and by arduous toil. What can
Madame de Bargeton give your brother in return for
all the hours which he spends at her feet? Lucien is too
proud to accept support from her, and we know him
too poor to continue to live in her society, the cost of
which is ruinous. Sooner or later that woman will abandon our dear brother, after making him lose the habit
of work, after developing in him a taste for luxury,
a contempt for our sober life, the love of enjoyment,
and his natural tendency to idleness, — that debauchery
of poetic minds. Yes, I tremble lest his great lady
make a plaything of him. Either she loves him sincerely, and will make him forget everything and so ruin
his career, or she does not love him, and will make him
wretched ; for he is madly devoted to her."

" You chill me to the heart," said Eve, standing still
beside the river. " But so long as my mother has
strength for her hard business, and so long as I live,
the proceeds of our work may be enough for Lucien's
expenses, and will enable him to wait the time when
his success will begin. I shall never fail in courage,
for the thought of working for one I love takes all the
bitterness and all the weariness out of toil," added Eve,
brightening. " I am happy when I think who it is for

whom I work so hard — if indeed it is hard. Yes, don't be afraid; we can earn enough money to keep Lucien in the great world. His chances are all there."

"And his destruction," said David. "Listen to me, dear Eve. The slow execution of works of genius requires either the possession of a considerable fortune, or the sublime cynicism of a life of poverty. Believe me, Lucien has so great a horror of the privations of poverty, he has smelt the aroma of feasts and the fumes of success with such satisfaction, his self-love has been so fostered in Madame de Bargeton's boudoir, that he will risk all rather than fail; and the products of your labor will never meet his needs."

"Oh, you must be a false friend!" cried Eve, despairingly. "Otherwise, how can you so discourage me?"

"Eve! Eve!" replied David, "I want to be Lucien's brother. You alone can make me that. Then he could accept everything from me; I should have the right to devote myself to him with the saintly love you put into your sacrifices, but with more discernment. Eve, dear love, do that which shall give Lucien a support of which he need not be ashamed. A brother's purse will be like his own. If you only knew the thoughts which Lucien's new position suggests to me! Should he insist on going to Madame de Bargeton's the poor lad must cease to be my foreman; he cannot live here in the suburbs; you must not be a working-girl; your mother must give up her business. If you will consent to be my wife all these difficulties will be overcome. Lucien can occupy the second story over us while I build him an apartment of his own above the shed in the courtyard, unless my father could be persuaded to raise the house. We should thus enable him to lead a life free of care, an independent life. My desire to further Lucien's prospects will give me a courage to make my fortune which I might not have had for myself; but it all depends on you, you must authorize my devotion. Perhaps he will one day go to Paris, the only place where success for him is to be had, and where his talents will certainly be appreciated and rewarded. But life in Paris is dear, and it will take the efforts of all three of us to support him there. Besides, you need, and so does your mother, some one to rely on. Dear Eve, marry me out of love to Lucien. Later you will love me, perhaps, when you see my efforts to serve him and make you happy. We are both simple in our tastes, — we need but little ; Lucien's welfare will be our chief concern, and his heart the treasure-house where we will put fortune, feelings, sensations, everything ! "

" But conventions separate us," said Eve, deeply moved by the great love which counted itself for so little. " You are rich, and I am poor. It needs much love to overcome so great a difficulty."

" And you don't love me enough to face it? " said David, sadly.

" But your father would oppose it," she began.

"Good, good ! " cried David ; "if there is only my father to consider, you are my wife. Eve, dear Eve, you make life easy for me to bear from this moment. My heart has been heavy enough with feelings I could not express. Tell me only that you will love me a little, and I will find the necessary courage to speak to you of certain matters."

."You make me ashamed," she said; "but since we are now speaking our real feelings I will tell you that I never in my life thought of any one but you. You have always seemed to me a man to whom a woman might be proud of belonging; but how could I think that I, a poor work-girl without a future, should have such a future given to me?"

"Oh, enough, enough," he said suddenly, sitting down on the cross-piece of the weir near which they were standing.

"What is the matter?" she asked, expressing for the first time the tender solicitude women feel for those who belong to them.

"Nothing but good," he replied. "Seeing my whole life made happy, my head seemed to turn, my soul was overwhelmed. Ah! why should I be the happiest?" he said half sadly. "But I know."

Eve looked at David with a coquettish air of doubt which asked an explanation.

"Dear Eve, I receive more than I give. I shall always love you more than you love me, for I shall have more reason to love you, — you are an angel, I am a man."

"I am not so learned in the matter," replied Eve, smiling; "but I love you truly — "

"As much as you love Lucien?" he asked, interrupting her.

"Enough to be your wife, to consecrate myself to you and try to give you no pain in the life — often a little hard — which we shall live together."

"Did you know, dear Eve, that I loved you from the day we first saw each other?"

" What woman does not know when she is loved?"
Eve answered.

" Now I must remove your scruples about my wealth.
Eve, I am poor. Yes, my father took pleasure in ruining me ; he speculated on my work, like many other
pretended benefactors. If I ever become rich it will be
through you. That is not a lover's speech, it is the reflection of a thinker. I ought to let you know my
defects, which are great in a man obliged to make his
own fortune. My character, my habits, the occupations
which give me pleasure unfit me for everything which
is business and speculation, and yet we can become
prosperous only by applying ourselves to some form of
industry. I might perhaps discover a gold mine, but I
should be singularly incapable of working it. But you,
who have learned, out of love for your brother, to
attend to small details, who have a genius for management and economy, and the patient attention of a true
merchant, you will gather the harvest that I shall sow.
Our situation — for you know, dear, I have long found
a home in the bosom of your family — fills my heart
with such anxiety that I spend days and nights in thinking how to make a fortune for us all. My knowledge
of chemistry, and my observation of the needs of commerce have put me on the track of a lucrative discovery.
We may be pinched for a few years, perhaps, but I shall
end by finding the practical means of using that discovery which will bring us.a great fortune. I have said
nothing about it to Lucien ; his eager nature might
spoil all ; he would convert my hopes into realities, and
live as a great lord and perhaps run in debt to do so.
Therefore keep my secret. Your dear and sweet com-

panionship can alone comfort me under the trials I see before me, just as the hope of enriching you and Lucien will give me constancy and a firm will."

" I was certain," said Eve, interrupting him, " that you were one of those inventors to whom a wife is necessary — as in the case of my poor father."

"Then you love me ! Ah, say it to me fearlessly, — to me who see in your name the symbol of my love. Eve was the only woman in the world, and what was materially true for Adam is morally true for me. My God ! do you love me ? "

" Yes," she said, lengthening the simple syllable by the way she pronounced it, as if to picture the extent of her feelings.

" Then let us sit down here," he said, leading her to a large log lying near the wheel of a paper-mill. "Let me breathe the evening air and listen to the tree-frogs, and watch the moonlight trembling on the water; let me grasp the nature in which I see my happiness as in a book ; it appears to me to-night for the first time in all its splendor, lighted by love, made beautiful by you. Eve, my dear love, this is the first moment of happiness, unalloyed, which fate has given me. I doubt if Lucien can ever be as happy as I am."

Feeling Eve's moist and trembling hand in his, a tear fell from David's eyes.

" Am I to know the great secret? " asked Eve in a coaxing tone.

" You have a right to, for your father busied himself with the same question, which is now becoming a serious one ; and I will tell you why. The fall of the Empire will make the use of cotton in place of linen almost universal on account of its cheaper price. At the present moment paper is made with rags of flax and linen, but these are dear, and their cost checks the great impetus which the French printing-press must inevitably feel. Now the production of rags cannot be forced. Rags depend on the use of linen, and the population of a country will use only a certain quantity. This quantity will increase only through an increase in the number of births. If, therefore, the need of paper is greater than the supply of rags produced by France, it becomes necessary, in order to keep paper at a low price, to find a means of manufacturing it from some other product than linen rags. This reasoning rests on a fact that is now occurring here. The paper manufacturers of Angoulême, the last who are making paper from linen rags, see that the use of cotton cloth is taking the place of that of linen with alarming rapidity."

In reply to a question of Eve, who knew but little of the subject, David gave her much information on the subject of paper-making, which may not be out of place in a work the material existence of which owes as much to paper as it does to print. But this long parenthesis between a lover and his mistress will not lose by being slightly abridged.

Paper, a product not less marvellous than the printed impression of which it is the base, had long been fabricated in China at a time when, by the subterranean paths of commerce, it reached Asia Minor, where, tradition says, a paper made of cotton, soaked and reduced to pulp, was in use about the year 750. The necessity for finding a substitute for parchment, the cost of which was excessive, led to the discovery, through an imitation of the "bombycian paper" (the name given to this cotton paper of the East), of the linen-rag paper, some say at Bâle in 1170 by Greek refugees ; others think at Padua in 1301 by an Italian named Pax. This paper was brought to perfection slowly and obscurely ; but it is certain that under Charles VI. a pulp for playing-cards was manufactured in Paris. After the Immortals, Faust, Coster, and Guttenberg had invented THE BOOK, artisans, forever unknown like so many of the great artists of that period, adapted paper-making to the needs of typography. In the vigorous and simple-minded fifteenth century, the names of the different sizes of papers, like the names given to types, bore the impress of the naïveté of the times. The Raisin, Jésus, Colombier, the "papier Pot," the Écu, Coquille, and Crown, took their respective names from the grape, the image of our Lord, the dove, crown, and pot, — in short, from the water-mark in the centre of each sheet ; where, in Napoleon's time, they stamped an eagle and called the paper by that name. In like manner the types were named Cicero, Augustine, Gros-Canon, from the liturgical and theological works and the treatises of Cicero, for which those types were first used. Italics were invented by the Aldini in Venice ; hence the name. Before the invention of machine-made paper, the length of which is unlimited, the largest sizes were the "Grand-Jésus" and the "Grand-Colombier," the latter being used only for maps and engravings. In fact, dimensions of printing-paper were regulated by that of the bed of the press. At the time when David was telling Eve these facts the manufacture of paper of continuous length was still problematical in France, though Denis Robert of Essonne had invented, in 1799, a machine for making it, which Didot-Saint-Léger afterwards perfected. Glazed white paper, invented by Ambroise Didot, only dates back to 1780. This rapid glance at paper-making shows incontestably that all the greatest acquisitions of industry and intellect are made with extreme slowness and by imperceptible accretions, as in the processes of nature. To attain perfection, writing, and also language, have groped their way with as many delays as typography and paper-making.

" Rag-pickers have collected throughout Europe old linen and the fragments of every kind of tissue," said David, ending his account. " These remnants, carefully sorted, are stored by the wholesale rag-dealers, who supply the paper-makers. To give you an idea of this business, mademoiselle, I must tell you that in 1814 the banker Cardon (owner of the mills at Buges and Langlée, where Léorier de l'Isle tried in 1776 to solve the problem which your father studied so long) had a lawsuit with a man named Proust about an error of two millions of pounds of rags in a matter of ten millions, representing four millions of francs. The manufacturer cleanses the rags and reduces them to a clear pulp, which is made to pass, exactly as a cook passes her sauces through a sieve, over an iron frame, the inside of which is filled with a metallic sheet, in the middle of which is the stamp of the mark which gives its name to the paper. The size of the ' form ' depends on the size of the paper. When I was an apprentice with the Didots, they were much concerned with this very matter, and so they are still ; for the perfection at which your father aimed has become in our day an imperious necessity. And I will tell you why. Though the lasting qualities of linen, compared to those of cotton, make linen in the long run as cheap, or cheaper, than cotton, yet, as the difficulty with the poor is to draw the immediate price from their pockets, they prefer to pay less rather than more, and so lose enormously in virtue of the *væ victis.* The bourgeois class follow the poorer classes in this. Consequently, the supply of linen rags is beginning to fail. In England, where cotton has taken the place of linen among three fourths of the population, they now make only cotton paper. This paper, which had, at first, the defect of tearing and splitting, is so easily dissolved in water that a pound of it, put to soak, would turn into liquid in a quarter of an hour, whereas a pound of the linen paper might stay in water two hours without change. The latter could be dried and ironed, and though rather yellowed, the text would still be readable and the work not destroyed. We have come to a period where fortunes are greatly diminished by equalization; every one is poorer; we now demand cheaper linen and cheaper books, just as we now want small pictures for want of space for larger ones. The result is that shirts and books don't last. Solidity and strength in manufactured products are disappearing everywhere. Therefore the problem now to be solved is of the greatest importance to literature and to science and politics. A lively discussion, at which I was present, took place one day in the Didot office as to the ingredients used in China for making paper. There, thanks to the supply of raw material, paper-making has from its earliest stages attained a perfection which ours has never reached. A

9

great deal was said on this occasion about Chinese
paper, and how our own could n't compare with it for
lightness and delicacy, — precious qualities which do not
hinder it from having substance, for, thin as it is, it is
never transparent. A corrector of the press, — there are
many learned correctors in Paris; Fourier and Pierre
Leroux are at this moment correcting in the printing-
offices of Lachevardière, but this was the Comte de
Saint-Simon, a proof-reader for the time being, — he
happened to come to the Didot office in the midst of the
discussion.   He told us that, according to Kempfer and
du Halde, brushwood supplied the Chinese with the
vegetable matter of their paper.   Another corrector declared that the material of Chinese paper was chiefly
animal, made from silk, which is very abundant in
China.   A bet was made in my presence.   As the
Didots are printers to the Institute, the matter was
naturally referred by them to certain members of that
learned assembly.   Monsieur Marcel, formerly director
of the Imperial printing-office, was chosen umpire, and
he sent our two proof-readers to the Abbé Grozier,
librarian of the Arsenal.   The latter decided that both
sides had lost the bet.   Chinese paper, the abbé said,
was not made of either silk or brushwood; its substance came from the fibres of the bamboo.   The Abbé
Grozier owned a Chinese book iconographic and also
technological, in which were numerous sketches exhibiting the manufacture of paper in all its phases; and he
showed us strips of bamboo piled in a heap in one of
these drawings.   When Lucien told me that your father,
with the sort of intuition which belongs to men of
genius, had foreseen a means of substituting for linen

rags a vegetable-matter that was extremely common
and could be used in the form of raw material, I began
to classify all the tentatives of my predecessors, and to
study the question seriously. The bamboo is a reed ;
I naturally thought of our own native reeds. Hand-
labor costs nothing in China, only three sous a day.
Therefore the Chinese are able, when they take their
paper from the ' form,' to lay it, sheet by sheet, between white porcelain slabs, well-heated, by means of
which they press it and give it the lustre, substance,
lightness, and satiny texture, which make it the best
paper in the world. Well, the thing to do was to discover a way of mechanically replacing the hand-labor
of the Chinese ; it can be done by machinery so as to
bring down the price to the same cheap cost. If we
succeed in producing a paper of the Chinese quality at
a low price, we shall diminish by more than half the
bulk and weight of books. A bound Voltaire, which
now weighs, in our heavy white paper, two hundred and
fifty pounds, will then weigh about fifty. That is certainly a great gain. The space required for libraries is
becoming a question of difficulty, especially in these
days when the tendency of men and things is to reduce
all compass, even in architecture. All the great man-
sions in Paris are gradually being demolished ; there
are no longer any fortunes in keeping with the fine old
dwellings of our forefathers. What a shame for our
century to be manufacturing books that will not last.
Another ten years and Holland paper, that is to say,
paper made of linen thread, will be a thing unknown !
Now, your brother communicated to me your father's
idea of using certain fibrous plants in the manufacture

of paper, and therefore, you see, if I succeed, you have
a right to — "

At this point, Lucien, having seen them from the
road, ran down to join them and silenced David's generous proposal.

" I don't know whether you have had a pleasant
evening," he said ; "to me it has been a dreadful one."

" My poor Lucien, what has happened ? " asked Eve,
noticing the excitement in her brother's face.

The angry poet related his grievances, pouring into
these loving hearts the flood of thoughts that assailed
his own. Eve and David listened in silence, grieved at
the torrent of distress, which showed an equal amount
of grandeur and of pettiness in the sufferer.

" Monsieur de Bargeton," said Lucien, concluding his
tale, " is an old man likely to be taken off any day by an
indigestion. I will bring those proud persons to submis-
sion by marrying Madame de Bargeton. I saw in her
eyes to-night a love that is equal to my own. Yes, she
felt my wounds, she calmed my sufferings ; she is as
grand and noble as she is beautiful and gracious. No,
she will never betray me! "

" Is not this the moment to promise him an easier
life ? " whispered David to his love.

Eve pressed his arm silently, and David, understanding her thoughts, hastened to tell Lucien all their plans.
The lovers were as full of their hopes as Lucien was of
his ; so eager were they to make their dear brother a
sharer in their happiness that Eve and David did not
notice the start of surprise with which the lover of Madame de Bargeton received the news of his sister's
betrothal to David. Lucien, who had been dreaming of

a fine alliance for Eve, when he himself had attained a position (meaning thereby to prop his ambition by the help of some powerful family), was shocked at the idea of a marriage which, it seemed to him, would put one more obstacle in the way of his social success.

" Madame de Bargeton might consent to be Madame de Rubempré, but she will never agree to be the sister-in-law of David Séchard ! " That sentence is a net formula of the thoughts that now tortured Lucien's heart. " Yes, Louise was right," he said to himself, bitterly ; " men with a great future before them are never understood by their own families."

If the news of the betrothal had reached him at any other moment than this, when he had killed off Monsieur de Bargeton with so much ease, it would have made him jump for joy. He would then have reflected on his actual situation and seen the probable fate of a beautiful and portionless girl, and the marriage would have seemed to him an unhoped-for good fortune. But he was now in the world of golden dreams, where youthful heroes astride of an " if " can jump all barriers. He had just beheld himself in fancy, mastering that insolent society, and to fall so soon into reality was cruel indeed. Eve and David only thought that their brother, overwhelmed by generosity, was unable to speak. To these noble hearts a silent acceptance showed the truest friendship. The printer began to picture with cordial, tender eloquence the happiness in store for all four of them. In spite of Eve's interjections, he furnished the new home with a lover's luxury ; with ingenuous good faith he built his second story for Lucien's benefit, and kept the room over the shed for Madame Chardon, to whom he intended to give a son's support. In short, he made every one so happy and his brother so independent that Lucien, charmed by his voice and by Eve's caresses, forgot, in that balmy atmosphere beside the calm and moonlit river, and beneath the starry skies, the wounding crown of thorns which society had thrust upon his head. Monsieur de Rubempré returned to his natural thoughts of David. The mobility of his character threw him back into the sentiment of the pure, work-day, bourgeois life of the family. He saw it beautified by the coming marriage, and himself released of cares. The echoes of the aristocratic world receded from him, so that when the trio reached the suburb the ambitious poet pressed his brother's hand and announced himself in unison with the happy lovers.

" Provided your father does not object to the marriage," he said to David.

" As if he cared one way or the other about me ! The old man lives for himself. But I shall go to Marsac to-morrow and see him, if only to get him to make the improvements we want to the house."

David accompanied the brother and sister to their home, where they found Madame Chardon, from whom he asked the hand of Eve with the eagerness of a man who could bear no delay. The mother took her daughter's hand and placed it in that of David joyfully, and the lover thus emboldened kissed the forehead of his beautiful Eve, who smiled at him and blushed.

" This is the betrothal of poor people," said the mother, raising her eyes as if to implore the blessing of God. " You have plenty of courage, my son," she

said to David ; " for misfortune is with us, and I tremble lest it be contagious."

" We shall be rich and happy," said David, gravely.
" For one thing, you shall no longer go out nursing ;
you must come and live with your daughter and son in
Angoulême."

The three young people hastened to tell their astonished mother of their charming plans, giving free rein
to one of those gay family talks in which young hearts
delight in gathering every seed, and in tasting, by an-
ticipation, every joy. It was necessary at last to turn
David out of doors ; he would fain have made that
evening eternal. It was striking one in the morning
when Lucien accompanied his future brother-in-law as
far as the Porte Palet. The worthy Postel, uneasy at
these extraordinary doings, was standing behind his
blinds ; he had opened his window and when he saw the
lights at this late hour in Eve's apartment, he said to
himself, " Something strange is happening at the
Chardons'."

" My lad," he said when Lucien returned, " is anything the matter? Can I be useful?"

" No, monsieur," answered the poet, " but as you
are such a friend I will tell you the secret; my
mother has just granted my sister's hand to David
Séchard."

For all answer Postel shut his window violently, in
despair at not having already asked for Mademoiselle
Chardon himself.

Instead of returning to Angoulême, David took the
road to Marsac. He walked along on his way to see
his father and reached the enclosed field adjoining

the house just as the sun was rising. The lover presently saw on the other side of the hedge beneath an almond tree the head of the old bear.

" Good morning, father," said David.

" Dear me ! is that you, boy? What chance has brought you here at this hour? Come in that way," said the old man, pointing to a little iron gate. " My vines are all through flowering, not a shoot frozen ! There 'll be twenty puncheons to the acre this year ; but then, just see how it was manured."

" Father, I came to speak of an important matter."

" Did you? well, how go the presses? you ought to be earning loads of money."

" I shall earn it, father : but for the present at least I am not rich."

" They tell me here I put too much manure," said the father. " These bourgeois, or rather Monsieur le marquis, Monsieur le comte, and Monsieur this, that, and the other, insist that I spoil the quality of the wine. What 's the good of education? only to muddle your brains. Just listen : those gentlemen get eight or ten puncheons to the acre, and sell them at sixty francs a puncheon ; which comes, at the most, to four hundred francs an acre in the good years. I get twenty puncheons, and sell at thirty francs. Who 's the silly there, I 'd like to know? Quality ! quality ! what do I care about quality? They can keep their quality to themselves ; as for me quality is francs. What were you going to say ? "

" I am going to be married, father, and I came to ask you —"

" Ask me ! for what? nothing at all, my lad. Marry

if you like ; I consent. But as for giving you anything, I have n't a penny for myself. For the last two years farming and taxes and expenses of all kinds have ruined me ; the government takes all. For the last two years we poor vineyard-owners have made nothing. This is n't a bad year so far, and yet my rascally puncheons won't bring more than eleven francs ; it is really working for the caskmakers. Why do you marry before the harvest ? "

" Father, I only came to ask your consent."

" Oh, very good, that 's another matter. Who is it that you are going to marry, if I may ask ? "

" Mademoiselle Eve Chardon."

" Who is she ? "

" The daughter of the late Monsieur Chardon, the apothecary at l'Houmeau."

" And so you marry a girl of the suburbs, — you, a bourgeois, printer to the king in Angoulême ! This comes of education ! Yes, yes, send our sons to school, indeed ! I suppose she 's rich, my boy ! " said the old fellow, with a sly look at his son. " If you marry a girl from the suburbs she ought to have hundreds and thousands. So much the better, she 'll pay my rent. Do you know, my lad, that it is now two years and three months since you have paid it, and that 's two thousand seven hundred francs that you owe me ; it will come in handy to pay for my puncheons. If you were not my son I should make you pay interest on it, for, after all, business is business. But I 'll let you off this time. Well, how much has she ? "

" The same that my mother had."

The old man was about to say : " She had only ten

thousand francs!" But remembering that he had refused all accounts to his son, he exclaimed: "Then she
has nothing!"

"My mother's fortune was her beauty."

"Go to the market and see what you'll get for
them! Heavens! what misery fathers do lay up for
themselves in sons. David, when I married I had a
paper cap on my head and two arms with which to
make my fortune. I was a poor bear; while you, with
the fine printing-office I *gave* you, and your chances
and acquaintances, you ought to marry a town bour-
geoise with thirty or forty thousand francs. Give up
this nonsense, and I'll marry you well. There's a
widow here, about thirty-two years old, keeps a flour-
mill, with a hundred thousand francs if she has a penny;
that's what you want. Her property and Marsac join
each other; we shall have a fine domain, and I'll manage the whole. They do say she is going to marry
Comtois, her head man, but you are better worth having. I'll look after the mill while she shows off at
Angoulême."

"Father, I am pledged."

"David, you don't understand business, and you'll
be ruined; you are very near it now. If you marry
that girl from l'Houmeau your accounts with me must
be settled; I shall summon you to pay up the rent, for
I see no prospect of your doing better. Ah! my
poor presses! my poor presses! Nothing but a good
year with the vines can console me for this."

"Why, father, I have never given you any cause of
annoyance."

"You have never paid any rent," said his father.

" I came to ask you," said David, " not only to consent to the marriage, but to help me to raise the second story of your house, and put a room over the shed."

" Not a bit of it! I have n't a sou, and you know that very well. Besides, it would be throwing money into the sea; what interest would it pay me? Ha, ha! so you got up at cock-crow to come out here and ask me to undertake buildings that would ruin a king. Though I did name you David, I have n't the treasures of Solomon. You 're crazy! or else they changed my son at nurse — There 's one that will bear well," he said, interrupting himself to show a vine-shoot to David; " that 's a child that won't betray the hopes of its parents; manure it, and you get your profits. Now look at me; I put you at the lyceum; I have paid enormous sums to have you educated; I apprenticed you to the Didots; and all this fine show ends in your giving me for a daughter-in-law a girl from the suburbs without a penny to clothe herself. If you had never studied, if you had stayed here under my own eye, you 'd have behaved to please me, and you 'd marry the widow with a hundred thousand francs besides the mill. Ha! and all your cleverness is worth is to make you believe I shall reward your fine feelings by building a palace for you! One would suppose, to hear you, that none but pigs had lived in that house for two hundred years, and that your girl from the suburbs was too fine to sleep in it. Hey, hey, the queen of France, is she?"

" Well, father, then I shall build the second floor at my own cost, and it will be the son who enriches his father," said David. " It seems to upset the order of things, but it does happen sometimes."

"How's that, my lad? Do you mean to say that you have got the money to build when you can't pay your rent? You scamp, you are cheating your father."

The question thus presented was difficult to answer, for the good man was delighted to get his son into a position which enabled him to give no help, and yet appear fatherly. David got nothing out of him except his consent to the marriage and permission to make the improvements he wanted to the house. The old bear, a type of the old-fashioned father, made it a favor not to exact the rent, and not to take from his son every penny he had managed to lay by, the existence of which he was foolish enough to let his father know. The poor fellow returned home sad enough ; he saw plainly that if misfortune ever happened to him he could not count upon his father's help.

Society in Angoulême rang with the bishop's speech and Madame de Bargeton's reply. The slightest events in that gossiping world were so distorted, exaggerated, and embellished that the poet became a hero for the time being. A few echoes from the upper sphere where the storm was raging reached the bourgeoisie. When Lucien passed through Beaulieu, on his way to Madame de Bargeton's, he could see the envious observation with which certain of the young men watched him, and he overheard a few sentences which puffed him up with pride.

"There's a fortunate young man," said a lawyer's clerk named Petit-Claud, Lucien's former schoolmate, towards whom he was in the habit of taking a patronizing air, and who was very ugly.

" Yes, that's true," said a young sprig of family who had been present at the reading ; " he's a handsome fellow and talented, and Madame de Bargeton is quite crazy about him."

" The handsomest woman in Angoulême is his," was another speech which stirred his vanity to its depths.

He impatiently awaited the hour when, as he knew, he could see Louise alone. He felt that he must make that woman, whom he now regarded as the arbiter of his fate, accept Eve's marriage. After what had taken place the evening before, Louise, he believed, would be more tender, and her tenderness might lead to his perfect happiness. He was not mistaken ; Madame de Bargeton received him with a gush of feeling which seemed to this novice in love a touching proof of the progress of passion. She allowed her poet, who had suffered so deeply the night before, to kiss her beautiful golden hair, her hands, her eyelids.

" If you could but have seen your face while you were reading ! " she said to him. " Sparks were emitted by those beautiful eyes ! I saw the golden chains by which all hearts are hung to poet lips issuing from that dear mouth. You will read me the whole of Chénier, will you not? he is the poet of lovers. Ah ! you shall suffer no more, I will not let you ! Yes, dear angel, I am the oasis in which you shall live your poet life, — active, inert, indolent, laborious, meditative, — all in turn. Never forget that if your laurels are due to me they are to me the noblest indemnity for the sorrows of my life, past and to come. Poor dear! the world will not spare you any more than it has spared me ; it takes its revenge for the joys it cannot share. My world is jealous, it envies me ; did you not see that yesterday? Those flies thirsting for blood hastened to suck it from the stings they gave. But I was happy, I lived at last ! It is a long, long time since my heart-strings sounded."

Tears ran down her cheeks. Lucien took her hand, and for all answer kissed it repeatedly. The vanity of the poet was flattered and coaxed by this woman as it had long been by his mother and sister and David. Every one who came about him assisted in heightening the imaginary pedestal on which he placed himself. Encouraged in his proud beliefs by all, by the jealousy of enemies as much as by the flattery of friends, he walked in an atmosphere of mirage. Youthful imaginations are so naturally influenced by praise and the sound of their own glory, all things do so concur and hasten to serve a handsome youth with a future shining before him, that it takes more than one cold and bitter lesson to dissipate such illusions.

" My beautiful Louise, you will be my Beatrice, — but a Beatrice who will let me love her?" he said, passionately.

She raised her beautiful eyes which she had kept lowered and said, contradicting her words with an angelic smile, " If you deserve it — later. Are you not happy? To obtain a heart that is all your own, to be able to feel yourself utterly understood — is not that happiness? "

" Yes," he answered, in the tone of a baffled lover.

" Child ! " she said, laughing at him. " Come, what were you going to tell me? you came in quite absorbed about something, my Lucien."

Lucien timidly confided to her David's love for his sister, that of his sister for David, and the projected marriage.

"Poor Lucien!" she said; "did he fear to be whipped and scolded as though it were he who was marrying? What do I care for your family, to whom you are an exception. If my father married his servant-woman you would not be unhappy. My dear child, lovers are alone, apart; their families are nothing to them. Have I any other interest in the world than my Lucien? Become great; win fame; that is your business — and mine."

Lucien was made the happiest man in the world by this selfish answer. Just as he was listening to the highflown reasons with which Louise was proving to him that they were alone together in the world Monsieur de Bargeton entered. Lucien frowned and seemed embarrassed; Louise made him a sign and begged him to stay to dinner and read André Chénier to her afterwards, till the usual guests and card-players arrived.

"You will give pleasure not only to Madame de Bargeton but to me," said her husband. "Nothing suits me better than to hear reading after dinner."

Flattered by Monsieur de Bargeton, cajoled by Louise, served by the servants with the respect they show to those who are in favor with their masters, Lucien remained at the Hôtel de Bargeton in all the enjoyment of the life-interest of a fortune. By the time the salon became full of guests he felt so secure in the crass stupidity of Monsieur de Bargeton and in the love of his beautiful mistress that he assumed an all-conquering air, which Louise encouraged. He tasted the delights

of Naïs' own despotism, which she made him share. In
short, during this evening he succeeded in playing the
part of the hero of a small town. Observing this new
attitude on Lucien's part several persons supposed that
he was, as they say, on the closest terms with the mistress of the house. Amélie, who had come with Monsieur du Châtelet, corroborated these suspicions in a
corner of the salon where the envious and the jealous
had congregated.

"Pray don't make Naïs responsible for the vanity of
a little young man who is puffed up with pride at finding himself in a society he could never have expected
to enter," said du Châtelet. "Don't you see how that
young fool mistakes the gracious speeches of a woman
of the world for advances. He does n't know how to
distinguish the silence which covers a passion from the
encouraging language which his beauty, youth, and
talent have naturally won for him. It would be too
hard on women if they were counted guilty of all the
desires they inspire. He is certainly in love, but as for
Naïs — "

"Oh, Naïs!" said the treacherous Amélie. "Naïs
is delighted with his passion. At her age the love of a
young man is bewitching! a woman becomes a girl
again, and puts on moral scruples and shy manners,
and nobody calls it ridiculous. But just see how the
son of an apothecary gives himself airs in Madame de
Bargeton's house."

"Love knows no distance," sang Adrien.

The next day there was not a single house in Angoulême where the question of the exact amount of intimacy between Monsieur Chardon, alias de Rubempré,

and Madame de Bargeton was not discussed. Guilty at the most of a few kisses, society accused them already of criminal happiness. Madame de Bargeton paid the penalty of her royal position. Among the oddities of social life have you never remarked the caprice of its judgments and the whimsicality of its requirements? There are persons to whom society grants the utmost license ; they may do the most unreasonable things ; in them everything is considered becoming, and that is what really justifies their actions. But there are others whom society combines to treat with extraordinary severity ; they are required to do right in everything ; never to be mistaken, never to fail, never to commit the smallest folly ; one might liken them to those admired statues which are taken from their pedestals and put away in winter lest the frost should crack a finger or chip a nose ; they are not allowed to be human ; they are expected to be perpetually perfect and divine. A single glance from Madame de Bargeton to Lucien counted for more than a dozen years of mutual happiness between Zizine and Francis. A pressure of the hand between the two lovers was about, as we shall presently see, to draw all the thunderbolts of the department on their heads.

10

V.

CATASTROPHES OF PROVINCIAL LOVE.

DAVID had brought from Paris a few savings, which he now proposed to use for the expenses of his marriage and the costs of building a second floor to his father's house. To enlarge that house was really, he thought, to benefit himself; sooner or later the house must come to him, and his father was then over sixty-eight years of age. He accordingly set to work on the apartment, building it of wood so as not to overweight the present walls of the old house. He took delight in decorating and furnishing the rooms on the first floor, where his beautiful Eve was to spend her life. It was a time of mirth and happiness without alloy to the two friends. Lucien, though disgusted with the mean proportions of provincial life, and weary of the sordid economy which made a five-franc piece a matter of immense importance, nevertheless endured without one complaint the close calculations of poverty and its privations. His gloomy melancholy was changed into a radiant expression of hope. He saw a star glittering above his head; he dreamed of a noble existence, basing his happiness on Monsieur de Bargeton's grave, — that gentleman having at times great difficulty with his digestion, and the happy mania of considering that an undigested dinner could be cured by a supper.

About the beginning of September Lucien ceased to be David's foreman ; he was Monsieur de Rubempré, lodged magnificently in comparison with the wretched garret in which " that little Chardon " had lived at l'Houmeau. He was a man of the suburbs no longer ; he lived in the upper part of Angoulême and dined three or four times a week with Madame de Bargeton. The bishop had taken a fancy to him, and he was often invited to the palace. His occupations now classed him among personages of the upper sphere ; in short, he was considered in a fair way to take his place among the distinguished men of France. Certainly, as he walked about his pretty salon and charming bedroom and study, arranged with so much taste, he might comfort himself for drawing thirty francs a month from the hard-earned wages of his mother and sister ; for he now saw every prospect that the historical romance at which he had been working for two years (" The Archer of Charles IX.") and a volume of poetry (entitled " Daisies ") would spread his name through the literary world and bring him sufficient money to pay back his indebtedness to his mother and sister and David. So, finding himself actually elevated, and listening for the echo of his name in the future, he accepted all their present sacrifices with superb confidence ; he smiled at his straits, and even enjoyed these last throes of poverty.

Eve and David had made their brother's happiness take precedence of theirs. Their marriage was delayed by the time the workmen took to finish the second floor ; in every respect Lucien's affairs were their first consideration. Any one who knew Lucien would not have been surprised at this devotion ; he was so fascinating,

his manners were so winning, he expressed his desires so charmingly, that he won his cause before he
even spoke of it. This fatal gift has been the ruin of
more young men than it ever benefited. Accustomed
to the consideration their sweet youth wins, relying on
the protection which society selfishly grants to those who
please it, just as it gives alms to a beggar who awakens
a sentiment, many of these children of a larger growth
enjoy their privilege and gain no advantage from it.
Deceived as to the real meaning and value of these
social relations, they fancy that the same smiles will
follow them through life ; and they find themselves bare,
bald, ragged, without worth or fortune, when, like old
coquettes and worn-out clothes, society leaves them in
the lurch at the door of a salon or consigns them to the
dust-hole. Eve had advocated the delay, partly because she wanted to prepare as economically as she
could the supplies necessary for the young household.
What could two lovers refuse to a brother who, seeing
his sister hard at work would say, in accents that came
from his heart: "Would that I could sew!" The
grave, observing David was a sharer in this devotion.
Nevertheless, ever since Lucien's success with Madame de Bargeton he was uneasy at the transformation
which was taking place in the poet; he saw that he
was in danger of despising a middle-class life. Wishing to test him, David would occasionally contrive to
put him between the family joys of home and the pleasures of the great world, and when it happened that Lucien sacrificed the enjoyments of his vanity David would
cry out joyfully : " There, they have not corrupted
him !" Several times the three friends and Madame

.Chardon made pleasure excursions, as they do in the provinces ; they went to walk in the woods which surround Angoulême and border the Charente ; they dined on the grass with provisions which David's apprentice brought to a certain place at a certain hour ; they came home at night, a little weary perhaps, and having spent but three francs. On great occasions when they dined at what was called a "restaurât" (a sort of country restaurant between the tavern of the provinces and the "guinguette," of Paris) they went to the extravagance of five francs, equally divided between David and the Chardons. David was infinitely grateful to Lucien for forgetting during these country holidays the gratifications he had at Madame de Bargeton's and the sumptuous dinners he enjoyed in her world ; for by this time every one was inviting the great man of Angoulême.

It was at this conjunction of affairs, when almost nothing was wanting to the establishment of the new household, and while David had gone to Marsac to invite his father to the wedding, hoping that when the old man saw his daughter-in-law he would contribute to the cost of arranging the house, that an event occurred which, as it happened in a small town, completely changed the face of things.

Lucien and Louise had a close spy in du Châtelet, who watched with the persistence of hatred mingled with passion and avarice for an occasion to expose them. Sixte wanted to make Madame de Bargeton commit herself. He took the part of her humble confidant ; but though he pretended to be Lucien's friend in her presence, he undermined him elsewhere. He obtained familiar entrance to Naïs' house, for she no longer distrusted her old admirer. But du Châtelet expected too much of the lovers, who continued to be strictly Platonic. There are, in fact, passions which start out well or ill, as it happens. Two persons plunge into sentimental tactics and talk instead of acting, and manœuvre in the open without ever coming to a siege. They contrive to surfeit both themselves and their desires with nothingness. Before long they reflect, and they judge. Often passions which have taken the field bravely accoutred, flags flying, and ardent for conquest, end by coming back without a victory, disarmed, ashamed, and altogether foolish at so much vain display. These mishaps are sometimes caused by the timidity of youth, and by the temporizations indulged in by women in their first love affairs ; for such deceptions are never practised by either coxcombs who know the business or coquettes accustomed to the manœuvres of allurement.

Provincial life is singularly antagonistic to the contentments of love, but it favors the intellectual discussion of passion ; moreover, the obstacles which it opposes to the tender intercourse of lovers are liable to drive ardent souls into extremes. The life is based on such minute and constant observation and such absolute transparency in all private affairs, it allows so little consoling intimacy without its virtue making an outcry, the purest relations are so unreasonably criticised that many women are held in provincial circles to be guilty who are really innocent. Some of them then regret that they never enjoyed the pleasures of a wrong the penalties of which are put upon them. Society, which blames or criticises without serious examination the facts which end a long and secret struggle, is often the original

cause of the crime; but most persons who declaim
against the so-called scandals provoked by women unjustly calumniated never think what the actual cause of
their final determination may have been. Madame de
Bargeton was about to find herself in the singular position of such women, who are not lost until after society
has unjustly accused them. The obstacles that are met
with at the beginning of a passion alarm inexperienced
persons; and those that our present lovers encountered
were very like the threads with which the Lilliputians
shackled Gulliver. A multiplicity of nothings made all
movement impossible and checked all violent desires.
Madame de Bargeton, for instance, was always visible.
If she had simply closed her doors at the hours when
Lucien was with her she might as well have fled with
him at once. It is true that she received him in a
boudoir, to which he was now so used that he thought
himself its master, but the doors were scrupulously left
open. All was virtuous to the last degree. Monsieur
de Bargeton roamed about the rooms like a beetle,
without the least idea that his wife would prefer to be
alone with Lucien. If he had been the only obstacle
Naïs could easily have sent him away or otherwise occupied him; but she was always overwhelmed with visitors, and they swarmed all the more now that their
curiosity was awakened. Provincials are naturally fond
of teasing; they like to annoy a dawning emotion.
The servants went and came about the house without
being summoned, a habit acquired at a time when their
mistress had nothing to conceal. To change the habits
of her household would be to admit a passion of which
Angoulême was still in doubt. Madame de Bargeton

could not set foot outside her own door without the whole town knowing where she went. To walk alone with Lucien in the environs would have been a decisive measure ; on the whole it was less dangerous to shut herself up with him at home. If Lucien had stayed one moment after midnight in the salon without other company all Angoulême would have chattered of it the next day. Therefore, within and without her own doors Madame de Bargeton lived in public. These details are representative of provincial life ; sins are either known or impossible.

Louise, like other women, led away by a passion without experience of such matters, saw one by one the difficulties of her position, and was frightened by them. Her alarm reacted on the amorous discussions which occupied the few delightful hours when she and Lucien were alone. Madame de Bargeton had no country-house to which she could carry her beloved poet, as many women, under various clever pretexts, bury themselves for a time. Tired of living in public, driven to extremities by the tyranny of society, the yoke of which was harder than her love was sweet, she bethought herself of Escarbas, and was meditating a visit to her old father, so irritated was she by the many annoyances in her way.

Châtelet did not believe in so much innocence. He discovered the hours at which Lucien went to the house, and would follow in a few minutes, usually accompanied by Monsieur de Chandour, the most indiscreet man of the coterie, whom he would send into the room before him, hoping that his eyes would see and his tongue report some questionable situation. His own rôle was

the more difficult, because he wished to remain neuter
and make others play the drama. In order to hood-
wink Lucien, whom he flattered, and Madame de Bargeton, who did not lack perception, he attached himself
apparently to the jealous Amélie. The better to spy on
Louise and Lucien he set up an argument with Monsieur de Chandour on the nature of their relations.
Du Châtelet insisted that Madame de Bargeton was
merely amusing herself; that she was much too proud
and too well-born to condescend to the son of a chemist.
This show of incredulity belonged to his part, which
was that of a defender. Stanislas, on the other hand,
maintained that Lucien was a successful lover. Amélie
spurred on the discussion because she really wanted to
know the truth. Each side gave his reasons. As often
happens in little towns, the intimates of the house of
Chandour would break in upon these conversations.
The adversaries would then seek partisans, asking opinions of the new-comers. Thus Madame de Bargeton and
Lucien were constantly before the minds of the coterie.
One day du Châtelet made the remark that whenever
he and Monsieur de Chandour called on Madame de
Bargeton and found Lucien there there was nothing at
all suspicious in their conduct to each other; the door
of the room was always open, the servants were going
and coming, there was nothing that mysteriously inti-
mated the charming crime of love. Stanislas, who was
not without a certain quantum of stupidity, fell into the
trap, and resolved to enter the next day on the points
of his toes, and Amélie encouraged him.

The next day Lucien happened to be in one of those
moods when young men tear their hair and swear to

themselves that they will not continue any longer in
the mortifying position of a supplicant. By this time
he had grown used to his privileges. The poet who
had timidly taken a chair in the sacred boudoir of the
queen of Angoulême was now metamorphosed into an
exacting lover. It had taken six months to make him
feel himself her equal ; he was now determined to be
her master. Accordingly he left home, resolved to be
perfectly unreasonable, even to the point of risking
his future ; he meant to employ all the resources of in-
flammatory eloquence ; to say that his mind was leaving
him, that he was growing incapable of thinking a
thought or writing a verse. Some women have a horror
of doing anything deliberately which does honor to
their delicacy ; they may yield to sudden temptation,
but not to agreement. As a general thing, no one likes
a regulated pleasure. Madame de Bargeton noticed on
Lucien's brow, in his eyes, in his whole countenance,
and in his manners, the excited air which betrays the
formation of a resolution ; and she resolved, partly in a
spirit of contradiction, and partly out of a really noble
sense of love, to baffle him. Exaggerating everything
as she did, she exaggerated the value of her own favors.
To her eyes, Madame de Bargeton was a sovereign, a
Beatrice, a Laura. She took her seat, as in the middle-
ages, under the dais of a literary tournament, and Lucien was only to win her after multiplied victories ; he
was to emulate and excel " l'enfant sublime," Lamartine, Walter Scott, Byron. As a noble woman, she
considered her love a vital principle ; the desires with
which she inspired Lucien were to be the incentive which
should lead him to fame. This female Don Quixotism

is a sentiment which gives to love its consecration ; it utilizes, it magnifies, it honors it. Firmly resolved to play the part of Dulcinea to Lucien's life for half a dozen years or more, Madame de Bargeton wished, like a good many other provincial women, to subject her lover to a species of servitude, during which time she could judge of his constancy.

When Lucien had opened the battle by one of those sulky exhibitions of temper at which a woman who is still free laughs, and none but those who are deeply in love are grieved, Louise assumed an air of dignity and began one of her long speeches, larded with pompous words.

" Is this what you have promised me, Lucien?" she said, in conclusion. " Do not put into so sweet a present a remorse which would poison my future life. Do not spoil that future. And — I say it with pride — do not spoil the present. Have you not my heart? What else do you need? Can it be that your love is influenced by the senses, when the noblest privilege of a beloved woman is to silence them? For whom do you take me? Am I no longer your Beatrice? If I am not more to you than a mere woman, then I am less than one."

" You could not say anything else to a man whom you did not love," cried Lucien, angrily.

" If you do not feel how much of deep, true love there is in my ideas, you are not worthy of me," she replied.

" You pretend to doubt my love to avoid replying to me," said Lucien, flinging himself at her feet in tears.

The poor lad really wept at seeing himself outside

the gates of Paradise. They were the tears of a poet who feels his power humiliated, the tears of a child to whom the toy it longs for is refused.

" You have never loved me ! " he cried.

" You do not believe what you say," she replied, flattered by his violence.

" Then prove to me that you are mine," said Lucien, beside himself.

Just then Stanislas arrived without being heard, saw Lucien half-kneeling, half-lying, the tears in his eyes, and his head on Naïs' knees. The tableau was satisfactory and sufficiently suspicious ; Stanislas turned hastily back to du Châtelet, who stood at the door. Madame de Bargeton sprang forward, but not in time to reach the spies, who retired precipitately, as if ashamed of their indiscretion.

" Who came in just now ? " she called to the servants.

" Monsieur de Chandour and Monsieur du Châtelet," said Gentil, her old footman.

She returned to the boudoir, pale and trembling.

" If they saw you as you were I am lost," she said to Lucien.

" So much the better ! " cried the poet.

Louise smiled at this selfish exhibition of his love.

In the provinces, such an adventure is certain to be magnified in the telling. In the twinkling of an eye every one knew that Lucien had been caught at Naïs' knees. Monsieur de Chandour, delighted with the importance such an affair was sure to give him, went first to the club with the great news and then on a round of visits. Du Châtelet hastened to say that, for his part, he had seen nothing ; but by putting himself thus aside he only incited Stanislas to talk the more, and to enlarge on details, adding something new at each relation. In the evening the whole social world of Angoulême flocked to Amélie's salon ; for by that time the most exaggerated versions were circulating through the aristocratic portion of the town, where each narrator had followed the example of Stanislas. Men and women were impatient to know the truth. The women who veiled their faces and cried shame were precisely Amélie, Zéphirine, Fifine, and Lolotte, who were themselves more or less smirched with illicit loves. The theme was varied in many keys.

" Well," said one, " that poor Naïs, you have heard about it? For my part, I don't believe the story ; she has an irreproachable life before her ; she is much too proud to be anything but Monsieur Chardon's patroness. But if it is really true, I do pity her with all my heart."

" She is all the more to be pitied," said another, " because the thing is so frightfully ridiculous ; she might be Monsieur Chardon's mother ; he can't be more than twenty-two, and Naïs, between ourselves, is n't a day less than forty."

" For my part." said du Châtelet, " I think the very situation in which Monsieur de Rubempré was seen proves Naïs' innocence. We don't go down on our knees to get that we have already had."

" That's as it may be ! " said Francis, with a frisky look, which earned him a reproving glance from Zéphirine.

" But tell us all about it," they said to Stanislas, forming a conclave in a corner of the room.

Stanislas had ended by composing a little tale full of improprieties accompanied by gestures and attitudes which fatally incriminated the pair.

" It is inconceivable ! " said one.

" At twelve o'clock in the day ! " said another.

" Naïs was the last woman I should have suspected."

" What will she do now ? "

Then followed commentaries and suppositions without number. Du Châtelet defended Madame de Bargeton, but so clumsily that he fanned the fire of gossip instead of extinguishing it. Lili, full of pious grief at the fall of the Angoulême angel, went in tears to report the affair to the bishop. When the whole town was undeniably in an uproar, the successful du Châtelet went to the Bargetons' and found only one table of whist. He asked Naïs, diplomatically, if she would not rather sit in the boudoir, where, accordingly, they took possession of the sofa.

" Of course you know," he said in a low voice, " what all Angoulême is talking of ? "

" No, I do not," she said.

" Well, then," he rejoined, " I am too much your friend to leave you in ignorance. I must give you an opportunity to deny these calumnies, invented, no doubt, by Amélie, who has the presumption to consider herself your rival. I came to see you this morning with that ape Stanislas, who was a few feet in front of me when he reached the door," pointing to that of the boudoir ; " and he insists that he *saw* you with Monsieur de Rubempré in a situation which prevented his entering the room. He turned back to me quite alarmed and dragged me away, without giving me time to think.

We had reached Beaulieu before he told me the reason of his hasty retreat. If I had known it in time I should not have left the house, and the matter could have been cleared up on the spot; but to come back later would have proved nothing in your defence. Now, whether Stanislas saw wrong, or whether he is right, is not the question; he must be *put in the wrong.* Dear Naïs, don't let your life, your future, your honor be at that fool's mercy. Silence him instantly. You know my situation here. Though I need the support of everybody, I am solely yours. Dispose of a life which belongs to you. Though you have repulsed my wishes my heart is ever yours; and on all occasions I only seek to prove to you how I love you. Yes, I watch over you like a faithful servant, without hope of recompense, solely for the pleasure I find in serving you, even without your knowing it. This morning I have said everywhere that I, too, was at the door of your salon and saw nothing. If any one asks you who told you of this gossip, make use of my name. I shall be only too proud to be your public defender, but, between ourselves, Monsieur de Bargeton is the only man who ought to demand an explanation from Stanislas. That little Rubempré may have committed some folly, but if so the honor of a woman ought not to be at the mercy of any heedless young fellow who flings himself at her knees."

Naïs thanked du Châtelet with an inclination of her head, but was silent and pensive. She was weary and disgusted with provincial life. At du Châtelet's first words her thoughts turned to Paris. The silence became embarrassing to her wily adorer.

" Dispose of me as you will, — I repeat it," he said.

" Thank you," she answered.

" What shall you do? "

" I will think about it."

Long silence.

" Do you really love that little Rubempré ? "

She smiled a superb smile, crossed her arms and looked at the curtains of her boudoir. Du Châtelet took his leave without being able to decipher the heart of the haughty woman. When Lucien and the four old gentlemen who had come to play their whist, regardless of the problematic gossip, had departed, Madame de Bargeton stopped her husband as he bade her good-night before going to bed.

" Come here, my dear, I want to speak to you," she said, with a sort of solemnity.

Monsieur de Bargeton followed his wife into the boudoir.

" Perhaps I am wrong," she said, " to have put such warmth into my protection of Monsieur de Rubempré, for it has been as ill-understood by the foolish people of this town as by Lucien himself. This morning he flung himself at my feet and made me a declaration of love. Stanislas came in at the moment when I was raising the foolish lad. Disregarding the duty of courtesy which a gentleman owes to a woman under all circumstances, he declares that he found me in an equivocal situation with that young man, whom I was really treating as he deserved. If the rash youth were to hear the calumnies to which his folly has given rise, he would, I am convinced, insult Stanislas and force him to fight a duel. Such an action would be a public avowal of his love. I need not tell you that your wife is pure; but you can easily see there would be something very dishonoring both for you and for me in Monsieur de Rubempré undertaking to defend me. Go yourself to Stanislas and ask him seriously for an explanation of the insulting things he has said about me; and do not let the affair be smoothed over until he retracts what he has said in presence of numerous and important witnesses. You will thus obtain for yourself and for me the respect of all decent people; you will behave like a man of intelligence and a gallant man; you will have every right to my esteem. I will send Gentil on horseback to l'Escarbas and summon my father, who must be your second. Notwithstanding his age, I know him to be a man who would trample under foot the puppet who dares to blacken my reputation. You will have the choice of arms; take pistols, for I am told you are an excellent shot."

"I will go," said Monsieur de Bargeton, taking his hat and cane.

"Ah, my friend," said his wife, much moved, "you are what men should be, what I love in a man, — you are a gentleman."

She offered him her brow, and the old man kissed it, proud of the privilege. This woman, who felt a sort of maternal sentiment for that grown child, could not repress her tears as she heard the *porte-cochère* close behind him.

"How he loves me!" she said. "The poor man clings to life, and yet he would lose it without regret for my sake."

Monsieur de Bargeton did not trouble himself about

11

meeting his adversary on the morrow and coldly facing the muzzle of a pistol; no, he was harassed by only one thing; he trembled as he went his way to Monsieur de Chandour at the thought, "What shall I say to him? Naïs ought to have told me what to say;" and he puzzled his brains to construct a speech which should not be ridiculous.

But those who live, like Monsieur de Bargeton, in a silence imposed by the narrowness of their minds and their want of outlook, do possess in the great crises of life a solemnity made to hand. Speaking seldom, they seldom say foolish things; reflecting much on what they ought to say, their extreme self-distrust leads them to study their words so carefully that they often express themselves as aptly as Balaam's ass. Monsieur de Bargeton now behaved himself like a very superior man. He justified the opinion of those who regarded him as a philosopher of the school of Pythagoras. He went to see Stanislas at eleven o'clock that night, and found a large party assembled at his house. He bowed silently to Amélie, and bestowed on the rest of the company, his vacant smile, which, under existing circumstances, seemed to them profoundly ironical. Then came a hushed silence, as in nature before a storm. Châtelet, who had gone there after leaving Naïs, looked significantly from Monsieur de Bargeton to Stanislas, whom the offended husband treated in the first instance politely.

Du Châtelet fully understood the meaning of a visit made at an hour when the old man was usually in bed. Naïs was evidently moving that feeble arm; and as du Châtelet's position in the Chandour household gave him a right to meddle in its affairs he rose, took Monsieur de Bargeton aside, and said, " Do you wish to speak to Stanislas ? "

" Yes," said the worthy man, glad of an interme- diary who would perhaps do the talking for him.

" Well, then, go into Amélie's bedroom, and I will send him to you," said du Châlelet, excited at the prospect of a duel, which might make Madame de Bargeton a widow, and prevent her from marrying Lucien, the cause of it.

" Stanislas," he said to de Chandour, " Bargeton has no doubt come here to ask you to give him satis- faction for the things you have been saying about Naïs. Come into your wife's room and behave, both of you, like gentlemen. Don't have any loud talking, affect politeness, — in short, assume the coldness of Britannic dignity."

Stanislas and du Châtelet went together into the room.

" Monsieur," said the offended husband, " if you do not retract your offensive speeches in presence of the company now assembled in your house I shall request you to choose your second. My father-in-law, Mon- sieur de Nègrepelisse, will call upon you to-morrow morning. The affair can only be settled in the manner I have just indicated. I am the offended party, and I choose pistols."

On his way thither Monsieur de Bargeton had rumi- nated over this speech. the longest he had ever made in the whole course of his life, and he made it without passion and in the simplest manner. Stanislas turned pale, and thought to himself. " What did I see, after all ? " But between the shame of denying his words

before all the world in presence of this dumb man who
could not see a joke, and fear, the hideous fear which
took him by the throat with scorching hands, he chose
the danger which seemed at the moment farthest off.

" Very good," he said. " To-morrow we will settle
it." hoping in this way that something might turn up to
arrange matters peacefully.

The three men returned to the salon, where the whole
company studied their faces ; du Châtelet smiled, Monsieur de Bargeton was absolutely the same as usual,
but Stanislas had turned livid. Seeing this, several
women guessed the upshot of the conference. The
words "They will fight!" ran from ear to ear. Half
the company thought Stanislas to blame, his pallor and
the discomposure of his face seemed indicative of falsehood ; the other half admired Monsieur de Bargeton's
demeanor. Du Châtelet played the grave and the
mysterious. After remaining a few moments and examining the faces of the company Monsieur de Bargeton withdrew.

" Have you any pistols?" whispered du Chatelet to
Stanislas, who trembled from head to foot.

Amélie understood the whole matter and was taken
ill ; the women present took her to her bedroom. Great
excitement prevailed ; everybody talked at once. The
men stayed in the salon and declared with unanimous
voice that Monsieur de Bargeton had the right of it.

" Who would have thought him capable of behaving
thus ? " said Monsieur de Saintot.

" But in his youth," said the pitiless Jacques, " he
was one of the best men of his day with weapons. My
father has often told me of his exploits."

" Pooh! put them at twenty paces and they are certain to miss each other if you give them cavalry pistols," said Francis to du Châtelet.

When the company had dispersed, du Châtelet reassured Stanislas and his wife by explaining how all could be made to go well, and that a duel between a man of sixty and one of thirty-six was certain to end in favor of the latter.

The next morning, while Lucien was breakfasting with David, who had returned from Marsac without his father, Madame Chardon came in quite terrified.

" Lucien! do you know what has happened? the news is all over the market. Monsieur de Bargeton almost killed Monsieur de Chandour this morning at five o'clock in Monsieur Tulloye's field. It seems that Monsieur de Chandour said he surprised you yesterday with Madame de Bargeton."

" It is false! Madame de Bargeton is innocent," cried Lucien.

" A countryman whom I heard giving the details saw the affair from his cart. Monsieur de Nègrepelisse was there as Monsieur de Bargeton's second ; he told Monsieur de Chandour that if anything happened to his son-in-law he must fight him next. An officer in a cavalry regiment lent his pistols, and Monsieur de Nègrepelisse tried them several times. Monsieur du Châtelet wanted to prevent his trying them, but the officer whom they chose as umpire said that unless they meant to behave like children the weapons they used ought to be in good condition. The seconds placed the two adversaries twenty-five paces apart. Monsieur de Bargeton, who was walking about quite unconcerned, fired first and put a ball in Monsieur de Chandour's throat, who fell without being able to return the fire. The surgeon of the hospital has since declared that Monsieur de Chandour will have his neck awry for the rest of his days. I came to tell you the result of the duel so that you may not go to Madame de Bargeton's, or show yourself in Angoulême, for the friends of Monsieur de Chandour will certainly try to pick a quarrel with you."

Just then Gentil, Monsieur de Bargeton's footman, brought the following note to Lucien, who read it hastily and slipped it into his pocket : —

"You have doubtless heard, my dear friend, the issue of the duel between my husband and Monsieur de Chandour. We receive no company to-day ; be prudent, do not show yourself in society ; I ask this in the name of the affection which you bear to me. Do you not feel that the best use you can make of this sad day is to come and listen to your Beatrice, whose life is completely changed by this event, and who has many things to say to you? "

"How fortunate," remarked David, "that my marriage is fixed for the day after to-morrow ; this will give you a reason for not going to Madame de Bargeton's."

"Dear David," replied Lucien, "she wishes me to go to her to-day ; I think I ought to obey her, for she must know better than we can how I ought to behave under existing circumstances."

"Is the house quite ready? " asked Madame Chardon.

"Come and look at it," cried David, delighted to show his mother-in-law the transformation he had made of the apartment on the first floor, where all was new and fresh. The very air gave forth the sweetness that fills a new-made home, where orange wreath and bridal veil still crown domestic life, where the springtide of love is reflected into things, and all is white, and fresh, and flowery.

"Eve will live like a princess," said the mother, "but you have spent too much money; you are very extravagant."

David smiled without answering, for Madame Chardon had unwittingly put her finger into a secret wound which made the poor lover suffer cruelly. The cost of his improvements had gone so far beyond his expectations that he had no money left with which to build the room above the shed. He could not therefore give his mother-in-law the apartment he had destined for her. Generous souls do suffer deeply when they cannot keep such promises which are, in a way, the little vanities of tenderness. But David was careful to hide his embarrassments so as to spare Lucien's feelings, thinking he might feel oppressed by the sacrifices his friend had made for him.

"Eve and her friends have been working too," said Madame Chardon. "The wedding clothes and the household linen are all ready. Her companions at the shop are so fond of her that without her knowledge they have covered all the mattresses in white fustian, edged with pink. It is very pretty! and makes one long to be married."

The mother and daughter had used their savings in supplying David's house with the things that young men do not think of. Knowing that he was buying luxuries (for there had been some question of a Limoges dinner-set) the two women had tried to make the things that they contributed in keeping with those that David bought. This little emulation of love and generosity had the result of involving the newly married pair and pinching them for want of means from the very beginning of their marriage, although they had all the outward appearance of middle-class competence, which might even pass for opulence in so backward a place as Angoulême.

No sooner did Lucien see his mother and David enter the bedroom, with its blue and white paper and the pretty furniture now well-known to him, than he slipped out of the house and hastened to Louise. He found her breakfasting with her husband, who, having gained an unusual appetite from his morning excursion, was eating his meal without a thought of what had happened. The old country-magnate, Monsieur de Nègrepelisse, an imposing figure, a relic of the French *noblesse*, was beside his daughter. When Gentil announced Monsieur de Rubempré the old man gave the latter the inquisitive glance of a father anxious to judge of a person his daughter patronized. Lucien's extreme beauty struck him forcibly, and he could not refrain from a look of approbation ; he seemed to regard the intimacy in the light of a fancy rather than a passion, — a caprice, not a lasting attachment. Breakfast was over and Louise, rising, left her father with Monsieur de Bargeton, and signed to Lucien to follow her.

" My friend," she said, in a voice that was sad and also joyous, " I am going to Paris ; and my father is to take my husband to Escarbas, where he will stay during my absence. Madame d'Espard, a Demoiselle

de Blamont-Chauvry, who is a relation of mine through
the d'Espards, the elder branch of the Négrepelisse, is
very influential in society at the present time. If she
deigns to recognize us at all, I intend to cultivate her;
she can easily obtain a government position for Bargeton if she chooses. I think the court might be induced
to express a wish for him as deputy; if so, it would
help his nomination here. It is you, my dear child,
who have unconsciously brought about this change in
my existence. The duel of this morning obliges us to
close our house here for a time, because some persons
will side with Chandour against us. Under our present
circumstances, and living as we do in a little town, an
absence is always useful in giving time for hatreds and
prejudices to die out. Either I shall succeed in these
plans, and never return to Angoulême, or else I shall
not succeed; in which case I should prefer to remain
in Paris during the winters, and go to Escarbas every
summer. It is the only life that is suitable for a woman
of character and position, and I ought to have taken it
before. To-day will suffice for my preparations, and to-
morrow I start after night-fall. You will accompany
me, will you not? I would rather you left Angoulême
before me. I will pick you up between Mansle and
Ruffec, and we shall soon be in Paris. There, dear Lucien, is the only true life for superior minds. We shall
feel at ease among our equals: here we can only suffer.
Paris, the capital of the intellectual world, will be the
theatre of your success. Spring boldly across the inter-
vening space; do not suffer your ideas to turn rancid
in the provinces; seek communion now, at once, with
the great men of the nineteenth century. Come nearer

to the throne and to power. Distinctions and dignities never seek the genius that stagnates in the provinces. Name me any truly noble work that provincial life has nurtured. On the contrary, behold that poor, sublime Jean-Jacques, irresistibly drawn by the moral sun which creates all fame and awakens intellect by the friction of rivalries. Ought you not to hasten to take your place among the Pleiades of your day? You hardly realize as yet how useful it is for a youth of genius to be brought into the light of the highest society. I will introduce you to Madame d'Espard; it is difficult to obtain an entrance to her salon. You will meet there all the greatest personages of the day, ministers, ambassadors, orators of the Chamber, distinguished peers, and many rich and influential persons. A man must be awkward indeed if he fails to obtain their interest and good-will when he is handsome and young and full of genius. Great talents have no littleness about them; they will give you their support. When you personally attain a high position, your works will acquire enormous value. For all artists, the great secret to solve is how to get into the public eye. Paris, Lucien, under these circumstances, offers you a thousand opportunities for making your fortune, obtaining a sinecure, or a pension from the Privy-purse. The Bourbons wish to encourage letters and the arts; therefore make yourself the religious poet and the royalist poet whom they want. Not only is it *right* that you should be that, but it will make your fortune. Does the Opposition, does liberalism give places, pensions, rewards? have they ever been known to make the fortune of a writer? Therefore choose the wise path and come with me to Paris,

where all men of genius gather. I have told you my
secret; but be silent about it, and get ready at once
to accompany me — Do you not wish it?" she added,
presently, astounded at the silence of her lover.

Lucien, bewildered by the rapid glance he had thrown
towards Paris as he listened to her persuasive words,
thought he had never until that moment used more
than half of his brain; it seemed to him that he was
suddenly developing another half, so immensely were
his ideas magnifying themselves; he saw himself in
Angoulême like a frog under a stone in the middle
of a bog. Paris and its splendors — Paris, which is to
provincial imaginations an Eldorado — stood before him
with her robe of gold, a circlet of royal jewels in her
hair, her arms wide open to embrace all talent. Illustrious men would hail him as a brother. In the great
city all things smiled on genius. No jealous sprigs of
countrified nobility would humiliate a writer with sting-
ing words or dull indifference to poesy. After reading
a few pages of his "Archer of Charles IX." publishers
would open their cash-box, and say to him: "How
much do you want for it?" Moreover, the thought
came into his mind that after such a journey, when
circumstances seemed to marry them. Madame de Bargeton would certainly be his and they would live together.

To the words, "Do you not wish it?" he answered
by a tear, caught Louise round the waist, pressed her to
his heart, and crimsoned her neck by the violence of
his kisses. Then he stopped short suddenly, struck by
a thought, and exclaimed: "Good God! my sister is
to be married that very day."

That cry was the last utterance of his pure and noble

youth. The powerful ties which bind young hearts to
their family, to their earliest friend, to all their primitive emotions, were now to be cut through as by an axe.

" Will you tell me," said the haughty woman, "what
the marriage of your sister has to do with the progress
of our love? Are you so desirous of dancing at a workman's wedding that you cannot sacrifice such noble
joys? A fine sacrifice!" she said, contemptuously.
" I sent my husband to fight a duel on your account,
and these are your sacrifices for me! Leave me; I am
deceived in you."

She fell half-fainting on the sofa. Lucien followed
her, entreating pardon, inwardly cursing David, his
sister, his family.

" I believed in you!" she said. "Monsieur de
Cante-Croix had a mother whom he idolized, yet to
obtain a letter from me in which I said, ' I am content
with you,' he died under fire. And you, when I ask
you to travel with me, you cannot forego a wedding
feast!"

Lucien was ready to kill himself, and his despair was
so genuine, so profound, that Louise forgave him, making him feel, however, that he would have to atone for
his crime.

" Well, well," she said at last, "be very discreet,
and wait for me to-morrow at midnight a short distance
beyond Mansle."

Lucien walked on air; he returned to David's house
followed by his hopes as Orestes by the Furies, for he
foresaw a crowd of difficulties, all of which might be
summed up in the one word " money." David's clear-
sightedness alarmed him so much that he shut himself

up in his pretty study to recover from the giddiness his
new prospects gave him. Must he leave these rooms
arranged for him at such a cost? should he let the sacrifice be useless? Perhaps his mother could live there,
and David would thus economize the building he proposed to make above the shed. His departure would
certainly benefit his family. In short, he found a hundred reasons to encourage his flight, for there is nothing so jesuitical as a wish. Having reached this point
in his mental discussion he rushed to l'Houmeau to find
his sister and tell her of his prospects, and arrange his
plans with her. As he passed Postel's shop the thought
occurred to him that if he could not otherwise find
means he would borrow from his father's successor the
sum he needed.

"If I live with Louise," he said to himself, "five
francs a day will be a fortune to me, and that is only a
thousand francs a year. Now in six months I shall
be rich."

Eve and her mother listened, under promise of secrecy, to Lucien's confidences. They both wept as
they did so, and when the ambitious youth asked why
they were so distressed they told him that all their savings were absorbed in the household linen and Eve's
trousseau and other expenses, which they had been glad
to pay, because David had settled upon Eve a promised
dower of ten thousand francs. Lucien then told them
his idea of borrowing from Postel, and Madame Chardon agreed to go and ask the apothecary for a thousand
francs.

"But, Lucien," said Eve, with a tightening of the
heart, "if you go you can't be at my wedding. Oh!

come back; I'll wait a few days. She will let you
come back in a fortnight after you have taken her
there. She can surely let us have you for a week or
so. I know the marriage won't turn out well unless
you are here— But will a thousand francs be enough?"
she said, interrupting herself suddenly. "Though that
coat of yours fits you divinely, it is the only one you
have! You have only two fine shirts, the rest are all
coarse linen; you've only three cambric cravats, the
other three are common jaconet; and your handkerchiefs are not nice. You won't have a sister in Paris
to wash your linen in the morning when you want it at
night, and therefore you ought to have more changes.
You have only had one new pair of nankeen trousers
this year; those of last year have shrunk. You must
get some new clothes in Paris, and Paris prices are not
those of Angoulême. You have only two waistcoats
that are fit to wear— I have mended all the others. I
advise you to take two thousand francs if you can."

David came in just then and seemed to have heard
Eve's last words, for he looked at the brother and sister,
who stopped speaking.

"Don't hide anything from me," he said.

"Well," said Eve, "he is going to Paris with
Madame de Bargeton."

"Postel," said Madame Chardon, coming in at the
moment without seeing David, "agrees to lend us one
thousand francs, but for six months only, and he wants
a note indorsed by your brother-in-law, for he says you
have no security."

She turned at the moment and saw David, and all
four persons were silent. The Chardon family knew

how much they had imposed on David's generosity; they felt ashamed of it.

"Then you cannot be at my marriage," said David, "and you will not live with us! and I have spent every penny I had! Ah, Lucien, I was bringing Eve her poor little wedding jewels, little dreaming that I should regret having bought them;" and he pulled the cases covered with morocco from his pocket and placed them on the table before his mother-in-law.

"Why do you do so much for me?" said Eve, with a smile that corrected her words.

"Dear mamma," said David, "go and tell Postel that I will indorse the note, for I see by your face, Lucien, that you are resolved to go."

Lucien bent his head softly and sadly, saying a moment later, "Don't think hardly of me, dear angels." He put his arms round Eve and David, drew them close to his heart, kissed them, and added, "Wait results, and you will then know how I love you. David, what would be the good of all our great thoughts if we were not above the conventional laws which hamper sentiment? My soul will be with you wherever I am; thought will unite us. I have a destiny to accomplish. Publishers will certainly take my 'Archer of Charles IX.' and the 'Daisies.' Sooner or later I must have done what I am going to do now; could I have done it under more favorable circumstances? Am I not making my fortune by the mere fact of entering Paris under the auspices of the Marquise d'Espard?"

"He is right," said Eve. "You yourself told me he ought to go to Paris."

David took Eve by the hand and led her into the

narrow little closet in which she had slept for the last seven years. " You say he needs two thousand francs, dear love," he whispered, " and Postel will only lend him one thousand."

Eve looked at her lover with an expression of pain that told her inward suffering.

" Listen to me, my own Eve ; we are going to begin life in a poor way. Yes, my expenses have eaten up nearly all I owned. I have but two thousand francs left, and half of that sum is absolutely necessary to carry on the printing office. To give a thousand francs to your brother is to give away our own bread and risk our peace and comfort. If I were alone I know what I should do, but we are now two ; you must decide."

Eve, overcome, flung herself into her lover's arms, kissed him tenderly, and whispered, as her tears flowed : " Do as if you were alone ; I can work to make it up."

In spite of the warmest kiss the lovers had ever yet exchanged, David left Eve deeply depressed, and returned to find Lucien.

" You shall have the two thousand francs," he said.

" Go and see Postel," said Madame Chardon, " for you must both sign the paper."

When the two friends returned they found Eve and her mother on their knees praying. Though they knew how many hopes this departure might realize, they could only feel at such a moment what they lost in this farewell ; happiness to come was dearly paid for by an absence which would break into their lives and fill their minds with perpetual anxiety about Lucien.

" If you ever forget this scene," said David in Lucien's ear, " you will be the most unworthy of men."

˙ The printer felt, no doubt, that solemn words were necessary. He dreaded the influence of Madame de Bargeton as much as he feared the fatal mobility of nature, which was quite as likely to cast Lucien into evil as into good.

Eve soon made ready Lucien's baggage. This literary Fernando Cortes took little with him. He wore his best surtout and best waistcoat and one of his two fine shirts. All his linen and the famous dress-coat, his other property and his manuscripts made such a small package that, in order to hide it from Madame de Bargeton's eyes, David offered to send it by diligence to his correspondent, a paper-maker, to whom he wrote, requesting him to keep the package till Lucien called for it.

Notwithstanding Madame de Bargeton's precautions and her efforts to conceal her departure, Monsieur du Châtelet heard of it, and was determined to find out whether she was going alone or whether Lucien accompanied her. He sent his valet to Ruffec to examine all carriages which stopped there to change horses.

" If she carries off her poet," thought he, " she is mine."

Lucien started the following morning at daybreak, accompanied by David, who hired a horse and cabriolet on pretence of driving out to do some business with his father, — a trifling fib, which, under existing circumstances, was likely enough to be true. The two friends did go to Marsac, where they spent a part of the day with the old bear. In the evening they drove on beyond Mansle, where they awaited Madame de Bargeton, who arrived towards morning. When Lucien saw the

12

antiquated sexagenary carriage he had often noticed in the coachhouse, he experienced one of the keenest emotions of his life. He flung himself into David's arms; the printer pressed him to his heart and said: "God grant that this may be for your good."

David got back into the old cabriolet and drove away with an aching heart; for he had horrible presentiments as to Lucien's fate in Paris.

NOTE. — The next part of "Illusions Perdues" gives the history of Lucien's life in Paris. This, as already explained, will form the second volume of the translation. It is enough to say here that Lucien and Madame de Bargeton no sooner reached Paris than they were disillusioned of each other. In the glamour of the great city, Lucien thought Louise old and dowdy; Louise perceived that an intimacy with Lucien would hinder her social success. They parted immediately. Lucien then plunged into various phases of literary and journalistic life in Paris, the history of which, under the title of "A Great Man in the Provinces in Paris," will be the second volume of "Lost Illusions."

PART II.

EVE AND DAVID.

I.

A BRAVE WOMAN.

AFTER Lucien's departure David Séchard — that ox, courageous and intelligent as the one which painters give to the Evangelist — set to work to make the great and rapid fortune which he had desired, less for himself than for Eve and for Lucien, that evening when he sat with Eve beside the river and she gave him her hand and heart. To put his wife into the sphere of comfort and elegance in which she was formed to live, to support with a powerful arm her brother's ambition, such was the programme written before his eyes in letters of fire. The newspapers, politics, the immense development of book-making and literature and science, the tendency to public discussion of all the interests of the nation, the whole social movement which took place as soon as the Restoration was firmly established, would, he was confident, create a demand for paper tenfold greater than the celebrated Ouvrard estimated, on a like basis, at the beginning of the Revolution. But in 1821 the paper-makers had become too numerous in France for any one man to hope for a monopoly of the trade, such as Ouvrard had when he bought up the principal factories and all their output.

Besides, David had neither the boldness nor the capital for such speculation. Just at this time the machinery required to manufacture paper of all lengths was coming into use in England. Nothing, therefore, was more desirable than the discovery of some means of adapting the manufacture of paper to the needs of French civilization, which threatened to carry discussion into everything, and to rest on the perpetual manifestation of individual thought, — a great misfortune; for the peoples that deliberate most, act the least.

Therefore, strange to say, while Lucien was being caught into the great machine of journalism at the risk of tearing into shreds his honor and his intellect, David Séchard, in the depths of his provincial printing-office, was becoming connected with the movement of the periodical press in its material aspects. He wished to put the means of printing on a level with the ends towards which the spirit of the age was tending. In this his judgment was good, he saw clearly that a fortune was to be made by the manufacture of paper at a low price, and subsequent events have justified his foresight. During the last fifteen years the patent office has received more than a hundred applications from persons claiming to have discovered a substance for the manufacture of cheap paper. More certain than ever of the utility of his discovery (inglorious as it was, but promising vast profits), he became, after his brother-in-law started for Paris, entirely absorbed in the problem he wanted to solve.

As his resources were exhausted by the preparations

for his marriage and the money he had given to Lucien
for his journey to Paris, David found himself, from the
day he became a married man, in actual distress. He
had kept a thousand francs for the needs of the printing-
office, and he owed the note of a thousand francs to
Postel, the apothecary. To this profound thinker, the
problem was a two-fold one. He must invent, and invent quickly ; he must adapt the profits of his discovery
to the needs of his household and his business. Now,
how shall we characterize a brain capable of shaking off
the painful preoccupations which arose from a poverty
that must be concealed, from the wants of a family lacking bread, from the daily requirements of a business as
minutely exacting as that of printing, all the while
searching the realms of the unknown with the ardor of
a scientist in pursuit of a secret which, day after
day, escapes the most subtle researches? Alas ! as we
shall see, inventors have many ills to bear, not counting
the ingratitude of the masses, the idlers, and the inca-
pables, who say of a man of genius : " He was born to
be an inventor, for he can't do anything else. He is
not to be thanked for his discovery any more than a
man should be thanked for being born a prince ; he
merely exercises his natural faculties, and he finds his
reward in the work itself. "

Marriage is a cause of great perturbations both moral
and physical to a young girl, but when she marries in
the bourgeois conditions of the middle classes she has,
in addition, to study new interests, and to initiate herself in the management of affairs ; hence comes a phase
in her life when she necessarily is on the watch to learn
before she can act. David's love for his wife unhappily

retarded this education ; he dared not tell her the state
of things, neither on the morrow of their marriage, nor
on the following days. In spite of the great distress to
which his father's avarice condemned him, the poor
printer could not bring himself to spoil his honeymoon
by teaching Eve a sad apprenticeship to his laborious
trade, or by training her to the duties of a business
man's wife. Consequently, the thousand francs, their
only means, which ought to have carried on the printing-
office, went chiefly to support the household. David's
recklessness and his wife's ignorance lasted three
months ! The awakening was terrible. When Lucien's
note to Postel, which David had indorsed, fell due,
there was. no money to meet it, and the cause of this
debt was so well known to Eve that she insisted on
sacrificing her wedding jewels and all her plate.

On the evening of the day when the note was paid
by these proceeds Eve tried to make David talk to her
about his affairs. Since the second month of their marriage David had spent the greater part of his time
under the shed in the courtyard, in a little room which
was used to cast his rollers. Three months after he
had taken the printing-office from his father, he had
substituted for the pads then in use ink-tables, with
cylinders, which distribute the ink by means of rollers
made of thick glue and molasses. This first improvement was so undeniably good that as soon as the
Brothers Cointet saw the result they adopted it. David
had built against the party-wall which formed the back
of this species of kitchen a furnace, with a wide copper
pan or boiler, under pretence of burning less coal
in re-casting his rollers, the rusty moulds for which

were ranged along the walls and were never used twice.
Then he not only put a thick oaken door, lined inside
with sheet iron, to this room, but he took out the dirty
panes of the sashes and replaced them with fluted glass,
which let in the light, but prevented those outside from
observing his occupations.

The moment Eve spoke to her husband about their
future, he looked at her uneasily, and stopped her with
these words : —

" My dearest, I know what you must think at the
sight of that empty workroom and the sort of commercial annihilation which has come over the business ;
but look there," he added, drawing her to the window
of their bedroom and showing her his mysterious retreat ;
" our fortune is there. We shall have to suffer for a
few months, but let us bear it patiently ; leave me to
solve the industrial problem I told you about, which
will put an end to all our troubles."

David was so good, his unselfish devotion so well
deserved to be trusted on his word, that the poor wife,
anxious, like all women, about the daily costs of the
household and the expenses of the printing-house, resolved to save her husband from all such cares. The
next day she left the pretty blue and white room, where
she was in the habit of sitting at work on some feminine occupation, and went down into one of the two
wooden cages in the press-room, determined to study
the commercial system of typography. Was not this
true heroism in a woman already pregnant? During
the last few months David's stagnant press-room was
gradually emptied of workmen required until then for
the business, but who had now departed, one after the

other. Overwhelmed with custom, the Cointet Brothers
employed, not only the workmen of the department,
attracted to their establishment by the prospect of full
days' work, but also printers from Bordeaux, among
them apprentices who thought themselves clever enough
to shirk the conditions of apprenticeship.

When Eve began to examine into the resources of
the firm of Séchard she found only three persons employed there : first, Cérizet, the apprentice whom
David had brought from Paris ; then Marion, attached
to the house like a watch-dog ; and Kolb, an Alsacian,
formerly man-of-all-work at the Didots'. Drafted into
the army, Kolb had turned up in Angoulême, where
David saw him at a review about the time his military
service was ending. Kolb went to see David and took
a fancy to the stout Marion, finding that she possessed
all the qualities a man of his class wants in a wife, —
the vigorous health that colored her cheeks, the masculine strength which enabled her to lift a form of type
easily, the religious honesty of which Alsacians think
so much, the devotion to her masters which revealed a
natural goodness, and lastly, that spirit of economy to
which she owed the possession of a thousand francs
besides household linen, gowns, and clothes of provincial nicety. Marion, tall and stout and thirty-six years
old, was flattered by the attentions of a cuirassier nearly
six feet tall, well-made, strong as a bastion ; and she
naturally advised him to become a printer. By the
time the Alsacian received his final discharge, Marion
and David between them had made him a respectable
" bear," who was, however, unable to read or write.

The work which came to the office was not so abundant during the last three months but that Cérizet sufficed to set it up. Compositor, clicker, and foreman, Cérizet realized in his own person what Kant calls a phenomenal triplicity ; he composed, corrected his composition, wrote down the orders, made out the bills ; but, as he usually had little to do, he spent most of his time reading novels in his cage, awaiting customers who brought in advertisements, posters, or wedding-cards. Marion, trained by old Séchard, made up the paper, damped it, helped Kolb to print it, stretched it, pared it, all the while minding her cooking and going by daybreak to market.

When Eve obtained from Cérizet the accounts for the last six months, she found that the receipts had been six hundred francs. The expenses, reckoning the wages of Cérizet at two francs a day and those of Kolb at one franc, amounted also to about six hundred. Now, as the cost of material required for the work done amounted to over a hundred francs, it was clear to Eve that during the first six months of their married life David had lost the interest on the property, due to his father in rent ; also that of the value of his material and his license ; also the wages of Marion, and the cost of the ink, and of the mass of things expressed in a printing-office by the word "stuff," — a term derived from the cloths and silks used to make the pressure of the screw less severe on the type, by inserting a square of some stuff, called the "blanket," between the plate of the press and the paper.

After getting a general idea of the means of the establishment and its proceeds, Eve discovered how few resources and how little chance it had, sucked dry

as it was by the competitive activity of the Brothers
Cointet, who had gradually made themselves paper-
makers as well as journalists, licensed printers to the
bishopric, and suppliers to the town and the prefecture.
The " Journal of Advertisements " which the Séchards,
father and son, had sold to the Cointets for twenty-two
thousand francs, was now returning eighteen thousand
a year. Eve saw plainly enough the scheme hidden
under the apparent generosity of the Cointets, who left
the Séchard printing-office just enough work to keep it
alive, and not enough to injure them. She now took
the management of its affairs into her own hands, and
began by making an exact inventory of all its property.
Then she set Kolb and Marion and Cérizet to work to
clear up the press-room, clean it, and put it in perfect
order.

One evening, when David returned from an excursion
into the fields, followed by an old woman bearing an
immense bundle wrapped in cloths, Eve asked his advice as to what she should do with a quantity of rubbish
accumulated and left on their hands by his father;
promising to attend to all the affairs of the printing-
office herself, and not to trouble him. By his advice,
Madame Séchard took all the remnants of paper she had
found, and sorted and printed on them, in two columns
and on single sheets, a variety of those popular legends
which the peasants delight in pasting on the walls of
their huts ; such, for instance, as the " Wandering
Jew," " Robert-le-Diable," " La Belle-Maguelonne,"
and the narrative of certain miracles. Eve turned
Kolb into a peddler. Cérizet went to work at once and
set up the type of these artless sheets and their coarse

illustrations, from morning till night. Marion printed them off. Madame Chardon took charge of the household, for Eve was busy coloring the illustrations. In two months' time, thanks to Kolb's activity and honesty, Madame Séchard sold, in a circuit of thirty miles around Angoulême, three thousand sheets, which cost her thirty francs to make, and brought her in, at two sous a sheet, three hundred francs.

But when all the cottages and taverns were papered with these legends, some other speculation had to be thought of, for Kolb was unable to leave the department. Eve, who had fairly rummaged the printing-house, found a collection of figures used in printing an almanac, called the "Shepherds' Almanac," in which things are represented by signs, figures, images, engraved in red, black, or blue. Old Séchard, who himself was unable to read or write, had formerly earned a great deal of money out of this work, which was intended for persons who could not read. It was sold at a sou, and consisted of one sheet folded sixty-four times, making one hundred and twenty-eight pages. Delighted with the success of her legends, Madame Séchard undertook the "Shepherds' Almanac" on a larger scale, putting her profits into it. The paper of this almanac, of which many millions of copies are sold annually in France, is coarser than that of the "Almanac Liégois," and costs about four francs the ream. When printed, this ream, which contains five hundred sheets, brings in, at a sou a sheet, twenty-five francs. Madame Séchard resolved on using one hundred reams for a first edition, which made fifty thousand almanacs to sell, and a profit of two thousand francs to earn.

However absorbed an inventor may be, David was surprised, as he glanced at his press-room, to hear the presses groaning, and to see Cérizet always standing and composing under Madame Séchard's direction. The day when he entered the room to give an eye to Eve's enterprises was one of triumph for the young wife, for he fully approved of everything and thought the idea of the almanac excellent. He promised his advice in the employment of inks of various colors, necessitated by the designs of the almanac, which spoke only to the eye. In fact, he offered to recast the rollers himself in his mysterious workshop, so as to help his wife as much as he could in her great little enterprise.

About this time letters began to arrive from Lucien describing his disappointments and distress in Paris, and the three hundred francs which Eve, Madame Chardon, and David combined to send him were a pure offering of their life's blood. Overcome by this news and distressed at earning so little in return for such labor and courage, Eve looked forward, with some dread, to an event which crowns with happiness a new-made home. Knowing herself on the point of becoming a mother, her mind was full of the one thought: "If my dear David does not succeed in his search before my confinement, what will become of us? who will manage the new business of the poor printing-office?"

The "Shepherds' Almanac" ought to have been ready before the first of January; but Cérizet, on whom the whole business of the composition depended, was extraordinarily slow, and this was the more annoying because Madame Séchard did not know enough of the mechanical process of printing to reprimand him; she could only watch his proceedings. He was an orphan from the great hospital of the "Enfant-Trouvés" in Paris, by which he had been apprenticed to the Didots. From the age of fourteen to seventeen he was devoted to David, who put him under the direction of the best workman, and made him his typographic page; for he was naturally interested in the lad's intelligence and soon won his affection by giving him pleasures and amusements which the boy was too poor to get otherwise. Cérizet had a rather pretty but pinched little face, with red hair, and eyes of a cloudy blue; he had brought the habits and ways of a *gamin de Paris* into the provinces. His sharp, sarcastic maliciousness made him feared. David did not look after him in Angoulême as he had done in Paris, partly because the lad was older and his mentor felt more confidence in him, and partly because he counted on provincial influence. The consequence was that Cérizet had become, unknown to his master, the Don Juan of three or four little grisettes, and was utterly depraved. His morality, obtained originally in Parisian wineshops, held that personal advantage was the only law. Moreover, he knew that in the coming year he should be drafted for military service and drop his present career; consequently, he ran in debt, reflecting that in six months he should be a soldier and his creditors could not follow him. David still had some hold over the lad, not as his master, nor yet because he had been kind to him, but because the ex-gamin felt him to be a man of high intellect.

After a time Cérizet fraternized with the workmen at

the Cointets', and there he lost what few good principles David had instilled into him. Nevertheless, when they laughed at him for the "sabots" of his master, — meaning the old wooden presses of the Séchards, — and showed him the fine iron presses, twelve in number, which did the work at the Cointets' (where the only wooden press was used for proofs), he still took David's part, and proudly declared in the faces of his tormentors : " With his old wooden presses my master will do greater things than yours with all their iron concerns, which turn out nothing but prayer-books. He is searching for a secret which will make every printing-house in France and Navarre bow down to him."

" You miserable little foreman at forty sous a day," the men would answer; " you 've got a washerwoman for your mistress."

" Well, she 's pretty," retorted Cérizet, " and that 's better to look at than the black muzzles of your masters."

Such speeches as these reached in time the ears of the Brothers Cointet; they discovered the situation of the Séchard business, learned of Eve's speculation, and judged it wise to nip in the bud an enterprise which might put the poor woman in the way of prosperity. " Let 's rap her fingers well and disgust her with business," said the brothers to each other. The one who managed the pressroom met Cérizet and proposed to him to read proofs for them at so much a proof, to relieve their corrector who found the work too heavy. By working several hours at night Cérizet earned more from the Cointets than he did from David for his day's work. Hence followed certain relations between the Cointets and Cérizet, in whom the brothers saw good faculties, and they openly pitied him for being in a position so unfavorable to his interests.

" You might," said one of the Cointets, " be foreman to a large establishment, where you would earn your six francs a day ; and with your intelligence you could soon get a share in the business."

" What good would it do me to be foreman?" said Cérizet. " I 'm an orphan, I am part of the contingent for next year, and if I am drawn who will pay for my substitute?"

" If you made yourself very useful," replied the prosperous printer, " why should n't some one advance the money to free you?"

" It would n't be my master who did that," answered Cérizet.

This remark was made in a way that raised the worst thoughts in the mind of the hearer ; moreover, Cérizet threw a glance at the printer which was full of very searching inquiry.

" I don't know what he is about," he went on cautiously, finding the other silent ; "but he is not a man to look for capitals in the lower case."

" Look here, my friend," said Cointet, taking six sheets of the Diocesan prayer book, " if you can correct that for us before to-morrow you shall have eighteen francs. We are not ill-natured ; we are quite willing to let our rival's foreman earn a little of our money. We might let Madame Séchard ruin herself on that almanac, but it is kinder to let her know that we are just bringing out a ' Shepherds' Almanac ' of our own ; you can tell her so, and warn her she won't be first in the field."

This explains why Cérizet was so slow in setting up the almanac.

Hearing that the Cointets were interfering with her poor little speculation, Eve was seized with terror ; she tried to see a proof of Cérizet's attachment in the warning he had given her hypocritically ; but she now detected in her only compositor the signs of a keen curiosity.

" Cérizet," she said to him one morning, " you are always watching at the door and waylaying Monsieur Séchard in the passage, to find out what he is concealing ; I have seen you looking about the courtyard when he leaves the workshop where he casts the rollers, instead of attending to your own work. All that is not right, especially when you see that I, his wife, respect his secrets, and put myself to a great deal of trouble to leave him free to give himself up to his occupations. If you had not wasted so much time the almanac would now be finished, Kolb would have sold a large number, and the Cointets could not harm us."

" Eh ! madame," replied Cérizet, " for the forty sous a day which I earn here you get a hundred sous' worth of composition ; is n't that enough ? If I had n't proofs to read at night for the Messieurs Cointet I should have to live on bran."

" You have learned to be ungrateful early ; you will make your way in life ! " replied Eve, less hurt by Cérizet's reproaches than by the rudeness of his tone and his threatening and aggressive look and attitude.

" I sha'n't make it with a woman over me," he said, insolently, " for then there 's more than thirty days to a month."

Thus insulted in her dignity as a woman, Eve gave

Cérizet a severe look and returned to her apartments. When David came to dinner she said to him, "Are you quite sure, my dear, of that little scamp Cérizet?"

"Cérizet?" he answered; "why, he's my own gamin; I made him myself; I taught him all he knows; he owes everything he is to me. You might as well ask a father if he is sure of his child."

Eve told her husband that Cérizet was reading proof for the Cointets in the evening.

"Poor boy! he has to live," answered David, with the humility of a master who feels himself to blame.

"Yes, but, my friend, just see the difference between Kolb and Cérizet. Kolb does fifty miles every day, spends fifteen or twenty sous, and brings us back seven, eight, sometimes nine francs for the leaves he sells, and never asks me more than one franc over and above his expenses. Kolb would cut off his hand sooner than pull a single bar of the Cointets' presses; he would never rummage among the scraps you throw into the court-yard if you were to offer him a thousand francs; whereas Cérizet picks them up and examines them."

Noble souls find it difficult to believe in evil, in in-gratitude; it takes more than one harsh lesson to teach them the extent of human unworthiness; and when their education in this line is completed they often show an indulgence which betrays the very last degree of contempt.

"Pooh!" cried David; "nothing more than a ga-min's curiosity."

"Then, my dear friend, do me the kindness to go down into the press-room and see the amount of work which your gamin has done during the last month, and

13

tell me whether he ought not during that month to have finished our almanac."

After dinner David went down and did admit that the almanac ought to have been finished in eight days. Hearing from Eve that the Cointets were preparing one like it, he came to the help of his wife, stopped Kolb's peddling of the legends, and directed the press-room himself. He got everything in readiness for one form, which Kolb and Marion were to work off, while he himself, with Cérizet, did the other, carefully over-looking the impressions, that were in inks of diverse colors. Each color required a separate impression. Four different inks took four impressions. Printed four times for one, the " Shepherds' Almanac " costs so much to bring out that it is made in provincial printing-houses only, where hand-work and the interest of capital used in the printing-business are of little account. This production, coarse as it is, is impossible for the great printing-houses which bring out fine works.

For the first time since old Séchard's retirement two presses were steadily at work in the old press-room. Though the almanac was, in its way, a masterpiece, Eve felt obliged to sell it for two farthings, because the Cointets were selling theirs to the peddlers at three centimes; she paid for the peddling, and earned on the sales made by Kolb; but the speculation was a failure.

Cérizet, seeing that his mistress distrusted him, be-came in his heart her enemy. He said to himself, " You suspect me; I will revenge myself." That is the gamin of Paris. He therefore accepted emoluments from the Cointet Brothers which were evidently larger

than his proper pay for correcting the proofs, which he
fetched every evening from their office and returned
in the morning. By talking with the brothers daily,
he grew familiar with them, and ended by perceiving
his chance, which was held out to him as a bait, of
escaping military service. Instead of having to corrupt
him, the Cointets did, in fact, receive from him the first
suggestion as to spying for the secret of which David
was in search. Uneasy at seeing how little she could
rely on Cérizet, and unable to find another Kolb, Eve
resolved to dismiss her only compositor, in whom her
second sight, that of a loving woman, detected treachery ; but as such an act would be the death of the
establishment, she determined to take an heroic course.
She sent to Métivier, David's correspondent in Paris,
also that of the Cointets and of other paper-makers in
the department, the following notice, requesting him to
insert it in the " Publishers' Journal " of Paris : —

" For sale, a printing-house, in active operation, with
material and license, situated in Angoulême. Address, for
terms of sale, Monsieur Métivier, rue Serpente."

When the Cointets read the number of the Journal
which contained this notice, they said to each other :
" That little woman has got a head ; we had better
now get possession of her printing-house, and give
her enough to live on ; otherwise, we shall have some
competitor in Séchard's place who will give us trouble."
Prompted by that thought, the Cointets went to talk
with David Séchard and his wife. Eve, whom they
first met, felt the keenest joy as she saw the instanta-
neous effect of her ruse, for they made no secret of their

wish that Monsieur Séchard should carry on the business for them ; they were overrun with work, they said ; their own presses did not suffice ; they had workmen coming from Bordeaux, and could manage David's three presses as well as their own.

" Gentlemen," said Eve, while Cérizet had gone to summon David, " my husband knew excellent workmen when he was at the Didots', and he can no doubt find a successor among the best of them.   It would be better for us to sell the establishment for twenty thousand francs, which would give us an income of a thousand francs to live on, than to lose a thousand a year through you.   Why did you envy us that poor little speculation of the almanac, which, after all, belonged by right to this office? "

" Ah, madame, why did you not let us know that? •We would certainly not have interfered with you," said the brother who was known as " the tall Cointet," graciously.

" Excuse me, gentlemen, but you did not undertake your almanac until after Cérizet told you I was making mine."

Uttering the words sharply, she looked straight at the tall Cointet, and made him lower his eyes.   She thus obtained good proof of Cérizet's treachery.

The tall Cointet, the manager of the paper-making department and the financial affairs of the house, was a far more able man of business than his brother Jean, who, however, managed the printing-office with much intelligence, though his capacity might be compared to that of a colonel, while the tall Cointet, named Boniface, was the general in whom Jean recognized his

commander-in-chief. Boniface, lean and lank, with a
wax-like, yellow face marbled with red splashes, pinched
lips, and eyes like those of a cat, was never angry ; he
could listen with the calmness of a saint to the worst
insults, and reply to them in gentle tones.   He went to
mass, confessed, and took the sacrament.   Beneath his
ingratiating manner and his outward man, which was
almost effeminate, lay the tenacity and the ambition of
a priest, and the greed of a merchant thirsting for riches
and honors.   From the year 1820 the tall Cointet
sought what the bourgeoisie obtained in 1830.   Filled
with hatred to the aristocracy, indifferent in matters of
religion, he was pious precisely as Bonaparte was democratic.   His spinal column bent with marvellous flexi-
bility before the nobility and the governing powers, to
whom he made himself humble, complying, and of no
account.   To picture this man by a single stroke, the•
meaning of which will be appreciated by those who are
in the habit of doing business, he always wore blue
spectacles, behind which he hid his glances, under pretence of saving his eyes from the glare of a town where
all the buildings are white and the intensity of light is
increased by the great elevation of the ground.   Though
his height was not much above the medium, he seemed
very tall because of his leanness, which told of a physical condition worn down by fatigue and a mental
state of continual fermentation.   The Jesuitical expression of his countenance was made complete by long,
gray hair, straight and flattened down and cut after the
fashion of an ecclesiastic's, and by his clothing, which
for the last seven years had consisted of black trousers,
black stockings, black waistcoat, and a "lévite" (the

name given in the south of France to a frock-coat) of
brown cloth. He was called "the tall Cointet," to distinguish him from his brother, who was called "the
stout Cointet," thus expressing the difference of the
shapes and capacities of the two brothers, who, in other
respects, were equally matched.

Jean Cointet, a good-natured, stout fellow with a
Flemish face, browned by a southern sun, short and
paunchy like Sancho, broad-shouldered, and with a smile
upon his lips, produced a striking contrast to his elder
brother. Jean differed from Boniface not only in appearance and mind, but he also professed opinions that
were almost radical, belonged to the "Left-centre,"
never went to mass except on Sundays, and was on the
best of terms with all the Liberal merchants. The tall
Cointet made clever use of the apparent good-humor of
his brother; he made a club of him. Jean was charged
with all the hard words, injunctions, and distrainings,
which were repugnant to the effeminate mildness of his
brother. Jean had the department of temper; he got
angry, blurted out impossible proposals which made
those of his brother seem more acceptable; and thus
they attained, sooner or later, their own ends.

Eve, with the natural tact of a woman, had perceived
the rôle of the two brothers, and she stood on her guard
in presence of such dangerous adversaries. David, who
knew of the whole matter from his wife, listened with
an abstracted air to the proposals of his enemies.

"Settle it with my wife," he said after a while, to
the two Cointets, leaving the office to return to his
little laboratory. "She knows more about the printing-
house than I do myself; I am busy with something

which will turn out far more lucrative than this poor business, by means of which I shall recover out of you the losses I have met with."

"How so?" said the stout Cointet, laughing.

Eve looked at her husband as if warning him to be cautious.

"You will be my dependants, — you and all others who want paper," replied David.

"What do you expect to discover?" asked Boniface.

When he asked the question in his soft, insinuating tones, Eve again looked at her husband to advise him not to answer, or to answer something that told nothing.

"I expect to discover a way to manufacture paper at fifty per cent below the present price."

So saying David went off, without observing the glance exchanged by the two brothers. "The man must be an inventor; he could n't have his build and be idle! Let us get this secret out of him," said the glance of Boniface. "How?" said that of Jean.

"David treats you as he does me," said Madame Séchard. "When I am inquisitive he is afraid of my name, and gives me some such reply as that, which is only evasion."

"If your husband can carry out that scheme he will certainly make his fortune more rapidly than he could by a printing-house, and I am not surprised that he neglects his business," said Boniface, looking into the press-room, where Kolb, seated on a wetting-board, was rubbing his dry bread with a clove of garlic; "but it won't suit us to see this establishment in the hands of an active, busy, ambitious competitor, and therefore, madame, perhaps we can come to some agreement. For

instance, would you lease your plant for a certain sum
to one of our men, who would do the work for us in your
name, as is often the case in Paris? We would give
this man sufficient work to enable him to pay you a
good rent and make some little profit for himself."

"That would depend on the sum offered," said Eve.
" What will you give?" she added, looking at Boniface,
in a manner which let him know that she saw through
his scheme.

" What do you want? " said Jean, quickly.

" Three thousand francs for six months," replied
Eve.

" My dear lady, you talked just now of selling the
whole place for twenty thousand francs," said Boniface,
gently. " The interest of twenty thousand francs is
only twelve hundred."

Eve was confounded for a moment, and saw the importance of discretion in business.

"But you will use our presses and type, with which,
as I have proved, a good deal can be made," she said ;
" and we have the rent to pay to old Monsieur Séchard,
who does not burden us with gifts."

After a struggle of two hours Eve obtained a rental
of two thousand francs for six months, of which one
thousand was to be paid in advance. After the agreement was made the brothers informed her that it was
their intention to give Cérizet the lease of the utensils.
Eve could not restrain a movement of surprise.

" It is much better to put in some one who understands your presses," said the stout Cointet.

Eve bowed, but made no answer, resolving to watch
Cérizet carefully.

" Well, so our enemies step into our shoes ! " said David, laughing, when she gave him at dinner-time the deeds to sign.

" Bah! " she said ; " I 'll answer for the devotion of Kolb and Marion ; they two will watch our interests. Besides, we are getting four thousand francs a year for a plant which was only costing us money, and I see a whole year before you in which to realize your hopes."

" You were born to be, as you told me that night by the river, the wife of an inventor," said David, pressing his wife's hand tenderly.

Though the inventor now had a sum of money suffi- cient to carry him through the winter, he soon found himself closely watched by Cérizet ; and he was, although he did not know it, at the mercy of the Cointets.

" We 've got them! " said the tall Cointet to his brother, as they left the establishment. " Those foolish people will get accustomed to receiving rent ; they will advance on it and make debts. In six months we 'll re- fuse to continue the lease, and then we 'll see what that genius has got in his pouch. If it is worth anything we will propose to help him out of his difficulties, on condi- tion that he agrees to make us partners in the sale of his discovery."

If any clever dealer had seen the tall Cointet as he uttered the words " *make us partners*," he would have felt that the dangers of marriage are less before the mayor than before the courts of commerce.

Was it not enough, and too much, that these ferocious hunters were scenting their game? Were David and his wife, with the sole help of Kolb and Marion, in a position to resist the schemes of a Boniface Cointet?

II.

• THE FIRST THUNDER-CLAP.

ABOUT the time of Madame Séchard's confinement came a note of five hundred francs from Lucien, which, added to Cérizet's second payment, sufficed for all expenses. Eve and her mother and David, who had thought themselves forgotten by Lucien, were filled with joy on receiving his letters confirming his first successes in journalism, the reports of which made as much noise in Angoulême as they had in Paris.

Lulled into false security, David shook in every limb when he received from his brother-in-law the following cruel letter : —

MY DEAR DAVID, — I have negotiated with Métivier three notes for a thousand francs each, which I signed in your name to my order. They fall due at one, two, and three months' sight. I had no choice between that and suicide; I was forced to choose this horrible resource, which I know will hamper you terribly. I will explain to you later the position in which I am ; and I will try to send you funds to meet the notes when due.

Burn my letter, and say nothing to my sister or my mother ; I own to having counted on your heroism, which I know so well.

Your despairing brother,

LUCIEN DE RUBEMPRÉ.

"Your poor brother," said David to his wife, who was just getting up from her confinement, "is in great straits; I have sent him three notes of a thousand francs each, payable in one, two, and three months. Write it down."

Then he left the room to avoid the explanations his wife was about to ask. But Eve, who had been made very anxious by Lucien's previous silence of more than six months, felt such painful presentiments after talking with her mother about David's speech, that she resolved to take one of those steps which are often prompted by extreme anxiety. Monsieur Eugène de Rastignac was then in the neighborhood of Angoulême, spending a few days with his family, and he had spoken of Lucien in sufficiently ill terms for his remarks, carried from mouth to mouth, to reach the ears of the mother and sister of the new journalist. Eve went to Madame de Rastignac and asked the favor of an interview with her son, to whom she told her fears, asking him to tell her the exact truth as to Lucien's situation in Paris. From him she heard the circumstances of Lucien's life, exaggerated by the witty dandy, who gave a covering of pity to his dislike and envy, taking a tone of friendly alarm about the future of a compatriot whose talents he said he admired sincerely, and who was now so painfully compromised. He spoke of the great faults Lucien had committed; faults which had cost him the protection of great personages and the gift of a royal ordinance conferring upon him the right to take the arms and name of de Rubempré.

"Madame," said Eugène de Rastignac, "if your brother had listened to good advice he would to-day

have been on the high road to fortune and the husband
of Madame de Bargeton, who is now a widow. But
instead of that, he chose to insult and desert her. She
loved Lucien, but she will now become Madame Sixte
du Châtelet, to her great regret."

" Is it possible?" exclaimed Madame Séchard.

" Your brother, madame, is an eaglet, blinded by
the first rays of luxury and fame that have dazzled him.
When an eagle falls, who knows the depths to which he
sinks? The fall of a great man is always in proportion
to the height he has attained."

Eve returned home terrified by this last sentence
which went to her heart like an arrow. Wounded in
the tenderest part of her soul, she nevertheless kept
silence ; but more than one tear rolled silently on the
cheeks and forehead of the child she was nursing at
her breast. It is so difficult to renounce the illusions
which family love justifies, and which are a part of life
itself, that Eve distrusted Eugène de Rastignac ; she
wanted the opinion of a true friend. In one of his
early letters Lucien had given her the address of Daniel
d' Arthèz, of whom he spoke with great enthusiasm.
To him Eve wrote a touching letter, and this is the answer she received : —

MADAME, — You ask me to tell you the truth about the
life which your brother is leading in Paris ; you wish to be
enlightened as to his prospects ; and in order to induce me
to answer you frankly, you tell me what M. de Rastignac
has said to you, and you ask me if such and such things are
true.

In all that relates to myself, madame, I must in justice to
Lucien rectify some of M. de Rastignac's statements. Your

brother expressed to me great remorse for his conduct. I accepted his regrets and understood his position. You ask me if Lucien still retains my friendship and esteem. There indeed, the answer is more difficult to make. Your brother is entering a career in which he will be ruined. At the present moment I pity him sincerely; before long I shall willingly forget him, — not so much for what he has done as for that which he will then do.

Lucien is a poetical being, but not a poet; he dreams, and does not think; he is emotional, not creative. In short, if you will allow me to say so, he is effeminate, he likes to pose — the vice of Frenchmen. Lucien will always sacrifice his best friend for the pleasure of exhibiting his wit. He would willingly sign a compact with the devil if it would give him a few years of a brilliant and luxurious existence. He has already done so by bartering his future for the passing delights of his life with an actress. Just now, the youth and beauty and devotion of that woman, who really loves him, prevents him from seeing the dangers of his situation, which neither fame, nor success, nor fortune, will make the world accept.

No, at every fresh temptation your brother will only see, as he does to-day, the pleasures of the moment. But there is one thing about which you may rest assured : Lucien will never commit crime; he has not the force; but he will accept a crime that has been committed, and share its profits, though he did not share its dangers. This seems horrible to every one, even to scoundrels. He will despise himself, he will repent, but whenever the occasion returns he will do the same thing over again, — for *will* is lacking to him; he is without strength against the allurements of pleasure, or against the satisfaction of his minor ambitions. Lazy, like all poetic natures, he thinks himself clever in shirking difficulties instead of facing them. He might have courage at one moment, at the next he would be a coward; and he deserves as little praise for his courage as blame for his cowardice.

Lucien is a harp, the strings of which tighten or stretch according to the variations of his atmosphere. He might write a fine book in a phase of happiness or anger, and not be conscious afterwards of its success, much as he desired it.

When Lucien first arrived in Paris he fell into the hands of a young man without any morality whatever, but whose success and experience in the difficulties of a literary life dazzled him. This juggler has completely seduced Lucien; he has led him into an unmanly life, over which, unfortunately for him, love has cast its glamour. To bestow admiration too readily is a sign of weakness; the poet and the acrobat should not be paid in the same coin. We have all been wounded by the preference Lucien has shown for literary intrigue and knavery over the courage and morality of those who advised him to face the struggle rather than filch success; to fling himself into the arena instead of becoming a mere trumpet in the orchestra.

Society, madame, is, oddly enough, extremely indulgent to young men of this nature; it likes them; it is won by the noble semblance of their outward gifts; from them, society asks nothing; it excuses all their faults, grants them the merit of matured natures, and treats them, in short, like petted darlings. By such conduct society, so violently unjust in appearance, is perhaps righteous. It finds amusement in buffoons; asks them for pleasure only, and then forgets them; whereas, before it bows the knee to greatness it demands divine credentials. To all things their own law: the indestructible diamond must be without a flaw; the ephemeral creation of a fashion has a right to be flimsy, fanciful, and without consistence. Therefore, in spite of his mistakes, Lucien may succeed in his own way; he may put to profit some happy vein, or find himself among good connections. But if he should fall into the hands of an evil angel he will go to the depths of hell. He is a brilliant assemblage of splendid qualities embroidered on too thin a material; time will wear away the flowers, the tissue alone will remain; if worthless, it is nought but rags. As long as Lucien is young he will please; but when he is thirty what position will he hold? That is the question which all those who sincerely love him ought to consider.

If I were alone in judging thus of Lucien I might, perhaps, have refrained from grieving you by my sincerity; but not only do I think it unfaithful to you (whose letter is a cry of anguish) to evade your questions by mere commonplaces, but all my friends who have known Lucien are unanimous in this judgment on him. I have therefore regarded it in the light of a duty to tell the truth, however terrible it may seem to you. Anything and everything may be expected of Lucien, either for good or for evil. Such is our opinion; and I give it to you thus formulated in a single sentence. If the chances of his life, which is now very miserable, very uncertain, should bring him back to you, use all your influence to keep him in the bosom of his family; for until his character has acquired some firmness Paris will always be dangerous for him. He called you — your husband and yourself — his guardian angels, and yet he has doubtless forgotten you; but he will bethink himself of you whenever, battered by the storm, he has no other shelter than his family. Keep him, therefore, in your heart, for he will need that haven.

Accept, madame, the sincere esteem of a man to whom your precious qualities are known, and who respects your sisterly anxiety too much not to render prompt obedience to your wishes, subscribing himself

Your devoted servant,

D'Arthès.

Two days after reading this letter Eve was obliged to take a wet-nurse; her milk dried up. After making a demigod of her brother, she saw him depraved through the exercise of his noblest faculties. To her mind, he was wallowing in the mire. This noble creature knew not how to compromise with integrity, with delicacy, with all the domestic faiths of the family hearth, which shine with so pure a lustre in the depths of the provinces. David had been right in his forebodings. When this grief, which cast its leaden shadows on that white brow, was confided by Eve to her husband in one of those limpid conversations in which two married lovers say all things to each other, David replied to her with comforting words. Though the tears came into his eyes when he knew that his wife's sweet breast was dried with grief and when he saw her despair in no longer being able to nurse her child, he reassured her mind and gave her several grounds of hope.

"Don't you see, dear, that your brother has gone wrong through his imagination? It is so natural to a poet to long for his mantle of purple and azure; he seeks the games with such eagerness. This bird of ours is caught by glitter, by luxury, in such simple good faith that God will pardon where society condemns."

"But he will ruin us!" cried the poor wife.

"To-day he does, but a few months ago he sent us the first fruits of his earnings," replied the good David, who had the sense to know that despair was leading his wife beyond reason, and that her love for Lucien would soon reappear. "Mercier said about fifty years ago, in his 'Tableau de Paris' that literature, poesy, letters, and science, in short, the creations of the brain, could not support a man; and Lucien, in his capacity as a poet, has chosen to disbelieve in the experience of five centuries. The harvests irrigated by ink are never gathered for ten or a dozen years after sowing, if indeed they ever are gathered; Lucien has mistaken the herb for the sheaf. He will at any rate have learned life. After being the dupe of a woman, he has now been the dupe of society and false friendships. The experience he has earned has been dearly paid for, that's all. Our ancestors used to say: 'Provided our son comes back with both ears and his honor safe all is well.'"

"Honor!" cried poor Eve. "Alas, how many virtues Lucien has lost! To write against his conscience! to attack his best friend! to accept the money of an actress! To be seen in public with her! to wring our last penny from us!—"

"Ah! that is nothing!" cried David; then he checked himself; the secret of Lucien's forgery was about to escape him. Unfortunately Eve, who noticed his manner, was seized with vague anxiety.

"Nothing!" she exclaimed. "How shall we ever pay that three thousand francs?"

"In the first place," replied David, "we shall renew the lease for the printing-room with Cérizet. For the last six months the fifteen per cent profit which the Cointets allowed him on the work done for them has given him six hundred francs, and he has earned five hundred by outside work he obtained from others."

"If the Cointets find that out they may not be willing to renew the lease; they will be afraid of him," said Eve; "for Cérizet is a dangerous man."

"Well, what does it signify?" said David. "In a few weeks we shall be rich! and as soon as Lucien is rich, my dear love, he will be virtuous."

14

"Ah! David, my friend, my friend, what a saying you have allowed to escape you! You mean that Lucien in the depths of poverty has no will or strength against evil! You think of him as Monsieur d' Arthèz thinks of him. There is no superiority without force of character, and Lucien is weak,— an angel who must not be tempted ; is not that your idea of him?"

"Well, his nature is fine in its own sphere only, its own heaven. Lucien is not made to struggle — I will spare him a struggle. My dear Eve, see! I am too near my great result not to show you this." He pulled from his pocket several sheets of paper of the size called in-octavo, waved them triumphantly over his head, and laid them on his wife's knee. "See! a ream of paper, royal form, won't cost more than five francs," he said, making Eve finger his samples, which she did with childlike surprise.

"Dear, dear! how did you succeed in making it?" she said.

"With an old hair sieve I got from Marion," he answered.

"Are not you satisfied yet?" she asked.

"The question now is not the means of manufacture, but the net cost of the pulp. Alas! my child, I have only just entered upon that difficult matter. In 1794 Madame Masson tried to convert printed paper into white paper, and she succeeded — at a monstrous cost. In England, about the year 1800, the Marquis of Salisbury attempted, as Séguin did in France in 1801, to use straw in the manufacture of paper. Our native reed, the *arundo phragmitis*, furnished the paper you hold in your hand. But I am going to try nettles, and thistles; for in order to keep down the cost of the fundamental material I must rely on vegetable substances which grow in marshes and waste lands; they, of course, cost little. My whole secret lies in a preparation which I apply to these substances. At present, the process is not enough simplified. However, in spite of this difficulty, I am certain to confer a benefit on the manufacture of paper in France by which all literature . will profit; I shall make it a monopoly of our country, as iron, pit-coal, and earthenware are monopolies of England. I mean to be the Jacquart of paper-making."

Eve rose, moved to enthusiasm and admiration by David's single-heartedness; she opened her arms to him and pressed him to her heart, laying her head upon his shoulder.

" You reward me as though I had really succeeded," he said.

For all answer, Eve showed her sweet face wet with tears, and was silent for a moment, unable to speak.

" I am not kissing the man of genius," she said, " but my comforter. In place of a fallen glory you show me a rising one. You soften the grief I feel at my brother's degradation by the knowledge of my husband's grandeur. Yes, you will be great! — great as the Graindorges, the Rouvets, the van Robais; as the Persian who discovered madder; as all those men of whom you have told me, whose names remain obscure because in bringing an industry to perfection they did great benefit to the world without display."

" What can they be about at this time of night?" Boniface Cointet was saying.

The tall Cointet was walking about the place du Mûrier with Cérizet, and he saw, as he spoke, the shadows of the husband and wife on the muslin window-curtains. Cointet was in the habit of coming there at midnight to talk business with Cérizet, who was charged with the duty of watching every action of his late employer.

" He is showing her, no doubt, the paper he manu-factured this morning," replied Cérizet.

" What substance did he use for it?" asked the paper-maker.

" Impossible to guess!" replied Cérizet. " I clam-bered on the roof and made a hole through it; I watched Séchard all night boiling his pulp in a copper pan ; I looked in vain at a heap of something he keeps piled up in a corner ; all I could find out was that the original material looked like a mass of tow."

" Don't go any farther," said Boniface to his spy, in a virtuous tone ; " it would be improper. Madame Séchard will probably propose to you to renew your lease. When she does so, tell her that you want to be-come a master printer ; offer her half the value of the license and the plant. If they accept, come and tell me. In any case, drag matters along ; they are now without money."

" Not a sou !" said Cérizet.

" Not a sou," repeated Cointet. " They are mine ! " he added softly to himself.

The firm of Métivier in Paris and that of the Cointets at Angoulême combined the business of banking with their other vocations, the one as agent for paper-makers, the other as paper-making printers. The Treasury has not yet found a way to control commercial business so as to force those who practise surreptitious banking to take out a banking license, which costs, in Paris for example, five hundred francs. But the brothers Cointet and Métivier, though they were what is called at the Bourse " marrons " (from the old word *marronner :* Anglicè, to maroon, — play the part of pirates and corsairs), did a business of their own, amounting to several hundred thousand francs quarterly, in the money markets of Paris, Bordeaux, and Angoulême. It happened that this very night the Cointet brothers had received from Métivier, in Paris, the three notes of a thousand francs each to which Lucien had signed his brother-in-law's name. The tall Cointet at once constructed, on the basis of this debt, a formidable scheme, directed, as we shall see, against the poor and patient inventor.

The next day, at seven in the morning. Boniface Cointet was walking up and down by the conduit which fed his paper-mill, the noise of which covered the words of those who were near it. He was waiting for a young man about twenty-nine years of age, who for the last six weeks had been practising as a lawyer in the courts of Angoulême ; the name of this man was Pierre Petit-Claud.

" You were in college at Angoulême at the same time as David Séchard, I think?" said the tall Cointet to the young lawyer, who had taken care not to miss his appointment with the rich merchant.

" Yes, monsieur," replied Petit-Claud, keeping step with Cointet.

" Have you kept up the acquaintance?"

"We have met only two or three times since his return. It could not be otherwise; I am buried in my office or engaged in the courtroom on common days, and on Sundays and feast days I study; for I have had to rely wholly on myself."

Cointet nodded his head in token of approval.

"When David and I did meet, he asked me what I had been doing. I told him I had studied law in Poitiers, and was afterwards head-clerk to Maître Olivet; and that I hoped to be able to buy that practice some day. I was much more intimate with Lucien Chardon, who now calls himself de Rubempré, the lover of Madame de Bargeton, our great poet, and now David Séchard's brother-in-law."

"You can, therefore, go to Séchard and tell him you have now bought the practice, and offer him your services," said Cointet.

"That is never done," said the young man.

"He has had no suit; he has never employed a lawyer; it can be done," insisted Cointet, who was closely examining the little practitioner under shelter of his spectacles.

Son of a tailor at l'Houmeau and despised by his schoolmates, Pierre Petit-Claud seemed to have had a certain amount of gall infused into his blood. His face had the dirty, muddy tints which indicate former illnesses, privations, nights of anxiety, and, nearly always, evil feelings. The fellow can be described by two words that are used in common parlance. — he was sharp and snappish. His cracked voice harmonized with his sour face, his pinched appearance, and the undecided color of his furtive eye, which was that of

a magpie. Napoleon declared that a magpie eye was
an unfailing indication of dishonesty : " Look at such
a one," he said to Las-Cases at Saint Helena (speaking
of one of his confidants whom he was forced to dismiss
for dishonesty) ; " I don't see how I could have trusted
him so long, for he has the eye of a magpie." So,
when the tall Cointet had fully examined the puny
little lawyer with scanty hair and a face pitted with
the small-pox, whose forehead and skull were becoming
one, when he had observed him resting his hand on
his hip wearily, he said to himself, " He is my man."
And, in fact, Petit-Claud, soaked in bitterness, filled
with scorn, eaten up by a corrosive desire to force his
way, had already had the audacity to buy the practice
of his employer for thirty thousand francs, without the
means to pay for it, trusting to a rich marriage to pay
it off, and relying also on his late employer to find him
a wife, — for the predecessor has always a personal
interest in marrying a successor, when the latter owes
for his practice. Petit-Claud, however, relied still more
upon himself; for he was not without a certain superiority, rare in the provinces, the mainspring of which
was his vindictiveness. Great hatred, great efforts.

There is a vast difference between city lawyers and
provincial lawyers, and the tall Cointet was much too
clever not to profit by the little passions which move
these little men. In Paris, a lawyer, if he is remarkable,
— and there are many such, — has several of the qualities which distinguish a diplomatist ; the number of his
cases, the magnitude of the interests and the breadth of
the questions that are brought before him, prevent his
regarding his business solely as a means of making a

fortune. Whether he is for or against, armed offen-
sively or defensively, a lawsuit is no longer to him, as
it once was, an object of lucre. In the provinces, on
the contrary, lawyers cultivate what they call, in the
legal regions of Paris, " kindling," — that is, a crowd of
little deeds and legal papers which swell the bill of
costs, use much stamped paper, and keep the pot a-
boiling. These trifles are valuable to the country lawyer ; he sees a charge to be made, where the Parisian
lawyer thinks only of a fee. The fee is what the client
owes to his lawyer over and above the costs for conduct-
ing, more or less ably, his case. The Treasury gets
half the costs, while the fees belong solely to the lawyer. Let us say it boldly : the fees paid are rarely in
keeping with the fees asked and justly due for the services of a good lawyer. The barristers, physicians, and
attorneys of Paris are, like courtesans with their tran-
sient lovers, constantly on their guard against the gratitude of their clients. The client before, and the client
after the suit is brought, might make two admirable
genre pictures worthy of Meissonnier, which would be
precious no doubt to many a feed lawyer.

There is another difference between the Paris lawyers and the provincial lawyers. The Parisian solicitor
seldom pleads ; he speaks sometimes before the judge
in chambers ; but in most of the departments in 1822
(since then barristers have swarmed) the solicitors
were barristers and pled their own causes. This double
life produced double work, which gave the country
solicitor the intellectual vices of a barrister, without relieving him of the weighty obligations of a
solicitor. The provincial solicitor became garrulous,

and lost that lucidity of judgment which is so important in the management of legal business. By thus doubling himself a superior man will sometimes make of himself two inferior men. In Paris a solicitor never wastes his faculties in words before the court, he seldom pleads for or against; consequently he retains the balance of his ideas. If the ballista of the law is under his control, if he ransacks the arsenal for methods which the contradictions of jurisprudence will put into his hands, he keeps his own counsel on the matter in behalf of which he is straining every nerve to prepare a triumph. Thought is much less intoxicating than speech. By dint of talking a man comes to believe what he says; whereas he who is silent can act against his thought without impairing it, and win a bad case without declaring it to be a good one, as the solicitor who pleads is forced to do frequently. An experienced Parisian solicitor makes a better judge than an experienced Parisian barrister.

It will be seen, therefore, that a provincial solicitor has many causes for being a second-rate man; he espouses the cause of petty passions, he manages petty affairs, he lives by bills of costs; he misuses the Code of proceedings, and — he pleads! In a word, he has a number of infirmities. Consequently, when we meet with a remarkable man among provincial lawyers we may set him down as really superior.

" Monsieur, I thought that you sent for me to talk business," replied Petit-Claud, making an epigram of his speech by the look which he darted at the impenetrable spectacles of the tall Cointet.

" Without circumlocution," replied Boniface Cointet, " I have this to say — "

After these words, big with confidences, Cointet sat down on a bench, and invited Petit-Claud to do the same.

" When Monsieur du Hautoy passed through Angoulême in 1804 to go to Valence as consul, he made the acquaintance of Madame de Sénonches, then Mademoiselle Zéphirine — by whom he had a daughter," went on Cointet, speaking in a low voice. " Yes," he continued, as Petit-Claud started, " and the marriage of Monsieur de Sénonches and Mademoiselle Zéphirine followed this clandestine birth almost immediately. This daughter, brought up in the country by my mother, is Mademoiselle Françoise de la Haye, now living with Madame de Sénonches who is, according to custom, her god-mother. As my mother, who was wife to the farmer of old Madame de Cardanet, grandmother of Mademoiselle Zéphirine, knew the secret of the only heiress of the Cardanets and the Sénonches of the elder branch, I was intrusted with the small sums which Monsieur Francis du Hautoy sent from time to time towards the support of his daughter. Her fortune was made by investing these small sums, which to-day amount to over thirty thousand francs. Madame de Sénonches will certainly give the trousseau, the silver, and ˙some furniture. I can get the girl for you, my lad," added Cointet, striking Petit-Claud on the knee. " By marrying Françoise de la Haye you will obtain the greater part of the aristocracy of Angoulême as clients. This alliance, in spite of the bar sinister, will open a splendid future to you. The position of a barrister and solicitor would, I suppose, be thought sufficient; in fact, I know that they expect no better."

"What can be done?" said Petit-Claud, eagerly. "You have Maitre Cachan for your lawyer — "

"Yes, and I shall not leave Cachan abruptly for you; you will only get my custom later," said Cointet, significantly. "You ask what can be done — why, David Séchard's business. The poor devil has three thousand francs to pay us, and he can't pay them. You must defend him; run up a huge bill of costs, and don't be afraid; go on, and pile up the items. Doublon, the sheriff, who will proceed against him under Cachan's direction, won't fail to strike hard. A word to the wise, you know? Now, young man? — "

He made an eloquent pause, during which the pair looked at each other.

"We have never seen each other, you and I," resumed Cointet. "I have never spoken to you; you know nothing of Monsieur du Hautoy, nor of Madame de Sénonches, nor of Mademoiselle de la Haye; only, when the time comes, say two months hence, you can ask for the hand of that young woman in marriage. When it is necessary that we should see each other, come here at night. We cannot write."

"You wish to ruin Séchard?"

"No, not wholly; but he must be kept in prison for some time."

"For what object?"

"Do you think me such a fool as to tell you? if you have sense enough to guess it you have enough to hold your tongue."

"Old Séchard is rich," said Petit-Claud, entering at once into Cointet's idea, and perceiving a cause of failure.

" As long as the father lives he won't give a penny to his son ; and that old ex-typographer is a long way yet from printing his funeral cards — "

" I agree ! " said Petit-Claud, deciding promptly ; " I ask you for no guarantees ; I 'm a lawyer ; if I am tricked I shall know how to bring you to account."

" That scamp will go far," thought Cointet, as he parted from Petit-Claud.

The day after this conference, April 3, the brothers Cointet caused the first of Lucien's forged notes to be presented. Unfortunately it was brought to poor Madame Séchard, who, seeing at once the imitation of her husband's handwriting, called David and said to him plainly, " You never signed that note?"

" No," he said, " your brother was so pressed he signed it for me."

Eve gave back the note to the Cointets' office-boy, saying, " We are not able to pay it."

Then, feeling that her strength was giving way, she went up to her room, where David followed her.

" My husband," said Eve in a faint voice, " go to the Cointets' ; they will surely have some consideration for you. Beg them to wait ; and besides, point out to them that by renewing Cérizet's lease they will owe you a thousand francs."

David went at once to his enemies. A foreman can always become a master-printer, but a clever printer is not always a business man. Consequently David, who knew little of business, was silent in presence of the tall Cointet when, having made his excuses awkwardly and preferred his request with a parched throat and a beating heart, he received the following reply : " This does not concern us; we have taken the note from Métivier, and he will pay us. Address yourself to Métivier."

"Oh!" said Eve, when David returned with this answer, " if the note belongs to Monsieur Métivier we need not be troubled."

III.

A LECTURE, PUBLIC AND GRATUITOUS, ON BILLS OF COSTS, FOR THE BENEFIT OF YOUNG MEN WHO CANNOT MEET THEIR NOTES.

THE next day Victor-Ange-Herménégilde Doublon, the sheriff, gave notice of the protest of the bill at two o'clock, an hour when the place du Mûrier is full of people; and in spite of the care he took to speak to Marion and Kolb at the side-door on the lane, the protest was none the less known to the whole business community of Angoulême before night. Besides, how could these hypocritical precautions of Doublon, who had been cautioned by the tall Cointet to show the utmost consideration, save Eve and David from the commercial disgrace of a suspension of payment? The following prosaic details will for once in a way seem only too short. Ninety-nine readers out of a hundred will be enticed along by them as they are by some piquant novelty in the shops. This will prove once more the truth of the axiom that there is nothing less known than that which everybody ought to know, namely, THE LAW.

Certainly to the vast majority of Frenchmen the mechanism of a wheel of the Bank of France, if properly described, would afford all the interest of a journey into a foreign country. When a merchant sends from

the town where he lives, a note of hand payable to a
person in another city, as David was supposed to have
done to oblige Lucien, he changes the simple transaction
of a payment made between merchants of the same town
for purposes of business into something which resembles
a letter of exchange drawn by one place on another place.
Therefore when Métivier accepted the three notes from
Lucien he was obliged, in order to touch their amount,
to send them to his correspondents in Angoulême, the
Cointet Brothers. That meant a loss for Lucien of so
much per cent mulcted from each note, beside the dis-
count, under the name of "commission for change of
place." The Séchard notes had now passed into the
category of banking affairs. You could hardly believe
how the quality of banker joined to the august title of
creditor changes the condition of a debtor. Therefore,
in banking (pay attention to that expression) whenever
a note, transmitted from the Paris money market to
the Angoulême money market, is unpaid the bankers
owe it to themselves to have recourse to what are
termed in law "bills of costs."

As soon as Doublon had registered his protest he
took it himself to the Cointets'. The sheriff kept an
account with these lynxes of Angoulême, and gave
them a credit of six months, which the tall Cointet pro-
longed into a year by his system of payment, all the
while saying from month to month to the sub-lynx,
"Doublon, do you want any money?" Boniface
Cointet now seated himself tranquilly at his desk, took
out a slip of paper stamped with thirty-five centimes,
all the while talking with Doublon on the real condition
of their various debtors.

" Well, are you satisfied with that little Gannerac?"
" He is not doing well; there 's a leak somewhere."
" Ah! the fact is he has too many drawing on him. They tell me his wife is expensive."
" His wife!" cried Doublon in a sarcastic tone.

The master-lynx, who had ruled his paper by this time, now wrote off in a round hand the following account, which is given verbatim : —

ACCOUNT RENDERED AND BILL OF COSTS.

To one note of ONE THOUSAND FRANCS, dated at Angoulême the tenth of February, one thousand eight hundred and twenty-two, drawn by Séchard Fils to the order of Lucien Chardon (otherwise called de Rubempré). passed to the order of Métivier and to our order, falling due on the thirtieth of April last, and protested on the first of May, one thousand eight hundred and twenty-two.

Principal	1,000 00
Serving notice of protest	12 35
Commission at one half per cent . . .	5 00
Commission on brokerage one quarter per cent	2 50
Stamps, return draft, and present account	1 35
Interest and postage	3 00
	1,024 20
Exchange at one and one quarter per cent	13 45
	1,037 45

One thousand and thirty-seven francs, sixty-five centimes, for which sum we have drawn at sight on Monsieur Métivier, rue Serpente, Paris, to the order of Monsieur Gannerac of l'Houmeau.

                                    COINTET BROTHERS.

Angoulême, May 2, 1822.

At the foot of this little bill, made out with the ease of a practised hand (all the while talking with Doublon), Cointet added the following declaration : —

We, the undersigned, Postel, master apothecary at l'Hou-meau, and Gannerac, carrier, inhabitants of the town of Angoulême, do hereby certify that exchange between the said town and Paris is one and one quarter per cent.

Angoulême, May 3, 1822.

" There, Doublon, be so good as to carry that to Postel and to Gannerac, and ask them to sign the declaration, and bring it back to me to-morrow morning."

Doublon, well versed in these instruments of torture, went off as if employed in the simplest every-day matter ; and all Angoulême was soon well aware of the unhappy condition of poor David Séchard's affairs. And what animadversions were then made against his apathy and incompetence ! some said his ruin was caused by his excessive love for his wife ; others by his blind affection for his brother-in-law. What folly to take other people's burdens upon him. Old Séchard was right in treating him harshly ; they admired his wisdom.

Now, all you who for any reason forget or are unable to keep your money engagements, examine carefully the strictly legal proceedings by which in ten minutes the bank exacts twenty-eight francs interest on a capital of one thousand francs.

The first item of the above account is the only incontestable one.

The second item concerns the Treasury and the sheriff. The six francs mulcted by the former (for registering

15

the debtor's misery and furnishing stamped paper) will prolong the life of this abuse for some time yet. You know, moreover, that this item covers a profit of one franc and fifty centimes to the banker for brokerage.

The commission of one half per cent which forms the third item is exacted under the ingenious pretext that not to receive a payment is equivalent, in banking, to discounting a note. Though it is precisely the reverse, giving a thousand francs seems to be considered the same as not receiving them cash in hand. Whoever has presented bills to be discounted knows that besides the six francs legally due, the broker deducts, under the humble name of commission, a percentage, which percentage being over and above the legal rate of interest enables him to make a further sum, which he loans at a profit. The more he earns, the more he demands. Therefore, do your discounting with fools ; it is cheaper. But are there any fools in a bank?

The law obliges the banker to furnish the certificate of a money-changer as to the current rate of interest. In places so unfortunate as not to have a Bourse, that is, an Exchange, this duty of the money-changer is performed by two merchants. The commission for brokerage due to this agent is fixed at one quarter per cent of the sum for which the note is drawn. It is customary to consider that this commission has been paid to the merchants who take the place of the money-changer, and the banker simply puts the percentage in his own cash-box. So much for the third article of this charming account.

The fourth item includes the cost of the stamped paper on which the various accounts and bills are written, and that of the stamp on what is so ingeniously called "la retraite;" that is to say, the new draft drawn by the banker on his brother banker to reimburse himself.

The fifth item includes the postage of letters and the legal interest on the sum in question during the time that elapses before it comes into the banker's hands.

And, finally, the change in the market, the very object of a bank, is made the reason of another payment.

Now, sift this account in which (as Polichinello computes in the Neapolitan song so delightfully sung by Lablache) "fifteen and five make twenty-two." Evidently the signature of Messrs. Postel and Gannerac was a matter of courtesy, and the Cointets certified for them in return when required; no charge either way. It was merely putting in practice the well-known proverb "Pass me the rhubarb, and I'll pass you the senna." The Cointets, having a current account with Métivier, were not obliged to draw a "retraite," that is, a new draft; a returned bill only required one line more to the credit or debit side.

This absurd account reduces itself in reality to the thousand francs due, the costs of the protest, and one half per cent interest for one month's delayed payment.

If a banking-house has an average of one unpaid note daily of the value of a thousand francs, it earns twenty-eight francs daily, by the grace of God and the constitutions of the bank, a formidable sovereignty invented by the Jews of the twelfth century, which to-day holds thrones and peoples in the hollow of its hand. In other words, one thousand francs bring in to one banking-house twenty-eight francs a day, or ten thousand two hundred and twenty francs a year. Triple that number of bills of costs, and you have a revenue of thirty thousand francs on fictitious capital. Consequently, nothing in banking is more lovingly cultivated than such accounts. If David Séchard had gone to pay his note on the 3d of May, or even on the very day it was protested, the Cointet Brothers would have said to him, " We have returned your note to Monsieur Métivier," though the paper might be still in their desk. This, in the language of the provincial banks, is called "making the francs sweat." Postage alone brings in twenty thousand francs a year to the Kellers, who correspond with the whole world ; and the proceeds of bills of costs' pay for the opera-box, carriage, and dress of Madame la Baronne de Nucingen. Postage is an abuse which is all the more flagrant because bankers dispose of a dozen matters of the same nature in a dozen lines of one letter. It is strange but true that the Treasury takes its share of this premium wrung from misery ; its coffers are swelled by commercial misfortunes. As to the bank, it flings to the debtor from the recesses of its counting-room this reasonable question : " Why are you not prepared to pay ? " to which, alas ! the unhappy victim has no answer. Thus the bill of costs is full of terrible fictions, for which debtors, if they do but reflect on this instructive history, will feel in future a salutary horror.

On the 4th of May Métivier received the return note and bill of costs from the Messrs. Cointet, with an order to prosecute to the utmost in Paris Monsieur Lucien Chardon, otherwise called de Rubempré.

Some days later Ève received in answer to the letter she had written to Métivier the following brief reply, which set her mind completely at ease : —

To MONSIEUR SÉCHARD FILS, PRINTER, ANGOULÊME.

I received in due course your esteemed favor of the 5th instant. I understand from your explanations relating to the unpaid note of the 30th of April last, that you have obliged your brother-in-law, Monsieur de Rubempré, who has spent so much money that it would be doing you a service to compel him to pay this note. His position is such that he will probably not delay doing so. Should your honored brother-in-law not take up this note, I shall rely on the credit of your long established house, and remain as before,

Your servant to command,

MÉTIVIER.

" Well," said Eve to David, " Lucien will know by this summons that we were unable to meet the note."

What a change in Eve's feelings was shown by this remark! The increasing love inspired by David's nature, as she came more and more to understand it, was superseding in her heart the old fraternal love. But, alas! to how many illusions was she forced to bid adieu.

Let us now follow the course of that returned note and bill of costs in Paris. A " third-holder " (the commercial name of one who holds a note transmissibly), is permitted by law to sue whichever of the divers debtors of the note offers the best or quickest chance of payment. In virtue of this legal right Lucien was summoned to pay by Métivier's sheriff. Here follow the different phases of this action. Métivier, behind whom were the Cointets, knew very well that Lucien was insolvent; but in the eye of the law insolvency *de facto* does not exist until it is legally declared. It was now in the following manner legally declared impossible to obtain payment of the protested note from Lucien.

Métivier's sheriff notified Lucien, May 5, that the note was protested in Angoulême and the return papers in his hands, and he summoned the poet before the Court of Commerce in Paris to hear a vast number of things, among others that he was liable to imprisonment as a merchant. When, at last, in the midst of his life as a stag at bay, Lucien read this scrawl, he also received notice that judgment had gone against him by default. He saw the meaning of it all, and the injury he had done to his family. Tears came to his eyes ; he pitied David ; he felt ashamed of his forgery and wished to pay the note. Naturally he consulted his friends ; but by the time Lousteau, Blondet, Bixiou, and Nathan had told him that poets ought to snap their fingers at courts of commerce, legal inventions meant only for shopkeepers, Lucien was already in the grasp of the law. His door bore the yellow poster which has such a stringent effect upon credit, carrying alarm to the mind of every tradesman, and freezing the very blood in the veins of a poet who has feeling enough to care for the bits of wood, the silken rags, the colored woollen stuffs, and the other knick-knackery which goes by the name of furniture. The author of "The Daisies" rushed to a friend of Bixiou, a lawyer named Desroches, who laughed at Lucien for being in such a fright about, as he called it, nothing at all.

"It is *nothing*, my dear fellow ; but I suppose you want to gain time ? "

" Yes, as much as possible."

" Well, then, you must apply for a stay of execution. Go and see a friend of mine, Masson, an attorney in the commercial courts. It can all be managed easily ;

you are a journalist of some note, you know. If you are summoned before the civil courts come to me; that's my affair."

On May 28 Lucien, summoned before the civil court, was condemned much more quickly than Desroches expected, for the creditors were urgent. When the new execution was put in and the yellow posters again appeared on the door, Desroches, who felt rather foolish at getting "'pinched'' as he said, in that way, moved a stay of proceedings, declaring with perfect truth that the furniture belonged to Mademoiselle Coralie (the actress with whom Lucien lived), and he referred the question to the judge, who rendered a decision that the property belonged to the actress. Métivier appealed, but his claim was overruled by a judgment rendered on the 30th of July.

August 7, Maître Cachan received by coach an enormous package of papers entitled, '' Métivier against Séchard and Chardon.''

The first document was the following little bill, the correctness of which is hereby guaranteed, for it is copied from the original : —

Note of April 30 last, drawn by Séchard Fils, to the order of Lucien de Rubempré, and bill of costs.

$$1,037 \text{ fr. } 45 \text{ c.}$$

May 5.	Notification of protest and return of note; with summons before the Court of Commerce in Paris for May 7	8 75
" 7.	Judgment, condemnation by default with arrest for debt	35 00
" 10.	Notification of judgment	8 50
" 14.	Procès-verbal of distraint	16 00

" 18. Procès-verbal of application of placards . 15 25
" 19. Insertion in newspaper 4 00
" 24. Procès-verbal of reading judgment to de-
fendant; containing appeal for stay of proceedings by the Sieur Lucien de Rubempré 12 00
" 27. Judgment of the court which, on appeal
duly repeated, sends the parties to the civil
courts 35 00
" 28. Summons without delay by Métivier, before
the civil court . . . . ' 6 50
June 2. Judgment after hearing, condemning Lucien
Chardon to pay the note, and bill of costs,
and the plaintiffs the costs before the Court
of Commerce 150 00
" 6. Notification of the above . . . . · . 10 00
" 15. Injunction 5 50
" 19. Procès-verbal of seizure, containing demurrer to seizure, by the Demoiselle Coralie,
who declares that the furniture belongs to
her, and demands to go before the judge
in chambers at once, in case the execution
must proceed 20 00
" 19. Order of the President sending the parties
into court 40 00
" 19. Judgment affirming that the property belongs to the said Demoiselle Coralie . . . 250 00
" 20. Appeal by Métivier 17 00
" 30. Decree confirming judgment 230 00

Total . 889 00

Note of May 31, and bill of costs . . . 1037 fr. 45 c.
Notification to Lucien Chardon 8 75

1,046 20

Note of June 30, and bill of costs 1,037 45
Notification to Lucien Chardon 8 75

1,046 20

This account was accompanied by a letter in which Métivier instructed Cachan, the lawyer at Angoulême, to compel David Séchard to pay by every means of law. Maître Doublon accordingly summoned Séchard before the Court of Commerce of Angoulême for the payment of the sum total of the three notes and the costs already incurred on the first ; namely, a sum total of four thousand and eighteen francs, eighty-five centimes, 4018 frs. 85c. The day on which Doublon brought to Madame Séchard the order compelling her to pay this enormous sum, Eve had received early in the morning this annihilating letter from Métivier : —

To MONSIEUR DAVID SÉCHARD, PRINTER, ANGOULÊME :

Your brother-in-law, Lucien Chardon, is a man of shameful dishonesty, who has put his property in the name of an actress, with whom he lives.

You ought, monsieur, to have honorably informed me of these circumstances, and not have allowed me to sue him uselessly, for you did not reply to my letter of May 10th last. You must not feel affronted if I demand of you immediate payment of the three notes and my expenses incurred thereon.

Accept, etc., etc.,

MÉTIVIER.

Having heard nothing more on the subject since Métivier's letter of May 10th, Eve, understanding nothing of commercial law, supposed that her brother had repaired his crime by paying the forged notes.

" David," she said to her husband, " go first of all to Petit-Claud ; explain to him our position and ask his advice."

" My dear friend," said the poor printer, hastily entering the private office of his comrade, " I little thought, when you came to tell me of your appointment and to offer me your services, that I should need them so soon."

Petit-Claud studied the fine face of the thinker as he sat opposite to him, for he did not need to listen to the details of an affair which he knew a great deal better than the man who was explaining them. Seeing that Séchard was anxious, he said to himself, "The trick works." This kind of scene often takes place in a lawyer's office. "Why should the Cointets persecute him?" thought Petit-Claud. Lawyers are as desirous of penetrating the minds of their clients as those of their adversaries; they feel the need of knowing the wrong side as well as the right side of the legal plot.

"You must gain time," said Petit-Claud, when Séchard had finished his tale. "How much do you want? Will three or four months do?"

"Oh! four months will save me!" cried David, to whose eyes Petit-Claud seemed a deliverer.

"Well, they can be prevented from touching your furniture or arresting you for three or four months; but it will cost you dear," said Petit-Claud.

"Well, that won't signify," cried Séchard.

"Do you expect remittances? are you sure of them?" asked the lawyer, somewhat surprised at the ease with which his client fell into the trap.

"In three months I shall be a rich man," said the inventor, with an inventor's confidence.

"Your father is still above ground," said Petit-Claud; "he clings to his vines."

"Do you suppose I am counting on my father's death?" said David. "I am on the track of an industrial secret which will enable me to manufacture paper without a thread of cotton, but quite as firm as Holland paper, at fifty per cent below the present net cost of the cotton pulp."

" There 's a fortune in it!" exclaimed Petit-Claud, understanding at once the Cointets' scheme.

" A great fortune, my dear friend, for ten years from now ten times the amount of paper that is used to-day will be wanted. Journalism is going to be the craze of our times."

. " Does any one know your secret? "

" No one but my wife."

" You have not told your plan — your prospects — to any one? to the Cointets, for example?"

" I think I did speak of it to the Cointets, but vaguely."

A flash of generosity passed through the embittered soul of Petit-Claud, and he tried to combine the interests of the Cointets and his own with that of Séchard.

" Listen to me, David," he said. " We are schoolmates ; I will defend you ; but remember, this defence against obvious law will cost you five or six thousand francs. Don't compromise your future. I think you will be obliged to share the profits of your invention with some manufacturer. You would think twice, I am sure, before you would attempt to manufacture paper yourself; besides, you will have to get a patent. All that will take time and money. The sheriff will be down upon you meanwhile, sooner or later, in spite of all our efforts to escape him."

" I hold to my secret!" replied David, with the simplicity of a student.

" Well, keep your secret; it will be your sheet anchor," returned Petit-Claud, repulsed in his first and loyal intention to avoid a lawsuit by a compromise. " I don't want to know it. But listen to what I say : work in the bowels of the earth, if you can ; let no one see or suspect your methods of execution, or your anchor will be stolen from you. An inventor is often a simpleton ; you think too much of your secrets to think of anything else. Before long some one will suspect the object of your researches ; and remember, you are surrounded by manufacturers. So many paper-makers, so many enemies ! You are like a beaver in the midst of the trappers, — don't let them get your skin."

" Thank you, my dear comrade, I have thought of all that myself," said David ; " but I am just as much obliged to you for showing me such forethought and solicitude. It is not really a question of myself in this matter. I could be satisfied with twelve hundred francs a year, and my father will certainly leave me three times as much some day ; I live by love and in my thoughts — a divine life ! But the question is for Lucien and for my wife ; it is for them I work."

" Well, sign me this power of attorney ; and think of nothing but your discovery. When the time comes for you to hide yourself to escape arrest, I will warn you the night before. And let me tell you again not to allow any one to come into your house whom you cannot trust as you would yourself."

" Cérizet does not wish to renew his lease, and that is why we are pressed for money to meet our daily expenses," said David. " There is no one now about the premises but Marion and Kolb, an Alsacian who is like a spaniel in his devotion to me and my wife and mother-in-law."

" Distrust that spaniel ! " said Petit-Claud.

" You don't know him," cried David ; " Kolb is another myself."

" May I test him ? "

" Yes," said Séchard.

" Well, good-bye ; but send Madame Séchard to me ; I must have a power of attorney from your wife as well. And, my friend," added Petit-Claud, warning him thus of the legal disasters which were about to overtake him, " remember that your affairs are all on fire."

" Well, here I am, one foot in Burgundy, the other in Champagne," thought Petit-Claud, after accompanying his friend David to the door of the office.

IV.

HARASSED by the annoyances caused by loss of money, distressed at the condition of his wife, who was overcome by Lucien's infamy, David still worked on at his problem. As he walked back to his own house from Petit-Claud's office, he was abstractedly chewing a stalk of the nettles he had been steeping in water in his attempts to discover a suitable material for his pulp. His desire was to find some equivalent to the various processes of maceration and webbing of all that becomes thread, linen, muslin. As he went along the streets, rather pleased at his conference with his schoolmate, he felt a wad of something sticking upon his teeth. He took it in his hand, smoothed it out, and found a pulp superior to any of the compositions he had hitherto obtained, — for the great difficulty with pulps made from vegetable matter is a want of cohesion; straw, for instance, gives a brittle paper, that is almost metallic and sonorous. Such luck as this falls only to the boldest searchers after natural causes. " I must now," he said, " contrive to do by machinery and some chemical agency what I have just done with my jaws."

He appeared before his wife in all the joy of his belief in a victory.

"Oh! my angel, don't be uneasy," he cried, seeing that his wife had been crying. "Petit-Claud guarantees us several months of tranquillity. It will cost me something ; but, as he said when we parted, all Frenchmen have the right to make their creditors wait, provided they end by paying capital, interest, and costs in full. Well, that is just what I shall do."

"And live meantime?" said poor Eve, who thought of everything.

"Ah! true," responded David, putting his hand to his ear, with an inexplicable gesture common to persons who are nonplussed.

"My mother can take care of little Lucien," said his wife, "and I will work."

"Eve! oh, my Eve!" cried David, taking his wife in his arms and pressing her to his heart. "Eve, a few miles away from here, at Saintes, in the sixteenth century, one of the greatest men of France — for he was not only the inventor of glaze, he was also the glorious precursor of Buffon and Cuvier and a geologist before them, the simple-minded soul! — Bernard Palissy suffered the passion of inventors ; but he had his wife, his children, and the whole neighborhood against him. His wife sold his tools. He wandered about the country, misunderstood, hunted, sneered at. But I — I am loved!"

"Deeply loved," said Eve, with the placid expression of a love sure of itself.

"Then I can suffer all the sufferings of poor Bernard Palissy, the maker of the Écouen porcelains, whom Charles IX. exempted from the massacre of Saint Bartholomew. That man gave at last, in the presence of all Europe, when he was old, rich, and honored, lectures on what he called the 'Science of Earths.'"

"As long as my fingers can hold an iron you shall want for nothing!" cried, the poor wife, in tones of the deepest devotion. "When I was forewoman at Madame Prieur's I had a good little friend, Postel's cousin. Her name is Basine Clerget. Well, Basine, who does our washing, told me just now, when she brought it home, that she is to take Madame Prieur's business; I will go and work for her."

"Ah! but not for long," replied Séchard. "I have discovered—"

For the first time Eve listened to that sublime faith in success which sustains inventors and gives them strength to push forward into the virgin forests of discovery with a smile that was almost sad. David dropped his head with a disheartened motion.

"Oh! my friend, I do not ridicule : I am not laughing at you ; I do not doubt," cried his beautiful Eve, throwing herself on her knees beside her husband. "But I see how right you are to keep silence about your hopes, your experiments. Yes, inventors ought to hide the painful travail of their glory from every one, even from their wives, — a wife is always a woman. Your Eve could not help smiling when she heard you say for the twentieth time within a month, ' I have discovered.'"

David began to laugh so heartily himself that Eve took his hand and kissed it sacredly. Her husband's grandeur of soul, the simplicity of the inventor, the tears she sometimes surprised in the eyes of that man of feeling and of poesy, developed in her a force of unspeakable endurance. She had recourse once more to a means which had already been successful. She wrote to Monsieur Métivier advertising the sale of the printing-office, offering to pay him out of the proceeds, and entreating him not to ruin David by useless costs. To this letter Métivier, as they say, played dead; his head-clerk answered that in the absence of Monsieur Métivier he could not take upon himself to arrest the course of law, for it was not his employer's custom to do so. Eve then proposed to renew the notes and pay all the accrued costs. This the head-clerk consented to, provided David's father would be his son's security. On this Eve walked out to Marsac, accompanied by her mother and Kolb. She braved the old man in his vineyard and was charming to him; she even succeeded in smoothing his frowning brow; but when, with a trembling heart, she spoke of the security, she saw a sudden and complete change come over that vinous countenance.

" If I allowed my son to lay a finger at the edge of my money-box he would soon turn it inside out, and grab every penny I have," cried the old man. " Children always prey upon a father. But I did n't; I never cost mine a farthing. Your printing-room is deserted, — the rats and mice do the printing. You are handsome, you, and I like *you;* you are a hard-working, careful woman; but my son! Do you know what David is? Well, he 's a do-nothing of a student. If I had drilled him as they drilled me, and not let him learn his letters, and made a *bear* of him like his father, he 'd own property now. Oh! that boy, I tell you, he 's my cross! And unhappily, he 's my only one, for I can't have another to take his place. He makes you unhappy." (Here Eve

16

protested with a vehement gesture of denial.) " Yes,"
he said, replying to her gesture, " you were obliged to
take a wet-nurse, for your milk dried up. I know everything, mind that ; you are up before the courts, and all
the town rings with it. I was nothing but a bear, I
was n't a learned man, nor foreman to the Didots, the
glory of typography, — no, I was n't any of that, but
never did I receive a bit of stamped paper. Do you
know what I keep saying as I walk about my vines,
trimming them and attending to my little matters? I
say to myself : ' Poor old fellow, you give yourself lots
of trouble ; you lay by crown after crown, and you'll
leave a fine property, but it will all go to sheriffs and
lawyers, or to rubbish, delusions, ideas ! ' Look here,
my dear, you are mother of that little boy who looked to
me to have his grandfather's nose when I held him at
the font with Madame Chardon ; well now, I want you
to think less of David, and more of that little scamp. I
have no confidence except in you. You can, some day
or other, prevent the waste of my property, — my poor
property ! "

" But, dear papa Séchard, your son will be your
glory ; you will see him rich by his own efforts with the
cross of the Legion of honor in his buttonhole."

" What will he do to get it?" demanded the old man.

" You will see. But, meanwhile, how could three
thousand francs ruin you? For that sum you could
prevent his arrest. Well, if you have no confidence in
him lend the money to me ; I will return it ; you can
put a lien on my dowry or my work."

" David Séchard in danger of arrest ! " cried the old
man, amazed to learn that what he supposed to be a

calumny was true. " This comes of knowing how to
sign his name! And my rent? Oh! I must go into
Angoulême, my girl, and see after my own safety, and
consult Cachan, the lawyer. You did well to come
here ; a man warned is forearmed."

After a struggle of two hours Eve was obliged to
come away defeated by this unanswerable argument :
"Women know nothing about business." Having gone
with a vague hope of succeeding, the poor soul walked
back to Angoulême almost fainting. She reached home
just in time to receive the notification of the decree
condemning Séchard to pay the whole sum to Métivier.
In the provinces the sight of a sheriff at a man's door
is an event ; and Doublon had been too often at David's
house for the neighborhood not to talk of it. Before
long, Eve was afraid to leave the premises, for she
dreaded the whisperings she heard as she passed along.

"Oh, brother! brother!" cried poor Eve, rushing
into the alley and upstairs into her bedroom. " I never
can forgive you, unless — "

" Alas, yes! " said David, who met her ; " he did it
to avoid suicide."

" Never let us speak of him again," she answered,
gently. "The woman who led him into that gulf of
Paris was very criminal, — and your father, David, is
very pitiless. Let us suffer in silence."

A discreet knock at the door stopped the tender
words on David's lips and Marion presented herself,
having in tow the tall, stout Kolb.

" Madame," she said, " Kolb and I see very well
that monsieur and madame are troubled ; and as we
own between us eleven hundred francs of savings, we

thought they couldn't be better placed than in madame's hands — "

" Madame's hands!" echoed Kolb, enthusiastically.

" Kolb," cried David, " you and I will never part.
Take a thousand francs on account to Cachan, the
lawyer, and ask for a receipt; we will keep the rest.
Kolb, let no human power get out of you one word as
to what I am doing, or about my absence from home,
or what you may see me bring back; and when I send
you to look for herbs — you know? — don't let any human eye watch you. . They will try, my good Kolb, to
make you betray me ; they may offer you a thousand,
perhaps ten thousand francs — "

" They may offer me millions and I sha'n't say one
word," replied Kolb. " Don't I know army regula-
tions?"

" I have warned you ; now go and ask Monsieur
Petit-Claud to assist in making the payment to Monsieur Cachan."

" Yes," said the Alsacian, " and I hope I'll some day
be rich enough to punch his head for him, that man of
law. I don't like his looks."

" Kolb is a good man, madame," said the stout
Marion. " He is strong as a Turk, and quiet as a
lamb. He's one to make a woman happy. It was he
who first thought of investing our savings this way ; he
calls them his 'cache.' Poor man ! if he speaks ill, he
thinks well ; and I know what he means all the same.
He thinks he had better go and work for others, so as
not to cost you anything."

" I would like to be rich if only to reward such faithful hearts," said David to his wife.

Eve thought it all simple enough; she was not surprised to meet with souls that were on the level of her own. Her way of taking this service would have explained the nobility of her character to the dullest and even to the most indifferent mind.

"You will be rich some day, monsieur; your bread is baked," cried Marion. "Your father has just bought a farm, and that will be a good income for you, sooner or later."

Under existing circumstances, this speech made by Marion to lessen the merit of her action shows an exquisite delicacy.

Like all things human, French legal procedure has its vices; nevertheless, the sword of justice being two-edged, it serves for defence as well as for attack. Besides, it has this advantage ; if two lawyers come to an understanding (and they can do that without words, simply by their comprehension of each other's method of proceeding in a given case), a suit may be made to resemble the warfare of the first Marshal Biron, the nature of which he defined when his son proposed, at the siege of Rouen, a plan by which the city could be taken in two days. "Why are you in such a hurry to go and plant your cabbages," said the marshal. Two generals can prolong a war indefinitely by bringing nothing to a crisis and sparing their troops ; like the Austrian generals whom the Aulic council never reprimanded for missing an important junction in order to let the soldiers eat their soup. Maitre Cachan, Petit-Claud, and Doublon now behaved even better than the Austrian generals ; they followed the example of an Austrian of antiquity, — Fabius Cunctator.

Petit-Claud, spiteful as a mule, had soon seen all the advantages of his position. After the payment of costs was secured to him by the tall Cointet, he determined to double on Cachan and make his own genius shine in the eyes of the paper-maker by creating incidents and items which should fall to the account of Métivier. Unhappily for the fame of this young Figaro of the buskin, the historian must pass over the ground of his exploits as though he were stepping on live coals. A single bill of costs, such as that already made in Paris, must suffice for this history of contemporaneous manners and customs. We must imitate the style of the bulletins of the Grand Army ; for the more rapidly Petit-Claud's performances are enumerated, the better this exclusively legal page will be.

Summoned, July 3, before the Court of Commerce of Angoulême, David did not appear. Judgment by default was notified to him on the 8th. On the 10th Doublon issued a writ, and on the 12th he attempted to put in an execution ; which Petit-Claud, on David's behalf, resisted, summoning in turn Métivier. On the other hand, Métivier, thinking the delay too great, summoned David again and obtained, on the 19th, a judgment which overruled David's opposition. This judgment, served on the 21st, authorized an injunction on the 22d, a notice of arrest on the 23d, and a *procès-verbal* of the execution on the 24th. This hasty execution was arrested by Petit-Claud, who lodged an appeal to the Royal Court. This appeal, renewed on the 25th, brought Métivier to Poitiers.

" Well," said Petit-Claud to himself, " here we shall stick for some time."

The storm having passed over to Poitiers into the hands of a solicitor of the Royal Court to whom Petit-Claud gave private instructions, this new defender with a double face made Madame Séchard summon David Séchard for a separation of property. To use an expression of the law courts he "diligented" the process of obtaining this decree of separation ; on the 28th of July he inserted it in the "Courrier de Charente," and on the 1st of August an affidavit was made before a notary of a schedule of Madame Séchard's accounts, which made her the creditor of her husband in the small sum of ten thousand francs, which David on his marriage had settled upon her, and for the payment of which he now made over to her the contents of his printing-room and the furniture of his house.

While Petit-Claud was thus protecting the family belongings he was putting forward successfully in Poitiers the claim on which he based his appeal. According to him, David was the less liable for the costs made in Paris on Lucien de Rubempré's account because the court there had put them on Métivier. This view, adopted by the court at Poitiers, was followed by a judgment reaffirming that of the court in Paris, by which David Séchard was condemned to pay all, less the six hundred francs of costs laid to Métivier. Petit-Claud opposed this judgment in the name of Madame Séchard, claiming the personal property and furniture as belonging to the wife, who was duly separated in estate from her husband. Moreover, Petit-Claud called as witness the elder Séchard, who had by that time become his client, ·as we shall now see.

The day after the visit of his daughter-in-law the old

man went to his lawyer in Angoulême, Maître Cachan, and demanded to know what means he should take to recover his rents, which he was in danger of losing through the difficulties his son had got into.

" I can't appear for the father while suing the son," said Cachan; "go and see Petit-Claud; he is very clever; he will probably serve you better than I could."

When Cachan met Petit-Claud in the courtroom he said to him: "I have sent you old Séchard; take charge of the case for me in exchange."

Lawyers often render such services to each other, both in Paris and the provinces.

The day after old Séchard had explained himself to Petit-Claud, Boniface Cointet came to see his accomplice, and hearing of the old man's visit remarked, "Try to teach that old Séchard a lesson. He is a man who will never forgive his son for costing him a thousand francs; this outlay will dry up any generous feeling in his heart — if he ever has any!"

" Go back to your vines," said Petit-Claud to his new client the next day; " your son is badly pinched — don't be too eager to eat from his plate. I'll send for you when the time comes."

Petit-Claud now claimed in the name of old Séchard that the presses themselves were fixtures, on the ground that the house had been used as a printing-office from the time of Louis XIV. Cachan denied the claim on behalf of Métivier, who, after finding in Paris that Lucien's furniture belonged to his mistress, now found in Angoulême that David's property belonged to his wife and father. Cachan then summoned the father and son before the court to settle such pretensions.

"We are resolved," he cried, "to unmask the frauds of these men who entrench themselves behind dishonest ramparts ; who turn the simplest and plainest articles of the Code into spiked walls, and for what? — to avoid paying three thousand francs ; how obtained? — stolen from Métivier ! And yet they dare to blame the brokers ! Such are the times we live in ! Let me hope that you will not by your judgment sanction a claim which would make the law immoral to the core ! "

The court of Angoulême, moved by Cachan's fine oratory, rendered a divided judgment, giving the ownership of the actual furniture to Madame Séchard, but denying the claim of the elder Séchard, and condemning him to pay four hundred and thirty-four francs sixty-five centimes costs.

"Old Séchard," said the lawyers to each other, laughing, "insisted on putting his finger into the pie, and he'll have to pay for it."

August 26 the notice of this judgment was served so that the presses and other implements of the printing-office might be seized on the 28th. Placards were affixed, and an order issued to sell the property on the premises. The announcement of the sale was inserted in the newspapers, and Doublon flattered himself he could proceed to the examination and auction on September 2. By that time David Séchard owed, legally, for notes and and costs, a sum total of five thousand two hundred and sixty-five francs and twenty-five centimes— not including interest. He owed besides to Petit-Claud twelve hundred francs and the fees, which were left to David's generosity, — with the noble confidence of cabmen who drive you briskly on expectation. Madame Séchard owed Petit-Claud three hundred and fifty francs and his fees. Old Séchard owed him four hundred and thirty-four francs for costs, and Petit-Claud asked him three hundred francs more for fees. Thus the whole sum owed by the Séchards amounted by this time to about ten thousand francs.

Apart from the utility of these details to foreign nations, who may here see how the artillery of French law is brought to bear, it is useful that the legislator (if indeed legislators have the time to read), should know the extent of these abuses. A law ought to be passed which should, in certain cases, forbid solicitors to run up bills of costs which often exceed the sum that is the object of the suit. The reader will comprehend, from this dry statement of the phases through which such cases pass, the meaning and value of the words, *form, legal justice, costs,* of which the majority of Frenchmen have little or no idea. The following will serve to show what in legal slang is called setting fire to a man's affairs. The type in the printing-room, weighing about five thousand pounds, was worth for recasting about two thousand francs. The three presses might bring six hundred francs. The rest of the utensils could only be sold for old iron or old wood. The household furniture would produce at the utmost a thousand francs. Therefore, on property belonging to David Séchard and amounting to about four thousand francs, Cachan and Petit-Claud claimed seven thousand, without estimating the future which promised fine fruits in bills of costs, as we shall presently see. Certainly the legal practitioners of France and Navarre, and even those of Normandy, ought to bestow their esteem and admiration on Petit-Claud ; though persons of better feeling may drop a tear of sympathy for Kolb and Marion.

During this legal warfare Kolb could be found whenever David did not want him, seated on a chair in the alley-way, fulfilling the duties of a watch-dog. He received the legal papers, which were always examined besides by a clerk of Petit-Claud's. When the placards were affixed to the house announcing the sale of the material of the printing-office Kolb pulled them down as soon as the bill-sticker's back was turned, exclaiming: "The scoundrels! tormenting such a good man! And they call that law and justice!" Marion earned ten sous during the morning by turning the crank in a neighboring paper-mill and she spent them on the daily expenses of the family. Madame Chardon returned without a murmur to the hard life of a monthly nurse and brought her daughter her earnings at the end of every week. She had made two neuvaines, and was amazed to find God deaf to her prayers and blind to the light of the candles she burned to him.

September 2 Eve received the only letter which Lucien wrote after the one in which he announced having put into circulation the three forged notes,— a letter which David Séchard never showed to his wife.

"This is only the third letter I have had from him since he left us," thought the poor sister, hesitating before she opened the fatal paper. At the moment she was feeding her child, whom she was now bringing up on a bottle, being forced to dismiss her wet-nurse on account of the expense. We can judge of the state into which the following letter threw her, and also David, whom she roused from his sleep; for after passing the night in making paper, the inventor had gone to bed at daybreak.

MY DEAR SISTER, —

Two days ago, at five in the morning, I received the last sigh of one of God's most beautiful creations, — the only woman who could love me as you love me, as David and my mother loved me; joining to those disinterested feelings that which a mother and a sister cannot give, the joys of love. After sacrificing everything for my sake my poor Coralie may perhaps have died for me — for me who have not at this moment enough to bury her. She consoled me in life; you alone, my dear angels, can console me for her death. This innocent girl was, I believe, forgiven by God, for she died a Christian death. Oh, Paris! — Eve, Paris is the glory but also the infamy of France; I have lost many of my illusions here; and I shall lose many more in begging for the paltry sum I need to lay the body of that angel in holy ground.

Your wretched brother,

LUCIEN.

P. S. I have caused you much unhappiness by my conduct: you will know all some day, and you will forgive me. You may feel easy about those notes; a worthy man to whom I have caused much cruel suffering, seeing Coralie and me so troubled, has promised to arrange everything.

" The letter is still moist with his tears," she said to David, looking at it with such pity that some of her old affection for Lucien shone in her eyes.

" Poor lad! he must indeed suffer if he was loved as he says he was," said the happy husband.

Husband and wife forgot their own troubles before that cry of anguish. Just then Marion rushed into the room exclaiming, " Madame! here they are! here they are! "

" Who? "

" Doublon and his men, the devils! Kolb is fighting them ; they have come to sell everything."

" No, no, they will not sell ; don't be anxious," said Petit-Claud, calling from the adjoining room. " I have given notice of an appeal. We must not remain passive under a judgment which convicts us of dishonesty. I thought best not to defend you in court here in Angoulême. To gain time I allowed Cachan to speechify ; but I am certain of success at Poitiers."

" But how much will that success cost?" asked Madame Séchard.

" Fees if you win, and a thousand francs in costs if we lose."

" Good God!" cried poor Eve, " the remedy is worse than the disease."

Hearing this cry of innocence suddenly alive to judicial wrong, Petit-Claud stood confused. Eve seemed to him very beautiful.

Old Séchard, for whom Petit-Claud had sent, now arrived. The presence of the old man in the bedroom of his children, where his grandson in the cradle was smiling at disaster, made the scene complete.

" Papa Séchard," said the young lawyer, " you owe me seven hundred francs for that demurrer, but you may claim them from your son and add them to the amount of the rent now due."

The old man caught the keen irony which Petit-Claud put into his tone and manner as he said the words.

" It would have cost you less had you given that security for your son when I asked you for it," said Eve, leaving the cradle of her child to come and kiss the old man.

David, overcome at the sight of the crowd collecting before the house, drawn there by the struggle between Kolb and the sheriff's men, held out his hand to his father without a word.

" How is it possible for me to owe you seven hundred francs? " said the old man to Petit-Claud.

" In the first place, because I appeared for you. As the matter concerns your rents you are conjointly liable with your son in paying me. If your son does not pay these costs you must pay them. But that's nothing; in a few hours David will be arrested and put in prison; will you allow that? "

"How much does he owe? "

" Something like five or six thousand francs; without counting what he owes to you, and what he owes to his wife."

The old man instantly became distrustful; he looked round on the scene before him in the blue and white room, — a beautiful woman weeping beside a cradle, David bending beneath the weight of his troubles, the lawyer, who had probably drawn him into a trap; and he felt convinced that his fatherly feelings were being worked upon; he believed they were taking advantage of his paternity.

" Hey! let David get out of his scrape as best he can. As for me, I think only of that child," cried the old grandfather, " and his mother will approve of that. David is so learned he ought to know how to pay his debts."

" I'll put the meaning of that into good French," said the lawyer, sarcastically. " Papa Séchard, you are jealous of your son. Listen to the truth: you have

brought David into his present position by selling him
your printing-house for three times what it was worth,
and by ruining him to get that usurious price. Oh yes,
you may shake your head, but the journal which you
sold to the Cointets, the money for which you pocketed
entire, was more than the whole value of the printing-
house. You hate your son not only because you have
despoiled him, but because you have made him a man
far above yourself. You pretend to love your grandson
to mask your unkindness to your son and daughter-in-
law, who would cost you something *hic et nunc*, whereas
your grandson only needs your *post-mortem* affection.
You love the little lad solely to appear to love some one
in your family and avoid being called unfeeling. That
sifts you out, Papa Séchard."

"Did you bring me here to listen to all that?" said
old Séchard in a threatening tone, looking at the lawyer
and his son and daughter-in law in turn.

"Oh, monsieur!" cried poor Eve, addressing Petit-
Claud; "have you sworn our ruin? My husband has
never, never complained of his father." The old man
looked at her askance. "He has told me a hundred
times that you loved him, after your own fashion," she
said to old Séchard, understanding his distrust.

Following Cointet's directions, Petit-Claud had managed to anger the father against the son in order to
prevent the old man from helping David out of the
cruel position in which he was.

"On the day when we get David into prison," Boniface Cointet had said to Petit-Claud, "you shall be
presented to Madame de Sénonches."

The instinctive intelligence which comes of deep

affection enlightened Madame Séchard about Petit-
Claud's treachery as it did, once before, about Cérizet.
We can imagine David's surprise at Petit-Claud's speech;
he could not understand how the lawyer knew his father
and his affairs so well. The honest printer knew nothing
of his counsel's intercourse with the Cointets; and he
was also ignorant that the Cointets were proceeding
against him in the skin of Métivier. His son's silence
was an offence to the old man. Under cover of his
client's astonishment Petit-Claud took leave.

" Adieu! my dear David," he said. " An arrest
won't be delayed by the appeal; it is the only course
open to your creditors, and they will take it. Therefore, get away at once. Or rather, if you will take
my advice, go and see the Cointets; they have capital,
and if your discovery is really made, if you are quite
sure about it, they are, after all, kindly men —"

" What discovery?" asked old Séchard.

" Do you think your son fool enough to neglect the
printing business unless he was thinking of something
else?" cried the lawyer. " He is on the high-road, so
he tells me, to make paper for three francs a ream
which is now costing ten."

" Another scheme to take me in!" cried the old
man. " You are all banded together like thieves at a
fair. If David has discovered that, he has no need of
me. He's a millionnaire. Adieu, my young friends,
and good-day to you."

So saying the old man departed down the stairs.

" Put yourself in hiding," said Petit-Claud to David,
as he started to overtake old Séchard and exasperate
him still further.

The little lawyer found him grumbling on the place du Mûrier, and walked with him as far as l'Houmeau, where he left him with the threat of putting in an execution on the old man's property if the costs were not paid within a week.

"I will pay you, if you will show me the legal means of disinheriting my son without injuring my grandson and daughter-in-law," said old Séchard, as they parted.

"How well Cointet knows people! Ha! he was right enough; those seven hundred francs will keep that old man from helping his son," said the little lawyer, as he climbed back to Angoulème. "Nevertheless I don't mean to be outwitted by that slyboots of a paper-maker; it is time to make him give me something more than words."

"Well, David, dear friend, what do you think of doing?" said Eve to her husband, when the old man and Petit-Claud had left them.

"Put your biggest pot on the fire, my girl," cried David, nodding to Marion; "I have my discovery in hand at last."

Hearing these words Eve put on her bonnet and shawl and shoes with feverish haste.

"Get ready," she said to Kolb, "and go with me; for I must and will find some escape from this hell."

"Monsieur," said Marion, when Eve had gone, "do be reasonable, or madame will die of grief. Earn enough money to pay what you owe, and then you can search for treasure at your ease."

"Hold your tongue, Marion; the last difficulty is just about to be overcome. I shall be able to get both a patent for invention and a patent for improvements."

17

The cross of French inventors is the patent for improvements. A man passes ten years of his life in seeking some industrial secret, — a machine, or some other discovery; he takes out a patent, and thinks himself master of his invention, whatever it is; he is followed by a competitor who, if he has not foreseen everything, will improve his invention with some screw or bolt, and get the whole value of the discovery out of his hands. Therefore, to invent a new pulp for making paper cheaply was far from being all that was necessary. Others could improve the process. David Séchard wished to foresee everything in order that a fortune pursued under so many difficulties might not be torn from his grasp. Holland paper (this name is still given to paper made of linen, though Holland no longer manufactures it) is slightly sized; but the size is applied, sheet by sheet, by manual labor, which of course increases the cost of the paper. If it could be made possible to size the pulp in the vat with some inexpensive size (such as that we now use, though that is still imperfect) there need be no fear of improvement. For a month past David had been seeking a method to size his paste. Two had occurred to him.

Eve had gone to see her mother. Madame Chardon was then nursing the wife of a deputy-magistrate who had just given an heir presumptive to the Minards of Nevers. Eve determined to consult this legal defender of widows and orphans on her position, and ask him whether she could free David from his embarrassments by taking them upon herself and selling her dower rights; she also hoped to discover the truth as to Petit-Claud's ambiguous conduct.

The magistrate, surprised by Madame Séchard's beauty, received her not only with the respect due to a woman, but with a sort of courtesy to which poor Eve was not accustomed. She saw in the eyes of this official an expression which, since her marriage, she had found in none but those of Kolb; an expression that, to women as beautiful as Eve, is the *criterium* by which they judge of men. When a passion, or self-interest, or age dims in the eyes of a man the sparkle of devotion which flames there in youth, a woman begins to distrust that man and to watch him. The Cointets, Petit-Claud, Cérizet, all men whom Eve had felt to be enemies, looked at her with cold, hard eyes; but now she suddenly felt at ease with this magistrate, though after receiving her courteously he destroyed in a few words all her hopes.

"It is not certain, madame," he said, "that the Royal Court will sustain the judgment confirming the transfer your husband made to you of his goods and chattels to pay your dower. Your privileges will not be allowed to cover a fraud. But as you will then be admitted under the head of creditor to share in the proceeds of the seizure, and as your father-in-law will have the same rights in view of the rent due, there will be matter for further litigation about what we call in legal terms a *Contribution* — in other words, the schedule by which the creditors are paid."

"Then Monsieur Petit-Claud is ruining us?" she said.

"The conduct of Petit-Claud," said the magistrate, "carries out your husband's desire to gain time. To my thinking, it would be better to desist from appeal-

ing, and to buy in, you and your father-in law, whenever the sale takes place, the necessary utensils to carry
on your business,— you, to the extent of what is legally
yours, he for the amount of his rent. But your lawyers will think this bringing matters to an end too
soon. They are running you up a bill of costs."

" I should then be in the hands of Monsieur Séchard,
the elder, to whom I should owe a rent for the utensils
as well as for the house ; my husband would still be
sued by Monsieur Métivier, who will have received
nothing."

" That is true, madame."

" Then our position would be worse than it is now."

" The law sustains the creditor. You received three
thousand francs ; it obliges you to return them."

" Oh ! monsieur, do not think that we — "

She stopped short, seeing the danger that her self-
justification might bring upon her brother.

" I know very well," said the magistrate, " that this
affair is obscure, both on the side of the debtors, who
are honorable, scrupulous, I may say grand, and on
the side of the creditor who is only a cat's-paw." Eve
looked at the magistrate in bewilderment. " You
must know," he went on, with a look of kindly shrewdness, " that we deputies have plenty of time to reflect
on what is passing before our eyes, while listening to
the pleadings of the lawyers."

Eve came home in despair at the uselessness of all
efforts.

At seven o'clock that evening Doublon brought the
notification of imprisonment for debt. The persecution
had reached its height.

" After to-morrow," said David, " I can go out only at night."

Eve and her mother burst into tears. To them it seemed dishonor to be in hiding. Kolb and Marion, learning of their master's danger, were all the more alarmed because they had long understood his guileless nature ; and they trembled for his safety so much that they went together to find Madame Chardon, Eve, and David, under pretence of asking whether they could do anything to assist him. They came into the room just as the wife and the mother, to whom life had hitherto been so simple, were weeping at the necessity of hiding David. How escape the invisible spies who, from this time forth, would watch every movement of this man, unhappily so absent-minded?

" If madame will wait one little quarter of an hour," said Kolb, " I 'll make a reconnaissance into the enemy's camp. She shall see what I can do ; for though I look like a German, I 'm a true Frenchman for tricks."

" Oh ! madame," said Marion, " let him do what he wants : his only thought is to save monsieur ; he has no other ideas in his head. Kolb is not an Alsacian, he is — well, there ! he 's a Newfoundlander."

" Go, my good Kolb," said David, " do what you like ; we have time enough before us to decide on a course."

V.

IMPRISONMENT for debt is, in the provinces, an extraordinary, abnormal fact, if there ever was one. In the first place all persons know each other too well to employ such odious means. Creditors and debtors have to see each other daily all their lives. When a bankrupt — to use the name given to the insolvent debtor in the provinces, where they do not mince matters about such legal theft — expects to fail heavily he takes refuge in Paris. Paris is the Belgium of the provinces ; men can find impenetrable hiding-places there, and a sheriff's warrant expires at the limit of his jurisdiction. Besides there are other hindrances equally invalidating. The law which maintains the inviolability of the domicile rules, without exception, in the provinces. The sheriff cannot, as he does in Paris, enter a house to seize a debtor. This law excepts Paris because of the number of families living in one house. But in the provinces a sheriff can enter the debtor's own house only after calling in the assistance of a justice of the peace. Now, as the justice holds the sheriff in his power, he usually gives his presence or withholds it as he pleases. To the honor of these justices it must be said that they dislike the office and will not pander to blind passions or revenge. There are other difficulties, not less real, which tend to modify the perfectly unnecessary cruelty of imprisonment for debt ; for instance, social customs, which often change the laws to the point of annulling them. In great cities there are always enough depraved and miserable creatures without restraint or faith who will act as spies, but in little towns every one is too well-known to hire himself to the sheriff. Thus the arrest of a debtor, not being, as in Paris and in other large centres of population, an object of individual interest to the guardians of commerce, becomes an exceedingly difficult proceeding, a combat of craft against craft between the debtor and the sheriff, which often furnishes amusing items to the newspapers.

The tall Cointet did not choose to show himself in the affair, but the stout Cointet, who said openly that Métivier had put the affair in his hands, went to Doublon's house with Cérizet, now the Cointets' foreman, and held a conference in the sheriff's private room, which was at the back of the front office, on the ground-floor of the house. The office was entered from a broad, paved passage which formed a sort of alley. The house had a single front-door, on each side of which were the official gilt scutcheons bearing in black letters the word "Sheriff." The two windows of the office looking on the street were protected by strong iron bars. Doublon's private room looked upon the garden, where the sheriff, a votary of Pomona, cultivated his wall-fruit with success. The kitchen was opposite to the office. This house was on a little street behind the new Law Courts then building and not finished till after 1830. These details are not useless to an understanding of what now befell Kolb.

The Alsacian had gone to Doublon's office with the intention of seeming to betray his master to the sheriff, in order to learn what traps were to be set for him, and thus thwart the arrest. The cook opened the door. Kolb told her that he wished to speak to Monsieur Doublon on business. Annoyed at being disturbed when busy, the woman merely opened the office door and told Kolb to wait there; then she went to the inner door and told her master that "a man" wanted to speak to him. That expression, "a man," implied a peasant, and Doublon called out, "Let him wait."

Kolb sat down near the door of the office.

"Well, how do you mean to proceed?" said the voice of the stout Cointet. "If we could lay hold of him to-morrow morning it is so much time gained."

"He is so absent-minded that you'll find it easy enough to take him." cried Cérizet.

Recognizing Cointet's voice, but, above all, enlightened by the two speeches, Kolb was immediately certain that they were talking of his master; his astonishment was great on distinguishing the voice of Cérizet.

"A fellow who ate his bread!" he muttered, horrified.

"My friends," said Doublon, "the thing to do is this. I will station men at intervals between the rue de Beaulieu and the place du Mûrier with orders to follow him if he comes out of his house. We shall thus, without letting him perceive it, track him to whatever house he hides in. If we leave him there in fancied security for some days we shall be sure to catch him out before long between sunrise and sunset."

"But what is he doing now?" said the stout Cointet. "Perhaps he will escape before to-morrow morning."

" He is at home," said Doublon ; " if he goes out I shall know it. I have one of my men on the place du Mûrier, another at the corner by the Law Courts, and a third within thirty feet of this house. If he comes out they will whistle, and he won't have gone ten steps before I know it by that telegraphic communication."

Kolb had not expected such luck. He stepped softly from the office and said to the cook : " Monsieur Doublon is busy ; I 'll come back to-morrow morning early."

The Alsacian, an old cavalry-man, was seized with an idea which he put in execution at once. He went to a livery-man of his acquaintance, chose a horse, had it saddled, and returned in all haste to his master's house, where he found Madame Eve in a state of despair.

" What is it, Kolb? " said David, noticing the joyful yet half-alarmed look on his follower's face.

" You are surrounded by scoundrels. Has madame thought of any place to hide monsieur? "

When the honest Kolb had explained Cérizet's treachery, the line of watchers about the house, the part taken by the stout Cointet, and the schemes that these men were plotting against his master, David was fatally enlightened as to his position.

" It is the Cointets who are persecuting you," exclaimed poor Eve ; " and that is why Métivier has been so hard. They are paper-makers, they want your secret."

" But how can he escape them? " cried Madame Chardon.

" If madame can find a little place in which to put monsieur," said Kolb, " I will promise to take him there safely without their knowing it."

" Wait till night and take him to Basine Clerget," replied Eve. " I will go and arrange with her. Basine is another myself."

" The spies will follow you," said David, recovering his presence of mind. " We must find some way of communicating with Basine without any of us going there."

" Madame wishes to go there," said Kolb. " This is my idea : monsieur and I will go out together; the spies will all follow us ; then madame can go to Mamselle Clerget, she won't be noticed. I've got a horse ; I take monsieur up behind, and the devil take me if they catch us."

" Well then, farewell, dear friend," cried the poor wife, throwing herself into her husband's arms. " None of us can go and see you, for fear they should find us out. We must say good-by for all the time this voluntary imprisonment lasts. We can correspond by post. Basine will mail your letters and I will write to you in her name."

When David and Kolb left the house they heard three whistles, and they led the spies as far as the Porte Palet, near which was the stable. There Kolb took his master behind him, exhorting him to hold fast.

" Whistle, oh yes, whistle away, my good friends I laugh at you," shouted Kolb. " Do you expect to catch a trooper? "

And the late calvary-man spurred his horse out into the country with a rapidity that not only made it impossible to follow them, but also impossible to discover where they were going.

Eve went to l'Houmeau to see Postel, under pretence

of consulting him. After enduring the mortification of
a pity that took no form but that of words, she left the
apothecary's shop and reached, without being noticed,
Basine's house; to this faithful friend she told her
troubles and asked her for help and protection. Basine, who by way of precaution had taken Eve into
her bedroom, opened the door of a small adjoining
room lighted by a skylight through which no human eye
could look. The two friends opened a little fireplace
the flue of which went up beside that of the ironing-
room, where the workwomen kept a fire to heat their
irons. Eve and Basine spread old coverlets over the
floor to dull all sounds if David made any. Then they
put in a flock bed, a furnace for his experiments, a
table and a chair, etc. Basine promised to carry food
to him every night, and, as no one could possibly enter
the room or know that any one was in it, David could
defy all enemies and even the police.

" At last," said Eve, " I can feel that he is safe."

Eve went back to Postel to clear up some doubt
which, she said, had brought her back to consult so
good a judge of commercial matters ; and she induced
him to walk back with her to her own home. " If you
had married me, you would not be where you are now,"
was the burden of Postel's remarks. On his return he
found his wife jealous of Madame Séchard's beauty
and furious with her husband for his politeness. But
he pacified her with an opinion that fair little women
were far superior to tall dark ones, who were, he said,
like fine horses, always in the stable. He no doubt
gave some proof of the sincerity of this opinion, for the
next day Madame Postel was very loving to him.

" We can be easy in mind now," said Eve to her mother and Marion, whom she found (to use an expression of Marion's) " all of a quiver."

" Oh! they 've gone," said Marion, when Eve looked mechanically into her bedroom.

" Which way shall we go?" said Kolb to his master, when they were three miles out on the road to Paris.

" To Marsac," answered David, " and as we have happened upon this road I will make one more attempt on my father's feelings."

" I 'd rather assault a battery any day — he has no heart, your father."

The old bear had no confidence in his son. He judged him, as the uneducated lower classes always judge, by results. In the first place, he did not admit he had robbed David; then, without considering the difference of the times, he kept saying : " I put him astride of a fine printing-house, just the position I had myself, and he, who knew a thousand times more than I did, could n't make it go." Incapable of understanding his son, he condemned him, and claimed a sort of superiority over his intelligence by thinking, "I am saving bread for him." Moralists will never succeed in laying bare all the influence which feelings exercise over self-interest. Every law of nature works two ways and in opposite directions. David, on his side, understanding his father, had the sublime charity to excuse him.

Reaching Marsac at eight o'clock David and Kolb found the old man in the act of finishing his dinner, which came of necessity very near his bed time.

" I didn't expect to see you again," said the father to the son with a crabbed smile.

" How should you meet, my master and you ? " cried Kolb, indignantly ; " he travels in the skies, and you are always among the vines. Pay what he needs, pay it — that 's your duty as a father."

" Come, Kolb, be off with you : put up the horse at Madame Courtois's, so as not to trouble my father ; and remember that fathers are always in the right."

Kolb went off growling like a dog who, being scolded by his master for his watchfulness, protests while he obeys.

David, without revealing his secret, now offered to give his father visible proof of his discovery, proposing to him a share in its profits in return for the sums that he required, first for his immediate liberation from debt, and next for the perfection of his invention.

" Hey ! how do you expect to prove that you can make fine paper for nothing ? " said the old bear, casting a vinous but shrewd, inquisitive, covetous look at his son. It seemed like a flash of lightning from a rainy cloud, for the old man, faithful to his traditions, never went to bed without a night-cap ; and that night-cap consisted of two bottles of excellent old wine which, according to custom, he sat and sipped.

" Nothing is easier," replied David. " I have no paper with me, for I came off in haste, to escape Doublon ; but finding myself on the road to Marsac, I thought it was better to come to you than go to a money-lender. I have nothing with me but the clothes I stand in. But shut me up in some retired place, where no one can enter and where no one can see me, and — "

" What ! " exclaimed the old man, with an angry

look at his son, "do you mean to say that I am not to see what you do?"

"Father," said David, "you have already proved to me that there is no fatherhood in business."

"Ha! you distrust the parent who gave you life."

"No, but I distrust him who has taken from me the means of living."

"Every man for himself; you are right enough there," said the old man. "Well, I'll put you in my distillery."

"Very good; I'll live there with Kolb. Let me have a caldron for my pulp," said David, not observing the glance his father gave him; "then, if you will send out and get me stems of artichokes, asparagus, nettles, and the reeds you cut on the banks of your little river, I will show you a magnificent paper to-morrow morning."

"If that is really so," said the bear, with a hiccough, "I will give you — perhaps — well, I'll see if I can give you twenty-five thousand francs, on condition that you earn that sum for me every year."

"Give me the chance, and I accept it," cried David. "Kolb, take the horse and go to Mansle; buy me a large horse-hair sieve, and some size at the grocer's, and get back as fast as you can."

"Here, drink something," said the old man, putting a bottle of wine, some bread, and the remnants of cold meat before his son. "Keep up your strength. I'll attend to your stock of green rubbish, — for they are green, those rags of yours; too green, I'm thinking!"

Two hours later, about eleven at night, the old man locked up his son and Kolb in a little apartment back-

ing on his storeroom, roofed with hollow tiles, in which
were stored all the utensils necessary for distilling the
wines of the province of Angoumois, which, as everybody knows, furnish the brandies which are called
Cognac.

" Oh, here's a manufactory made to hand!" cried
David. " Plenty of pans and fuel."

" Well, then, I bid you good-bye till to-morrow," said
old Séchard. " I shall lock you in and let loose my
two dogs, so as to make sure that no one brings you
any paper. Show me the sheets to-morrow, and I
promise I will be your partner, and then things will
be well-managed."

Kolb and David let him lock them up; then they
spent two hours in breaking and preparing the stalks,
using two pieces of joist. The fire burned, the water
boiled. Towards two in the morning Kolb, less preoccupied than David, heard a sigh suspiciously like a
hiccough. He took one of the two candles and looked
about. Presently he perceived the purple face of the
old man filling a little square opening cut in the wall
above the door of communication between the storeroom and the distillery, which was usually blocked by
empty casks. The crafty old fellow had put his son
into the distillery by the outer door. This inner door
enabled him to roll his casks into the storeroom from
the distillery without going round by the courtyard.

" Oh, father!" cried David, looking up at Kolb's
exclamation.

" I came to see if you wanted anything," said the
bear, half-sobered.

" And your interest in us made you bring a ladder!"

said Kolb, pushing aside an empty cask and opening the door, which revealed the old man, in his night-shirt, perched on a short ladder.

"How can you risk your health?" said David.

"I walk in my sleep," said his father, getting down. "Your distrust of me has made me dream; I fancied you had dealings with the devil, who showed you how to do impossible things."

"The devil, indeed!" cried Kolb. "It was your greed for gold that brought you."

"Go to bed, father," said David; "lock that door if you like, but spare yourself the trouble of coming back. Kolb will stand sentinel."

The next day, at four in the afternoon, David issued from the distillery, after destroying all traces of his operations, bringing with him a dozen or more sheets of paper, the fineness, whiteness, texture, and strength of which left nothing to be desired; they bore as a water-mark the threads of the sieve, some being heavier than others. The old man took the specimens in his hand and applied his tongue to them, as a well-trained bear, accustomed from early youth to make his tongue the test of paper, should do. He felt them, rubbed them, folded them, submitted them to every test to which printers subject paper, but though he found nothing to find fault with, he would not admit that he was vanquished.

"I must first see how that works in the press," he said, to avoid praising his son.

"Queer old man!" ejaculated Kolb.

"I will not deceive you, father," said David. "I consider that that paper is still too dear, and I must solve the problem of sizing the pulp, — that is the only improvement to be made."

" Ha! you are only trying to trick me."

" No: let me tell you! I can size the pulp in the caldron, but so far the size does not permeate the pulp evenly; I have to give the paper a touch of the brush."

" Well, discover how to size it in the caldron and you shall have the money."

" My master will never see the color of your money," growled Kolb.

The old man was evidently determined to make David feel the mortification he had himself been made to feel in the night.

" Father," said David, sending Kolb away, " I have never felt hardly to you for selling me your printing-house at an exorbitant price, and one of your own appraising. I have always looked upon you as a father. I have said to myself: ' He is an old man, who has worked hard, and brought me up better than I had any right to expect; let him enjoy in peace, and in his own way, the fruit of his labor.' I have even allowed you to keep my inheritance from my mother; I have borne without a murmur the embarrassments you saddled upon me. I vowed I would make my way to fortune without asking any help from you. Well, this secret of mine, I have discovered it in the midst of want, without bread to feed my family, and tortured by debts which are not my own. Yes, I have struggled patiently until now, when my means are all exhausted. Perhaps it might be said that you owe me help, — but do not think of me; think only of that woman and child" (David could not restrain his tears), " — help them, protect them! Would

18

you be less to them than Kolb and Marion, who gave me their savings?" cried the son, seeing that his father was as cold as the slab of his press.

"And even that did n't suffice you!" cried the old man, lost to all sense of shame; "why, you would soon lay waste all France! Good-bye to you; I 'm too ignorant to dabble in schemes in which I 'm the one who is schemed against. The monkey can't devour the bear" (using the press-room terms). "I 'm a farmer, not a banker. Besides, business between father and son always turns out ill. Eat your dinner here; you sha'n't say that I let you go without giving you anything."

David's nature was one of those profoundly deep ones which drive back their sufferings to the depths and keep them a secret from their nearest and dearest. With such natures, when their anguish forces its way to the surface and makes an appeal, the effort is a mighty and supreme one. Eve had thoroughly understood the noble character of the man. But the father saw in this wave of anguish rising from the depths the common trick of children who want "to work upon" their fathers, and he took the excessive depression which overcame his son for the shame of failure. They parted on bad terms. David and Kolb returned about midnight to the neighborhood of Angoulême, where they dismounted and entered the town on foot, with as many precautions as thieves would take for their robberies. About one in the morning David was safely inducted by Mademoiselle Basine Clerget into the impenetrable hiding-place selected by his wife. There the poor man was now to be watched and tended by the most ingenuous and simple-hearted of all pities, that of a grisette.

The next day Kolb openly boasted of having saved his master on horseback, and of not leaving him until he saw him safely in the suburbs of Limoges. A great provision of David's raw material was already stored in Basine's cellar, so that Kolb, Marion, Madame Séchard, and her mother had no need to communicate with Mademoiselle Clerget.

Two days after this scene with his son, old Séchard, who had three weeks to spare before the business of the vintage began, went to live in his daughter-in-law's house, led there by greed. He could not sleep for thinking and wondering if this discovery had really any chances of profit in it. He must watch the grapes, he said. Accordingly he betook himself to the apartment of two rooms which he had reserved for himself in the attic of David's house ; and there he lived, shutting his eyes to the bareness and poverty which now afflicted his son's household. They owed him rent, consequently they were bound to feed him, and he took no notice of the pewter forks and spoons with which the meals were served.

" I began that way myself," he replied, when his daughter-in-law excused herself for having no silver.

Marion was obliged to run in debt for the food the old man consumed. Kolb was employed by a mason at twenty sous a day. Before long only ten francs remained to poor Eve, who, in the interests of her child and David, sacrificed one by one her last resources to make the old man comfortable. She hoped by her pretty ways, her respectful attentions, her quiet resignation, to touch the old miser's feelings ; but she found him always the same, utterly insensible. She tried to study his character and divine his intentions, but it was labor lost. Old Séchard made himself impenetrable by keeping, as the saying is, between two wines. Intoxication is a good veil. Under cover of his drunkenness, often more pretended than real, the old man tried to worm David's secret from Eve. Sometimes he cajoled her, sometimes he frightened her. When Eve assured him that she was wholly ignorant, he would answer, " I 'll use up my whole property ; I 'll buy an annuity." These humiliating struggles wore out the poor victim, who, not to seem wanting in respect to her father-in-law, ended at last in saying nothing. But one day, driven to extremities, she made answer, " Father, there is a very easy way to find out everything. Pay David's debts, let him come home, and you will soon come to an understanding together."

" Ha ! that 's what you want to get out of me ! " he cried ; " I'm glad to know it."

Old Séchard, who would not believe in his son, believed in the Cointets. He went to consult them, and they purposely dazzled him, telling him there might be millions in his son's discovery.

" If David can prove that he has succeeded I should not hesitate to take your son into the partnership of my paper factory on equal terms, counting his discovery as of equal value with the property," said the tall Cointet.

But the suspicious old bear made so many inquiries while drinking with the workmen, he asked so many questions of Petit-Claud, pretending stupidity, that he ended by suspecting that the Cointets were the real movers in the matter, behind Métivier, and that their object was to ruin the Séchard printing-house, and decoy him into paying the notes by this talk of a discovery; for the old peasant suspected nothing of Petit-Claud's complicity, nor of the deep plot laid to get possession. sooner or later, of this valuable industrial secret. Finally, one morning, the old man, exasperated at not being able to conquer his daughter-in-law's silence, nor even to discover from her where David was hiding, resolved to force the door of the foundry in the shed. after discovering the fact that his son was in the habit of working there. He got up very early in the morning and began to pick the lock.

" What are you doing there, papa Séchard?" cried Marion, who got up at daybreak to go to her factory, and now bounded to the door of the workshop when she saw the old man.

" I am in my own house, Marion," said Séchard, confused.

" Ha! do you mean to be a thief in your old days? You won't get anything by it. however. I shall go and tell all this to madame, red-hot."

" No, don't do that, Marion. See here ; " and the old man pulled two crowns of six francs each from his pocket.

" I 'll say nothing," said Marion, pocketing the money ; " but don't try it again," shaking her finger at him, " or I 'll tell it to all Angoulême."

As soon as old Séchard had gone out Marion rushed up to her mistress.

" See here, madame! I have got twelve francs out of your father-in-law ; there they are."

" How did you do it?"

" He wanted to have a look into the shed and see

what tools and provisions monsieur had there. I knew there was nothing there ; but I frightened him well, and told him he wanted to rob his son, and he gave me those crowns to hold my tongue."

Just then Basine came in joyously with a letter from David, written on magnificent paper, which she gave to her friend secretly.

MY ADORED EVE, — I write to you *first*, on the first sheet of paper obtained by my process. I have succeeded in solving the problem of sizing the pulp in the vat. A pound of pulp will cost (even supposing the products I employ to be cultivated on good ground) five sous. Thus the ream of twelve pounds takes three francs' worth of sized pulp. I am certain to lessen the weight of books by at least one half. The envelope, letter, and samples enclosed are all different fabrications.

I kiss you, dear wife ; we shall now be happy in riches, the only thing lacking to us.

" See," said Eve to her father-in-law, holding up the samples. "Give your son the profits of your vintage and let him make his fortune ; he will return you tenfold what you give him, for he has succeeded at last ! "

VI.

A CRISIS, WHEN THE DOGS STAND AND LOOK AT EACH OTHER.

OLD Séchard had no sooner got the paper into his own hands than he hurried to the Cointets. There each sample was assayed and examined minutely. Some were sized, others unsized; the price was ticketed on each, from three to ten francs a ream; some were of almost metallic purity, others soft as Chinese paper; all possible shades of white were among them. The eyes of Jews appraising diamonds never gleamed with a keener light than those of the Cointets and old Séchard.

" Your son is on the right road," said the stout Cointet.

"Very good; then pay his debts," said the bear.

" Willingly, if he will take us for partners," replied the tall Cointet.

" You are thumb-screwers," cried the old man. " You are persecuting my son under the name of Métivier, and you want me to buy you off. Thank you, I'm not such a fool as that! "

The brothers looked at each other, but they managed to conceal their surprise at the perspicacity of the old miser.

" We are not yet millionnaires enough to dabble in discounts," replied the stout Cointet. " We think ourselves lucky if we can pay our current bills, and we still give notes to our dealers."

" The experiment must be tested on a larger scale." said the tall Cointet, coldly. " A thing that succeeds in a saucepan may fail when it comes to a vat. Free your son, and let him try it."

" Yes, but will my son allow me to be his partner if I set him at liberty? "

" That is not our affair," said the stout Cointet. " Do you suppose, my good friend, that when you have paid ten thousand francs for your son, that's the whole of it? A patent of invention costs two thousand francs, and involves journeys to Paris in order to get it. Then, before making any outlay it will be prudent, as my brother says, to manufacture a thousand reams, and risk the loss of whole batches so as to know what can be counted on. There's nothing more to be distrusted than inventors."

" As for me," said the tall Cointet, " I want my bread all baked."

The old man passed the night in turning over and over in his mind the following dilemma : " If I pay David's debts he is at liberty, and once at liberty he is not forced to make me a partner in his enterprise. He knows that I got the better of him in that first transaction, and he won't try a second. It is my interest, therefore, to keep him in prison."

The Cointets knew old Séchard well enough to be certain they could hunt in couples. The three men said in words : " Before we form a company on this discovery we must have larger experiments; to make these experiments David Séchard must be at liberty." But all concerned had private thoughts of their own. Petit-Claud said to himself: "After I am married I'll take my neck out of the Cointet yoke; but till then I hold them." The tall Cointet was thinking: "I would rather see David under lock and key; I should then be master of the situation." Old Séchard was saying to himself: "If I pay his debts my son will just give me a nod of thanks and that's all."

Eve, harassed by the old man, who threatened to turn her out of the house, still refused either to reveal her husband's refuge or propose to David to return under promise of safety. She was not certain of being able to hide him so successfully a second time, and she therefore replied to all her father-in-law's requests: "Liberate your son, and you will know all." None of these four interested men, standing, as it were, before a festive table, dared to touch the food, so fearful were they of having it snatched from them; they all watched each other with keen distrust.

Some days after David Séchard's concealment Petit-Claud went to see the tall Cointet at his paper factory.

"I have done my best," he said. "David has voluntarily made himself a prisoner, we don't know where, and he is no doubt quietly improving his process. If you have not obtained your object the fault is not mine. Do you intend to keep your promise to me?"

"Yes, if we succeed," replied Cointet. "Old Séchard has been here several times; he asks questions about the manufacturing of paper; the old miser has scented his son's invention, and he wants to profit by it.

There is, therefore, some hope of forming a company. You are the lawyer of father and son — ”

“And you want the Holy Spirit to get the better of them?” said Petit-Claud, smiling.

“Yes,” said Cointet. “If you succeed either in putting David in prison, or in our hands through a deed of partnership, you shall be the husband of Mademoiselle de la Haye.”

“Is that your ultimatum?”

“Yes,” replied Cointet.

“And this is mine,” rejoined Petit-Claud, in a curt tone: “Give me something positive to rely upon; in other words, keep your promise, or I will pay David’s debts and make myself his partner by selling my practice. I will not be cheated. You have spoken plainly, and I use the same language. I have kept my word to you; do you keep yours to me. You have got everything out of me, I have nothing out of you. If I do not at once have proofs of your sincerity I check-mate you.”

The tall Cointet took his hat and umbrella and put on his Jesuit air; then he left the house and signed to Petit-Claud to follow him, saying : —

“You shall see, my dear friend, whether or not I have prepared the way for you.”

The shrewd and wily merchant had instantly seen his danger; he saw too that Petit-Claud was one of those men with whom it was wisest to play aboveboard. He had already, by way of preparation or to acquit his conscience, said a few words in Monsieur du Hautoy’s ear under pretence of giving an account of Mademoiselle de la Haye’s financial position.

" I have found an excellent marriage for Françoise," he said. " Of course with a *dot* of only thirty thousand francs a girl can't be exacting in these days."

" We will talk it over," replied Francis du Hautoy. " Since Madame de Bargeton's departure the position of Madame de Sénonches has changed very much. We might now be able to marry Françoise to some old country noble."

" If you do she will disgrace herself," said Cointet, coolly. "Better marry her to a young man ambitious and capable, whose future you could help, and who would put his wife in a good position."

" We will see about it," Francis had replied ; " the godmother must be consulted first of all."

On the death of Monsieur de Bargeton his wife had sold his property in Angoulême. Madame de Sénonches, who was poorly housed, persuaded her husband to buy the Bargeton mansion, — the cradle of Lucien's ambition, where this history began. Zéphirine de Sénonches had formed a plan to succeed Madame de Bargeton in the sort of sovereignty the latter had once exercised, — to "hold a salon," as it is called ; to be, in short, the great lady of the place. A schism had taken place in the upper ranks of Angoulême society at the time of the duel between Monsieur de Bargeton and Monsieur de Chandour ; some declaring for the innocence of Louise de Nègrepelisse, others for the calumnies of Stanislas de Chandour. Madame de Sénonches declared for the Bargetons and made an immediate conquest of all the adherents of that party. Then, after she was fairly installed in her new house, she profited by the old habits of those who had come there so many years, to win them back again. She received every evening, and soon carried the day over Amélie de Chandour, who posed as her rival. The hopes of Francis du Hautoy, now at the heart of Angoulême society, went so far that he thought of marrying Françoise to Monsieur de Séverac, whom Madame du Brossard had not been able to capture for her daughter.

The tall Cointet, who had his Angoulême at his fingers' ends, appreciated this difficulty, but he resolved to get round it by one of those audacities which a Tartufe alone can venture on. The little lawyer, a good deal surprised at the loyalty of his partner in quibbling, left him to his own thoughts as they walked from the factory to the house in the rue du Minage, where, on the landing, the importunate pair were stopped by the words: "Monsieur and Madame are breakfasting."

"Announce us all the same," said the tall Cointet. They were at once admitted, and the merchant presented the lawyer to the affected Zéphirine. who was breakfasting with M. Francis du Hautoy and Mademoiselle de la Haye; Monsieur de Sénonches having gone, as usual, to a meet at Monsieur de Pimentel's.

"This, madame, is the young lawyer who will take charge of the arrangements on the coming of age of your beautiful ward."

Francis du Hautoy examined Petit-Claud, who, on his side, glanced furtively at the "beautiful ward." Zéphirine's surprise at this address — for Francis had not said a word to her on the subject — was so great that the fork dropped from her hand. Mademoiselle de la Haye, a shrewish-looking girl with a glum face, a thin, ungraceful figure, and dull, fair hair, was, in spite of a rather aristocratic air and manner, very difficult to marry. The words " father and mother unknown " in her certificate of birth forbade her the sphere where the affection of her godmother and Francis du Hautoy would fain have placed her. Mademoiselle de la Haye, who was herself ignorant of her position, was difficult to please ; she had rejected more than one rich merchant of l'Houmeau. The significant grimace which she made at the puny aspect of the little lawyer was reflected on the latter's lips, and Cointet saw it. Madame de Sénonches and Francis seemed to be consulting each other with their eyes as to how they could get rid of Cointet and his protégé. Cointet, who saw everything, begged Monsieur du Hautoy to give him a few moments' private conversation, and the pair then passed into the salon.

" Monsieur," said Cointet plainly, " don't let paternity blind you. You will have difficulty in marrying your daughter, and in the interest of all concerned I have committed you irrevocably to this marriage ; for I love Françoise as though she were my own ward. Petit-Claud knows all. His extreme ambition will guarantee the happiness and comfort of your dear girl. Besides, Françoise can make anything she likes of her husband ; with your influence he will soon be *procureur du roi*. Petit-Claud will sell his practice ; you can easily obtain for him at once the position of second assistant-*procureur ;* after that he will soon make himself *procureur*, president of the court, and deputy."

When they returned to the dining-room Francis was very polite to his daughter's suitor. He looked at

Madame de Sénonches in a certain way, and ended the scene by inviting Petit-Claud to dinner on the following day to talk business. Then he went with them as far as the courtyard, saying to Petit-Claud that he was disposed, on the recommendation of Cointet, and so was Madame de Sénonches, to confirm all that the guardian of Mademoiselle de la Haye's fortune had arranged for the happiness of that dear angel.

"Heavens! how ugly she is!" cried Petit-Claud, when they were off the premises, "and I am caught!"

"She has a very distinguished air," said Cointet; "and if she were handsome do you suppose they would give her to *you?* Hey! my dear fellow, there's more than one small land-owner to whom thirty thousand francs and the influence of Madame de Sénonches would be very acceptable; all the more because Monsieur Francis du Hautoy will never marry and this girl is his heir. Your marriage is settled."

"Settled! how so?"

"This is what I have just told Monsieur du Hautoy," replied Cointet, who now related his audacious proceeding. "My dear fellow, Monsieur Miland is, they say, about to be made *procureur du roi.* Sell your practice, and in ten years from now you'll be Keeper of the Seals. You are bold enough not to shrink from any service the court may ask of you."

"Well, I'll meet you to-morrow at half-past four on the place du Mûrier," replied the lawyer almost beside himself at the probability of such a future. "I shall then have seen old Séchard and planned a partnership in which both father and son shall belong to the Holy Spirit of the Cointets."

On the following day three men, each remarkable in his way, bearing with their whole weight upon the future of the poor voluntary prisoner, namely, old Séchard, the tall Cointet, and the puny little lawyer, were standing on the place du Mûrier. Three men! three greeds! each greed as different as the men themselves. One was conspiring against his son, another against his client, and Cointet was buying these infamies, resolved, in his own mind, not to pay for them.

It was about five o'clock and many of those who were on their way home to dinner stopped to look for a moment at the three men.

"What the devil can old Séchard and the tall Cointet have to say to each other?" thought the most inquisitive.

"There is probably something between them about that wretched David, who has left his wife and child and mother-in-law without bread," replied some one.

"See what it is to send your sons to Paris to learn a trade!" remarked a wise man of the provinces.

Just then old Séchard caught sight of the venerable priest of his own parish of Marsac, who was making his way across the place du Mûrier.

"Hey! monsieur le curé, what are you doing here?" he cried in astonishment.

"Ah! Monsieur Séchard, is that you?" replied the Abbé Marron. "I have come on business to your family."

"Something about my son," thought Séchard.

"It will not cost you much to make everybody happy," said the priest, pointing to a window where Madame Séchard's beautiful face had just appeared between the curtains. Eve was hushing the child's cries by tossing him in her arms and singing to him.

" Have you brought news of my son ? " said the father, " or money? — for that's what he wants most."

" No," said the Abbé Marron. " I bring news to Madame Eve Séchard of her brother."

" Lucien ! " exclaimed Petit-Claud.

" Yes. That poor young man has come from Paris on foot. I found him at Courtois's, dying of fatigue and starvation," replied the priest. " He is very unfortunate."

Petit-Claud took Cointet by the arm, saying aloud : " We dine with Madame de Sénonches ; it is time to dress." Then when they had reached a little distance he added in a low voice, " Catch the cub, and you have the mother. We have David."

" I 've married you, do you marry me," returned Cointet, with a treacherous smile.

" Lucien was my schoolmate ; we were *chums*. In a week I shall get everything out of him. See that my banns are published and I will promise to put David in prison. My mission ends when the bolt is drawn on him."

" Ah ! " said the tall Cointet, softly. " The best thing to do would be to take out the patent in our own name."

Hearing those words the puny little lawyer shuddered.

At this moment Eve saw her father-in-law entering the house with the Abbé Marron.

" Here, Madame Séchard," said the old bear, " here's our vicar who has fine news to tell you of your brother."

" Oh ! " cried poor Eve, struck to the heart, " what has happened to him now ? "

This exclamation showed so many sufferings already borne, so much anxiety of so many kinds, that the abbé hastened to say: "Do not be alarmed, madame, he is living!"

"Would you be kind enough, father," said Eve, addressing old Séchard, "to call my mother; she must hear what monsieur has to tell us about Lucien."

The old man went to find Madame Chardon, to whom he said: "You are to go down and have a scene about your son with the Abbé Marron; he is a good man, though he is a priest. Dinner will no doubt be late. I shall be back in an hour."

And the old bear, indifferent to all that did not ring or glitter gold, left the poor mother without paying any heed to the effect of the blow he had given her. The misfortunes which weighed on her two children, the failure of the hopes she had set on Lucien, the change she had so little foreseen in a character she had always believed to be upright and energetic, — in short, all the events which had happened during the last eighteen months had made Madame Chardon almost unrecognizable. She was not only noble by birth, but she was noble in heart, and she worshipped her children; consequently she had suffered more during the last six months than ever before during her widowhood. Lucien she knew had had the chance to become a Rubempré by letters-patent from the king, to revive her family, the title, the arms, to become a noble! — and he had lost it; he had fallen into the mire! More severe than his sister, she had considered Lucien as lost from the day she first heard of the forged notes. Mothers sometimes choose to deceive themselves; but they know well the children they have suckled, from whom they are never really parted even by distance ; and in the many discussions between David and his wife as to Lucien's chances in Paris Madame Chardon, while apparently sharing her daughter's illusions, trembled lest David were right, for he spoke that which her mother's conscience told her was true. She knew too well the sensitiveness of her daughter's sympathy to burden her with her own distress ; she had therefore borne it in that silence which only mothers who love their children are capable of preserving. Eve, on the other hand, saw with terror the ravages which grief was making in her mother ; she saw her going from old age to decrepitude and threatening to pass away forever. Mother and daughter were acting towards each other one of those noble lies that do not deceive. In the life of this mother the brutal speech of the old miser was the drop that overflowed the cup of her afflictions ; Madame Chardon was heart-struck.

Therefore, when Eve said to the priest ; " Monsieur, this is my mother," and when the abbé looked in that worn face, pallid as that of a nun, framed with hair that was wholly white and yet made beautiful by the calm and tender air of a woman piously resigned, who walked, as they say, by the will of God, he understood the whole life of these two beings. The priest felt no more pity for the executioner, for Lucien ; he shuddered as he became aware of the tortures his victims had evidently endured.

" Mother," said Eve, " my poor brother is very near us ; he is at Marsac."

" Why is he not here ? " asked Madame Chardon.

The Abbé Marron related the circumstances which had brought Lucien from Paris, and the misery of his last days there. He described the anguish of the poet when he discovered the effects of his conduct on his unfortunate family, and his fears as to the greeting he might receive in Angoulême.

" Has he reached the point of doubting us? " said Madame Chardon.

" The unfortunate young man came all the way on foot," said the abbé, " enduring the utmost privations ; he returns to his home disposed to enter upon the humblest way of life ; he desires to repair his faults."

" Monsieur," said the sister, " in spite of the harm he has done us I love my brother as we love the body of a friend who is dead ; and in loving him thus, I still love him better than many sisters love their brothers. He has made us very poor ; but let him come, and we will share with him the morsel of bread that he has left us. Ah ! if he had never left us, monsieur, we should not have lost our dearest possessions."

" Can I in any way be useful to you in your painful situation? " said the worthy abbé, wishing to take leave with a suitable speech.

" Ah ! monsieur," said Madame Chardon, " the wounds of money are not mortal, they say, but wounds of that sort can have no other remedy than the disease."

" If you had enough influence over my father-in-law to induce him to help his son," said Eve, " you would save a whole family."

" He does not believe in you ; he seemed to me greatly exasperated against your husband," said the abbé, who had been made to feel by the paraphrases of the old miser that the Séchard affairs were a wasp's-nest into which he had better not set his feet.

The priest's mission accomplished, he went to dine with his grand nephew Postel, who dispelled the small amount of good-will felt by his uncle towards Eve and David by taking, as did all Angoulême, the part of the father against the son.

" You may do something to reform a spendthrift," said Postel, " but those who make inventions and experiments are certain to ruin themselves."

The abbé's curiosity was completely satisfied; and curiosity is, in all the provinces of France, the principal cause of the excessive interest the inhabitants take in one another. That evening when he returned to Marsac and saw Lucien, he told him what was happening at the Séchards', and let him know that his errand there was dictated by the purest charity.

" You have saddled your sister and her husband with a debt of ten or twelve thousand francs," he said in conclusion, " and no one, my good sir, has that amount of money to lend to a friend. We are not rich in Angoumois; I had no idea when you spoke to me of those notes that the sum was so large."

Thanking the abbé for his efforts, the poet added: " The word of pardon which you bring is, to me, the real treasure."

VII.

THE RETURN OF THE PRODIGAL BROTHER.

THE next day Lucien started at daylight for Angoulême, which he entered at nine in the morning, carrying a cane in his hand and wearing a small frock-coat rather damaged by his journey, and trousers with black and white lines. His worn-out boots told plainly enough that he belonged to the hapless class of foot-passengers. He did not conceal from himself the effect that would certainly be produced on his townsmen by the contrast between his return and his departure. But, his heart still panting with remorse caused by the abbé's picture of his home, he accepted at the moment his punishment, resolving to face the eyes of his former acquaintance. He said to himself, " I am heroic ! " All such poetic natures begin by first duping themselves.

As he walked through l'Houmeau his soul struggled between the shame of his return and the poesy of his recollections. His heart beat as he passed by Postel's shop, where, fortunately for him, the apothecary's wife was alone with her infant. He saw with pleasure that his father's name had been effaced. Since Postel's marriage the shop had been repainted, and above the door, as in Paris, was the word " Pharmacy." As Lucien climbed the stairway of the Porte Palet he felt the influence of his native air; the burden of his misfortunes fell from him, and he said in his heart joyfully, " I shall see them once more! "

He reached the place du Mûrier without having met a single person whom he knew; a happiness he hardly expected,— he who had once like a conquering hero walked about his town. Kolb and Marion, standing sentinels at the door rushed up the stairs crying out: " He is coming! " Lucien saw once more the old press-room, the old courtyard; on the stairs he met his sister and his mother, and they kissed each other, forgetting for a moment in that close clasp the sorrows that were upon them. In family life we almost always compound with sorrow; we make our bed, and hope enables us to bear its hardness. Though Lucien was the image of despair, he was also the embodiment of its poesy. The sun had browned his skin during his long and weary journey; the deepest melancholy, stamped on every feature, cast its shadows on that poetic brow. This change in his bearing told of so much suffering that the only feeling possible in those who saw the traces left by misery on his countenance, was pity. The ardent imagination which had let him go in hope found on his return a sad reality. In the midst of her joy, Eve's smile was that of a martyred saint. Grief often renders the face of a very beautiful woman sublime. The gravity which Lucien saw on his sister's features, in place of the tranquil innocence they had worn when he left her, spoke too eloquently to his heart not to pain it. So, the first effusion of their feelings, keen and natural as they were, was followed on both sides by reaction; each feared to

speak. Lucien's eyes could not help seeking the one
who was missing from the meeting. The look was understood by Eve, and she burst into tears, as did Lucien. Madame Chardon continued as before, pallid and
apparently impassible. Eve rose, to spare her brother
the painful answer to his look, and went to find Marion
and say to her: "Lucien likes strawberries — can we
get some?"

"Oh! don't trouble. I thought you would want to
welcome Monsieur Lucien, and I've got a nice little
breakfast for him, and a good dinner, too."

"Lucien," said Madame Chardon to her son, "you
have much to repent of here. Pledged to be an object of pride to your family, you have plunged it
into the worst distress. You have almost destroyed
the opportunity your brother had to make a fortune
for his new family. And that is not all you have
destroyed," added the mother. A painful pause
succeeded; Lucien's silence seemed to imply acceptance of his mother's blame. "You entered a career
of toil," went on Madame Chardon, more gently. "I
do not blame you for wishing to revive the old family
from which I came; but such an enterprise needed
both fortune and noble principles; you had neither.
Our belief in you is changed by your own actions to
distrust. You have destroyed the peace of this hard-
working, patient family, whose way was already difficult. But the first wrong-doing should receive forgiveness. Do not do wrong again. We are now in very
difficult circumstances; be prudent; listen to your
sister's advice; misfortune is a teacher whose lessons,
harshly given, have borne their fruit in her; she has

become serious, she is a mother, she bears the whole
burden of the home and its affairs out of devotion to
our dear David ; and she has now become, through your
wrong-doing, my only comfort."

" You might be more severe," said Lucien, kissing
his mother. " I accept your forgiveness, because it is
the last I shall ever receive."

Eve returned ; seeing her brother's humiliated attitude, she knew that Madame Chardon had spoken.
Her loving-kindness put a smile upon her lips, to which
Lucien answered by repressed tears. The bodily presence has a charm ; it changes the most hostile feelings
of those who love, whether as lovers or with family
affection, however strong may be the causes of discon-
tent. Is it that affection lays a path in the heart which
we love to re-enter? Can it be that this phenomenon
belongs to the domain of magnetism? Does reason
tell us we must either never meet again, or we must
forgive each other? Whether it be reason, or a physical cause, or an action of the soul that produces this
effect, certain it is that every one's experience will tell
him that the motions, gesture, and look of a beloved
being revive in those he has most ill-used, grieved, or
offended, the vestiges of tenderness. The mind may
have difficulty in forgetting, self-interest may still suffer,
but the heart, in spite of everything, returns to its alle-
giance. So the poor sister, listening until breakfast-time
to her brother's confidences, was no longer mistress of
her eyes as she looked at him, nor of her tones when she
suffered her heart to speak. Beginning to understand
the elements of literary life in Paris, she also understood
how it was that Lucien had succumbed in the struggle.

The poet's joy in fondling his sister's child, his own childlike ways, the happiness he showed at returning to his land and his people, mingled with his bitter grief at David's disaster, the melancholy which sometimes overshadowed him, his emotion when he noticed that his sister had remembered his love for strawberries, — all these things, even to the difficulty of lodging the prodigal brother, made this day a festive one. It was like a pause in the midst of misery. Old Séchard did his best to drive back the feelings of these poor women by saying to them: " You welcome him as if he brought you hundreds and thousands."

" What has Lucien done that he should not be welcomed?" cried Madame Séchard, anxious to conceal her brother's shame.

Nevertheless, after the first flow of tenderness had passed, shadows of the truth reappeared. Lucien soon perceived in Eve a difference between her old affection and that she now bore him; David was deeply honored, while Lucien was loved in spite of all, as we love a mistress notwithstanding the disasters she has caused. Esteem, the necessary basis of all true sentiments, and the solid material which gives them the security by which they live, was now felt to be wanting between the mother and son, the sister and brother. Lucien felt himself deprived of the perfect confidence they would have had in him but for his lapse in honor. D'Arthez' opinion of him had become that of his sister, and unconsciously it showed itself in her looks and tones and gestures. Lucien was pitied ; but as to being the glory, the honor of the family, the hero of the hearth, all such fine hopes were gone without recall. His instability was such that they even feared to tell him the place of David's refuge. Eve, unmoved by his caresses, — for he wanted to see his brother, — was no longer the Eve of l'Houmeau, to whom, in former days, a mere glance from Lucien was an irresistible command. Lucien talked of repairing the wrongs he had done, and boasted of being soon able to rescue his brother. To this Eve replied: " Don't meddle in the matter; our adversaries are the ablest and most perfidious men in town." Lucien threw up his head, as if to say: " I have battled with Parisians ; " to which his sister replied with a look which meant, " And you were worsted."

" I am no longer loved," thought Lucien ; " for my family, as well as for the world, I ought to have succeeded."

After the second day, when he thus explained to himself the evident want of confidence in his mother and sister, the poet was seized with a feeling that was not anger, but grief, — he was hurt. He applied the axioms of Parisian life to the restrained provincial life of his family, forgetting that the patient mediocrity of the home, sublime in its resignation, was his work. " They are only tradespeople, they cannot understand me," he thought; thus separating himself from his sister and mother and David, being unconsciously aware that he could no longer deceive them as to his character, or his future.

Eve and Madame Chardon, in whom the divining sense had been awakened by so many shocks, so many misfortunes, were aware of Lucien's secret thoughts ; they felt themselves misjudged, and saw him gradually withdrawing from them : " Paris has changed him towards us," they said to each other. They gathered the fruits of the selfishness they themselves had cultivated. On both sides this first leaven of estrangement was certain to ferment; and it did ferment, but chiefly on Lucien's side, for on that lay the wrong. As for Eve, she was one of those sisters who can say to faulty brothers : " Forgive me *thy* sins." But, when any union of souls has been perfect, as it was at the dawn of life between Eve and Lucien, all that injures that ideal feeling kills it. Where ordinary humanity recovers from the thrust of a dagger, the hearts that love are parted irrevocably by a word, a look. The secret of inexplicable separations may be found in the memory of some perfection lost to the life of the soul. We can live with distrust in our hearts when the past offers no memory of a pure and cloudless love ; but, to two beings once absolutely united life becomes, when look and word are guarded, intolerable. Thus the great poets kill their Paul and Virginia in adolescence. Conceive of a Paul and a Virginia estranged !

Let us here remark, to the honor of Eve and Lucien, that self-interests, harshly wounded as they were, did not aggravate this estrangement. In the faultless sister as in the faulty brother all was feeling, unalloyed ; therefore, the least misunderstanding, the slightest quarrel, any new disappointment in Lucien, might at once disunite them, or lead to one of those partings which are irrevocable. Matters of money can be settled ; feelings are unrelenting.

A few days after his arrival Lucien received a copy of the " Journal d'Angoulême," and turned pale with

pleasure on seeing himself made the subject of a leading
article in that estimable paper, which resembled the
well-brought-up young lady mentioned by Voltaire, who
never got herself talked about. We give the entire
article : —

" Let Franche-Comté take pride in having given birth
to Victor Hugo, Charles Nodier, and Cuvier ; Brittany, for
possessing Chateaubriand and Lammenais ; Normandy, as the
parent of Casimir Delavigne ; Touraine, of the author of
' Eloa.' To-day our own Angoulême (where, in the days of
Louis XIII., the illustrious Guez, better known under the
name of Balzac, became our compatriot), Angoulême, we
say, has no need to envy those provinces, nor Limousin
which has produced Dupuytren ; nor Auvergne, the country
of Montlosier ; nor Bordeaux, which may boast of giving
birth to so many great men ; for we ourselves now have our
poet ! The author of the noble sonnets entitled ' Daisies,'
unites with the glory of a poet that of a prose writer ; for to
him is due that fine romance of ' The Archer of Charles IX.'
The day will come when our sons will be proud of having
for their compatriot Lucien Chardon, a rival of Petrarch ! ! !
[In the provincial newspaper of this period notes of exclamation were like the ' hurrahs ' which greet the speeches at
an English public meeting.] In spite of his dazzling success
in Paris our young poet did not forget that the Hôtel de
Bargeton in his native town was the cradle of his triumphs,
and that the Angoulême aristocracy were the first to applaud
his poems ; he remembered that the wife of our present prefect, Monsieur le Comte du Châtelet, encouraged his first
steps in the career of the Muses, and he has returned to us !
All l'Houmeau was agitated when early yesterday morning
our Lucien de Rubempré presented himself. The news of
his return has produced the liveliest sensation. It is certain
that the town of Angoulême will not allow her suburb to

surpass her in the honors paid to one who has so gloriously, both in the press and in literature, represented our town in Paris. Lucien has dared to brave the fury of faction as a religious poet and a royalist. He has come, we are told, to rest, after the fatigues of a struggle which might well weary stronger athletes than men of poetry and imagination.

" With an eminently wise political forethought, which we applaud (it is said that the Comtesse du Châtelet was the first to whom the idea occurred), it is proposed to restore to our poet the title and name of the illustrious family of Rubempré, the only heiress of which is Madame Chardon, his mother. To revive thus, by means of genius and fresh fame, the names of ancient families about to become extinct, is another pledge from the immortal author of the Charter of his constant desire, expressed in the two words, Union and Oblivion !

" Our poet is staying with his sister, Madame Séchard."

An "item" in another part of the paper was as follows :

" Our prefect, Monsieur le Comte du Châtelet, lately appointed Gentleman of the Bedchamber in ordinary to his Majesty, has just been made Councillor of State, for special service.

" Yesterday all the municipal authorities called on the prefect.

" Madame la Comtesse Sixte du Châtelet will receive every Thursday.

" The mayor of Escarbas, M. de Nègrepelisse, representing the younger branch of the d'Espard family, the father of Madame du Châtelet, who was recently made a count and Peer of France and Commander of the royal order of Saint-Louis, is, they say, selected to preside over the electoral College of Angoulême at the coming elections."

" There ! " said Lucien to his sister, giving her the paper.

After reading the article attentively, Eve gave the sheet back to Lucien with a thoughtful air.

"What do you think of it?" asked Lucien, amazed at a caution which seemed to him coldness.

"Brother," she answered, "that newspaper belongs to the Cointets ; they control absolutely everything that goes into it ; they cannot be forced to insert anything, unless by the prefect or the bishop. Do you suppose that your former rival, now prefect, is generous enough to sing your praises? Have you forgotten that the Cointets are suing us under the name of Métivier, hoping, no doubt, to force David to let them profit by his discoveries? From whatever · quarter that article comes, I think it alarming. When you were here you excited only dislike and jealousy ; they calumniated you on the principle of the proverb that ' a prophet is of no honor in his own country ; ' and yet everything is now changed in the twinkling of an eye ! "

"You don't know the self-love of towns, of provinces," replied Lucien. "In one of the small southern towns the inhabitants went to the gates to receive in triumph a young man who had won the prize of honor at the 'grand concours,' for they saw in him the germ of a great man."

"Listen to me, my dear Lucien ; I don't want to preach to you, but let me say it all in one word : distrust everything, even the smallest things, here."

"You are right," said Lucien, surprised to find his sister so little enthusiastic.

The poet himself was at the summit of happiness at finding his mean and humiliating return to Angoulême transformed into a triumph.

"You do not choose to believe in the slight amount of fame which has cost us so dear!" cried Lucien, after an hour's silence, during which time a storm had been gathering in his heart.

For all answer Eve looked at him, and the look made him ashamed of his accusation.

A few minutes before the dinner hour a servant from the Prefecture brought a note addressed to Monsieur Lucien Chardon which seemed to justify the self-satisfaction of the poet whom, as it now appeared, society desired to welcome.

The note contained the following invitation : —

Monsieur le Comte Sixte du Châtelet and Madame la Comtesse du Châtelet request the honor of Monsieur Lucien Chardon's company at dinner on the 15th of September next.

R. S. V. P.

With this note came a card bearing the words : " Le Comte Sixte du Châtelet, Gentleman of the Bedchamber in ordinary to the King, Prefect of the Charente, Councillor of State."

" You are in favor," said old Séchard ; " I hear people talking about you as if you were a great personage. They say l'Houmeau and Angoulême are wrangling over the honor of twisting wreaths for your head ! "

" My dear Eve," said Lucien, in a low voice, " I am absolutely as I was that day at l'Houmeau when I was invited to Madame de Bargeton's — I have no clothes in which to dine at the prefect's."

" Do you mean to accept his invitation?" cried Eve, terrified.

On this an argument began between the brother and
sister as to the expediency of going or not going to the
Prefecture. The common-sense of the provincial
woman told Eve that Lucien ought not to appear in
society unless with a smiling face and a perfectly irreproachable dress; but the real anxiety that filled her
mind she kept to herself; it was this : " What will be
the result to Lucien of this dinner? What can the
great world of Angoulême want of him? May it not be
some plot against him?"

Lucien finally said to his sister before he went to bed,
" You do not know what my influence is. The wife of
the prefect is afraid of the journalist; besides, in the
Comtesse du Châtelet I can always find Louise de
Nègrepelisse. A woman who has just attained so high
a position can save David. I will tell her of the great
discovery my brother has made, and it will be nothing
for her to obtain a succor of ten thousand francs from
the ministry."

At eleven o'clock that night the whole household
were aroused by music in the streets; the place du
Mûrier was crowded with people. A serenade was
given to Lucien Chardon de Rubempré by the young
men of Angoulême. Lucien went to his sister's window and said, after the last piece and in the midst of
the deepest silence : " I thank my townsmen for the
honor they have done me ; I shall endeavor to make
myself worthy of it ; they will forgive me for not saying
more ; my emotion is so great that I cannot continue."

" Long live the author of ' The Archer of Charles
IX. !' " " Long live the author of ' The Daisies !' "
" Long live Lucien de Rubempré !"

After three salvos of cheers, shouted by many voices, three crowns and bouquets were adroitly flung through the open window of the room. Ten minutes later the square was empty and silence reigned.

" I 'd rather have ten thousand francs," growled old Séchard, fingering the bouquets with a very contemptuous air. " You gave them daisies, and they give you nosegays. You appear to deal in flowers ! "

" So that 's your estimate of the honors my fellow-citizens bestow upon me? " cried Lucien, whose countenance now wore an expression of radiant satisfaction, without a trace of melancholy. " If you knew men, papa Séchard, you would know that there are not two moments like these to be met with in a lifetime. Nothing but true enthusiasm can bestow such triumphs! This, my dear mother and my good sister, will efface all griefs." Lucien kissed his mother and Eve as people kiss in those rare moments when joy wells up in waves so mighty that we feel impelled to fling ourselves upon the hearts of friends. (In default of friends, said Bixiou one day, an author drunk with success embraces his porter.) " My dear sister," cried Lucien suddenly, " why do you weep? Ah ! I see, — for joy."

" Alas," said Eve to her mother when they were alone before going to bed, " I do believe there is, in a poet, a pretty woman of the worst kind."

" You are right," said the mother, shaking her head, " Lucien has already forgotten not only his misfortunes, but ours."

The mother and daughter separated without daring to put their whole thought into words.

20

VIII.

THE MACHINERY OF AN OVATION.

IN countries consumed by that spirit of social insubordination which underlies the word *equality*, any triumph is one of those miracles which, like certain miracles of past times, will not work without a manipulator. Out of ten ovations obtained by ten men and awarded in the midst of their fellows, nine are the result of causes entirely foreign to the man glorified. The triumph of Voltaire on the boards of the Théâtre-Français was that of the philosophy of his period. No one can triumph in France unless the crown fits the heads of all who acclaim him. Thus the two poor women had cause for their presentiments. This ovation to the great man of the province was too antipathetic to the stagnant ways of Angoulême not to have been put in motion either by self-interests or by the hand of some eager admirer. Eve, like most women, was distrustful through instinct, without being able to explain to herself the causes of her distrust. She was still thinking as she went to sleep that night, —

" Who in Angoulême admires Lucien enough to have stirred the whole town in this way! He has not yet published 'The Daisies ; ' why is he congratulated on a success he has not obtained?"

This excitement was in fact the doing of Petit-Claud. On the day when the abbé told him of Lucien's arrival at Marsac, the lawyer dined for the first time with Madame de Sénonches, who was then to receive his formal demand for the hand of her goddaughter. It was one of those family dinners the solemnity of which is shown by the style of the gowns rather than by the number of the guests ; it may be domestic, but it has a purpose, the meaning of which can be discerned on the faces of all present. Françoise was dressed for exhibition. Madame de Sénonches flew the flag of her most elegant toilet. Monsieur du Hautoy wore a black coat. Monsieur de Sénonches, to whom his wife had written of the arrival of Madame du Châtelet (who was to dine with her on this occasion) and of the formal reception of a suitor for Françoise, had returned to town from Monsieur de Pimentel's preserves. Cointet dressed in his best brown coat, ecclesiastically cut, presented to the eyes of all a six-thousand-franc diamond in his shirt-frill, — the revenge of a rich merchant on these poor aristocrats. Petit-Claud, though brushed and combed and well-soaped, had not been able to get rid of his dried-up look. It was impossible to avoid comparing the skinny little lawyer squeezed into his clothes to a torpid viper ; but hope had so increased the sharpness of his magpie eyes, he affected such indifference, he curbed himself so tightly, that he attained to all the dignity of an ambitious little *procureur du roi.*

Madame de Sénonches had requested her intimates not to speak of this first meeting of her goddaughter and the suitor, nor of the fact that Madame du Châtelet would be present, so that she had every reason to expect that her rooms would be filled. The prefect and his wife had already made their official visit by means of cards, reserving the honor of a personal one for this occasion. The aristocracy of Angoulême were so devoured with curiosity on the subject that several persons in the Chandour camp proposed to spend the evening at the hôtel Bargeton, — for they persisted in not calling it the hôtel de Sénonches. The rumor of Madame du Châtelet's position in Parisian society woke many ambitions ; moreover, it was said that she had changed for the better wonderfully, and every one wished to judge of this improvement for themselves. Learning from Cointet that Zéphirine had obtained permission to present him to Madame du Châtelet as the future husband of her dear Françoise, Petit-Claud determined to get some profit out of the embarrassing position in which Lucien's return had placed the late Madame de Bargeton.

Monsieur and Madame de Sénonches had taken so much upon them by the mere purchase of the house that, like true provincials, they refrained from the expense of altering it. So the first words of Zéphirine, as she advanced to meet Madame du Châtelet, were : " My dear Naïs, see ! you are once more at home ! " pointing, as she spoke, to the little chandelier, with the glass pendants, the panelled walls, and the furniture which had once so fascinated Lucien.

" That, dear, is what I least care to remember," said the prefect's wife graciously, casting a glance about her to examine the company.

Every one agreed that Louise de Nègrepelisse was no longer like her former self. Parisian society, in which

she had spent the last eighteen months, the first pleasures of her marriage which had transformed the woman
as much as Paris had transformed the provincial, and
the sort of dignity which power gives, made Madame du
Châtelet a woman who resembled Madame de Bargeton
as a girl of twenty resembles her mother. She wore a
charming little head-dress of lace and flowers, carelessly
fastened on her head by a diamond pin. Her hair was
in curls, which suited her face and rejuvenated it by
masking its outlines. She had a foulard gown, made
with a pointed waist gracefully fringed, the cut of
which (due to the famous Victorine) became her figure.
Her shoulders, covered with a blonde fichu, were
scarcely visible beneath a gauze scarf cunningly wound
about her throat, which was too long. She toyed with
one of those pretty trifles the manipulation of which is
a rock of disaster to provincial women ; a crystal scent-
bottle was fastened to her bracelet by a chain, and in
one hand she held her fan and her handkerchief without
appearing to be the least embarrassed by them. The
taste displayed in every detail of her dress, her pose
and manners (copied from Madame d'Espard) proved
that Louise had been an apt pupil of the faubourg
Saint-Germain. As to her husband, the old beau of the
Empire, marriage had ripened him like those melons
which are green one day and turn yellow in a single
night. Finding on the glowing face of the wife the
freshness which Sixte had lost, many provincial sarcasms went round from ear to ear ; all the more because
the women, furious at the new superiority of the former
queen of Angoulême, made the husband the scape-goat
of the wife.

Except for the absence of Monsieur de Chandour and his wife, Monsieur de Pimentel, and the Rastignacs, the salon was filled with about the same persons as on the day when Lucien read there for the first time; even the bishop arrived, followed by his grand-vicars. Petit-Claud, much impressed by his first sight of the Angoulême aristocracy, to the heart of which he had never expected to penetrate, felt his hatred against the upper classes getting much subdued. He thought the Comtesse du Châtelet ravishing as he said to himself: "There's the woman who can get me appointed assistant-procureur!"

Towards the middle of the evening, after talking for about the same length of time to all the women present, varying the tone of the interviews according to the importance of the individual and the course she had taken at the time of the flight with Lucien, Louise retired into the boudoir with the bishop. Madame de Sénonches then took the arm of the suitor, whose heart beat violently, and led him into the boudoir where Lucien's troubles had begun, and where they were now to be consummated.

"This is Monsieur Petit-Claud, my dear," said Zéphirine to Naïs. "I commend him to you all the more warmly because whatever you can do for him will benefit my goddaughter."

"Are you a lawyer, Monsieur?" said the daughter of the Nègrepelisse, looking at the little man as if from a height.

"Alas, yes, Madame la comtesse." (Never before had the tailor's son had the opportunity of uttering those last three words, and his mouth seemed full of them.)

" But," he continued, " it depends on Madame la comtesse to advance me. Monsieur Milaud is, they say,
going to Nevers — "

" But," said the countess, " are you not required to
be second assistant before you are made first? I should
be very happy to see you first assistant at once if it
could be done. But before I do anything to obtain
this favor for you I should like some assurance of your
devotion to legitimacy, to religion, and above all to
Monsieur de Villèle."

" Ah, madame," said Petit-Claud, approaching her
and whispering in her ear, " I am a man who is rever-
ently obedient to the king."

" That is what *we* need in these days," she replied,
drawing back to let him know he was not to whisper in
her ear again. " If you and Madame de Sénonches are
agreed, you may count on me," she added, making a
regal gesture with her fan.

" Madame," said Petit-Claud, who saw Cointet at the
door making a sign to him. " Lucien is here."

" Monsieur ! " said the countess, in a tone which
would have stopped the words in the throat of an ordinary man.

" Madame la comtesse does not understand me," continued Petit-Claud, speaking in his most respectful manner. " I desire to offer her a proof of my devotion to
her person. How does Madame la comtesse wish that
the great man she herself has made should be received
in Angoulême ? "

Louise de Nègrepelisse had never thought of this
dilemma, in which she was evidently more interested
on account of the past than of the present.

" Monsieur Petit-Claud," she said, with a stately and dignified manner, " you wish to belong to the government. Remember that its first principle is never to be in the wrong ; women have, even more than governments, the instinct of power and the sentiment of dignity."

" So I supposed, madame," he answered eagerly, all the while watching the countess with an attention which though deep, was scarcely visible. "Lucien has returned in a state of abject misery. If he should receive an ovation I can oblige him, for that very reason, to leave Angoulême, where his sister and brother-in-law, David Séchard, are just now harassed by a law-suit."

Madame du Châtelet's proud face showed a slight emotion produced by the repression of her satisfaction. Surprised at being understood, she looked at Petit-Claud and opened her fan. Françoise de la Haye coming into the room at the moment gave her time to choose her answer.

" Monsieur," she said, with a smile, "you will soon be *procureur du roi.*"

Surely that was saying all, without compromising herself.

" Oh, madame !" cried Françoise, "I shall owe you the happiness of all my life." Then she stooped to Madame du Châtelet's ear and whispered, with a girlish gesture, " I should die by inches as the wife of a provincial lawyer."

If Zéphirine thus threw herself upon Naïs it was because Francis, who was not without a certain knowledge of bureaucracy, urged her.

" Remember," he said, " that in the first days of an

accession to power, whether it is that of a prefect, a
dynasty, or a speculation, men are eager to render services ; but they soon find out the annoyances of patron-
age and freeze over. To-day Madame du Châtelet will
make an effort for Petit-Claud which three months hence
she would not make for your husband."

"But has Madame la comtesse thought of what an
ovation to our poet involves? He will have to be received at the Prefecture during the nine days the won-
der lasts."

Louise made a sign with her head dismissing the little lawyer ; then she rose and went to the door of the
boudoir to speak to Madame de Pimentel who was just
arriving. Astonished at the elevation of old Monsieur
de Nègrepelisse to the peerage, the marquise felt that
she had better court a woman who was clever enough to
have increased her influence by making a sort of quasi
false step.

" Do tell me, my dear, why you took the pains to
put your father in the Upper Chamber," said the marquise, in the midst of a confidential conversation, in
which she was figuratively on her knees before the superiority of her " dear Naïs."

" My dear, they bestowed that favor because my
father has no children and will always vote for the
crown ; but if I have sons I count on getting the title
and arms and peerage transferred to the eldest."

Madame de Pimentel sadly perceived that she could
never persuade a woman whose ambition extended to
her unborn children, to help her to realize her ardent
desire of getting Monsieur de Pimentel raised to the
peerage.

" I have won the prefect's wife," said Petit-Claud to
Cointet as they left the house, " and I promise you that
partnership. In a month I shall be first assistant-procureur and you — you will be David Séchard's master.
Try to find me a purchaser for my practice, which I have
made, in five months, the best in Angoulême."

" It only needed to put you on horseback," said
Cointet, half jealous of his own work.

We can now understand the cause of Lucien's triumphant reception in his own town. Like the King of
France, who would not avenge the Duke of Orleans,
Louise would not remember the wrongs done in Paris
to Madame de Bargeton. She resolved to patronize
Lucien, to crush him with her protection, and get him
out of the place *honorably.* Petit-Claud, who knew in
part what had happened in Paris, relied on the perennial hatred women bear to men who have not had the
wit to love them at the moment when they wanted to be
loved.

The day of the ovation (which was also to justify the
past of Madame de Bargeton) Petit-Claud, for the purpose of turning Lucien's head still more, arrived at
Madame Séchard's with six young men of the town,
all old schoolmates of Lucien. This was a deputation
sent by the rest of the schoolmates to the author of
" The Archer of Charles IX." and " The Daisies," requesting him to be present at the banquet they wished
to give to a great man who had issued from their ranks.

" That's you, Petit-Claud," cried Lucien.

" Your return here," said Petit-Claud, " has stimulated our vanity ; it is a point of honor. We have
clubbed together and we are preparing a magnificent

feast for you ; the head of the college and all the pro-
fessors are coming, and as things look now, we shall
have some of the authorities."

" What day is it? " asked Lucien.

" Next Sunday."

" Then I can't be present," replied the poet. "I
can't accept anything for the next ten days ; but after
that I will, gladly."

" Well, just as you say," said Petit-Claud. " So be
it, — in ten days."

Lucien was charming to his comrades, who treated
him with an admiration that was almost reverential.
He talked for half an hour with much brilliancy, for he
felt himself on a pedestal, and he wished to justify the
opinion of the community. He put his thumbs in the
armholes of his waistcoat, and talked like a man who
saw things from the eminence on which his fellow-citizens had placed him. He was modest, and a good
fellow, as became a genius in his off moments. His
tone was that of an athlete fatigued with the arena of
Paris, above all, disenchanted, disillusioned ; he congratulated his comrades on never having left their
worthy provinces. They departed one and all delighted
with him. Then he called to Petit-Claud and detained
him to ask the truth about David's affairs, reproaching
him for ever letting things come to the pass of obliging
his brother-in-law to conceal himself. Lucien intended
to be deeper than Petit-Claud. Petit-Claud endeavored
to make his former schoolmate think him a little provincial lawyer without either faculty or shrewdness. The
constitution of modern society, which is infinitely more
complicated in its running-gear than the societies of

ancient times, has had the effect of sub-dividing the faculties of mankind. In the olden time eminent men, forced to be universal, appeared in small numbers, like torches among the nations of antiquity. Later, though faculties were specialized, their application was still to the general whole. Thus a man " rich in cunning," as Louis XI. called it, applied his cunning generally. But to-day the quality itself is sub-divided. For example : so many professions mean so many different forms of cunning. A wily diplomatist may be tricked in the provinces by a very common lawyer or by a peasant. The most crafty of journalists can be fooled in a matter of commercial interests, and Lucien was fitted to be and did become the plaything and tool of Petit-Claud. That malicious little lawyer had himself written the article which announced that the town of Angoulême felt it due to its own dignity to receive its great man. Lucien's fellow-citizens who assembled on the place du Mûrier were the workmen in the printing-house and paper factory of the Cointets, accompanied by the clerks in the offices of Petit-Claud and Cachan, together with a number of their schoolmates. By making himself at once Lucien's intimate, Petit-Claud thought, with good reason, that sooner or later he should get from him the secret of David's retreat. If David were betrayed through Lucien the latter could certainly not remain in Angoulême.

" What would n't I have done to assist David," said the lawyer, in reply to Lucien's reproaches, " if only for the sister of my old friend ? but in law, you understand, there are positions to which every thing must be sacrificed. David asked me on the 1st of June to guarantee him three months tranquillity ; he is not in any danger

till September, and, moreover, I have managed to secure all his property from his creditors, — for I shall
certainly gain the suit before the Royal Court; I shall
get a judgment that the rights of the wife are absolute,
and that in this case they cover no fraud. As to you,
my dear friend, you have come back poor, but you are a
man of genius." (Lucien made a gesture as if the incense
were swung too near his nose.) " Yes, dear Lucien,"
continued Petit-Claud, " I have read ' The Archer of
Charles IX.,' and it is more than a book, it is a work of
genius. There are but two men in France who could
have written that preface, — Chateaubriand and you ! "

Lucien accepted the compliment and refrained from
saying that the preface was written by Daniel d'Arthèz.
Out of one hundred French authors, ninety-nine would
have done the same.

" Well, here in your native town no one seemed to
know you," continued Petit-Claud, pretending indigna-
tion. " When I saw the general indifference, I took it
into my head to revolutionize opinion. I wrote the
article you read — "

" You ! did you write it? " cried Lucien.

" I, myself. Angoulême and l'Houmeau were made
rivals ; I collected those young men, your old schoolmates, and organized the serenade last night; then,
once launched into enthusiasm, we subscribed for the
dinner. I said to myself, ' Never mind whether David
is still in hiding, Lucien shall be crowned at any rate.'
Besides this, I have done my best in other ways," continued Petit-Claud. " I have seen the Comtesse du
Châtelet, and I have made her understand that she owes
it to herself to pull David out of danger ; she can do it,

and she ought to do it. If David has really made the discovery he told me about, the authorities ought to sustain him ; and what a thing it would be for the new prefect to share in the honor of so great an invention by affording protection to its discoverer. Everybody would talk of him as an enlightened administrator. Your sister is afraid of our judicial musketry ; she is frightened by the smoke. Legal warfare costs as much as that on the battlefield ; but David has maintained his position, — he is master of his secret ; he can't be arrested, and he will not be arrested."

" Thank you, my dear fellow," said Lucien, " I see I can trust you with my plan, and you will help me to carry it out." (Petit-Claud looked at Lucien, giving to his gimlet nose the appearance of an interrogation mark.) " I wish to save David," continued Lucien, with an air of importance. " I am the cause of his misfortunes ; I shall repair all ; I have more influence over Louise — "

" Louise ! who is she ? "

" The Comtesse du Châtelet." (Petit-Claud gave a start.) " I have more influence over her than she herself is aware of," continued Lucien ; " only, my dear fellow, though I may have a secret power in your government, I have no clothes — "

Petit-Claud made a movement as if to offer his purse.

" Thank you, no," said Lucien, pressing his friend's hand, " In ten days from now I shall call on Madame du Châtelet, and then I will return your visit."

They separated with a hearty shake of the hand like comrades.

" He ought to be a poet," thought Petit-Claud, " for he is crazy."

"They may say what they like," thought Lucien, "but in the matter of friends there are none to compare with old schoolmates."

"Dear Lucien," said Eve when he talked to her of his friend, "what has Petit-Claud been saying to make you feel thus? Beware of him!"

"Of him?" cried Lucien. "Listen, Eve," he went on, apparently following out some reflection, "you no longer believe in me; you distrust me; you also distrust Petit-Claud unjustly; but in twelve or fifteen days you will change your opinion," he added, with a conceited smile.

Then he retired to his room and wrote the following letter to one of his journalistic friends in Paris : —

MY DEAR LOUSTEAU, — Of us two, I am probably the only one who remembers that I lent you a thousand francs. But I know, alas too well, the situation in which you are sure to be when you open this letter not to say at once that I don't ask for them back in gold and silver,— no, simply in credit. You and I have the same tailor, you can therefore order for me, on your credit and with the briefest delay, a complete fit-out. Without being precisely in the dress of Adam, I cannot show myself. Here, the honors of the department due to a distinguished Parisian await me — to my great surprise. I am the hero of a banquet, for all the world as though I were a deputy. Now you see the absolute necessity for a black coat. Promise payment; have the things charged to you; invent some new Don Juanism, for I must have clothes at any price — I am in rags! Here it is September; weather magnificent; *ergo* be sure that I receive, by the end of this week, a charming morning suit, to wit: small frock coat, green-bronze, dark ; three waistcoats, — one, sulphur color ; another, fancy material, Scotch pattern ; third, all white ; next, three pairs of trousers *to kill the women,* — one, English stuff, white ; the second, nankeen ; the third, thin black cassimere ; and finally, a black coat and a black satin waistcoat for evening wear. If you have replaced Florine by another of her kind, I petition her for two cravats.

But all this is nothing ; I know I can rely on you, or your cleverness ; I am not uneasy about the tailor. But there is something else ! My dear friend, how many times have you and I deplored that the intellect of poverty (which certainly is the most active poison that destroys the man of men, the Parisian !),— that our intellect, the activity of which surprises Satan himself, has, so far, been unable to find a way to get a hat on credit. When fashion gives to the world hats that are worth a thousand francs we shall be able to get them on credit, but till then, we must have enough money in our pockets to pay for them. I feel, I profoundly feel the diffi-culties I put upon you by this request. Add a pair of boots, a pair of pumps, six pairs of gloves to be sent by the tailor. It is requiring the impossible, I know that. But is n't lit-erary life itself the impossible ?

May I suggest one thing ? Perform this prodigy by writing some great article or doing some small infamy, and I will re-lease you from that thousand francs and discharge the debt. Remember, it was a debt of honor, and has been running now twelve months ; you would blush, I know, if you could blush !

My dear Lousteau, joking apart, I am in serious circum-stances. You will understand this when I tell you that the Cuttle-fish has grown fat, and has married the Heron, and the Heron is now prefect of Angoulême. This dreadful couple can do much for my brother-in-law, whom I have placed in a frightful position ; the sheriff is trying to arrest him ; he is in hiding ; it is all about those notes of hand. I must reap-pear to the eyes of the *prefect's wife,* and recover my influ-ence over her at any price. Is n't it frightful to think that David Séchard's future depends on a handsome pair of boots, gray silk stockings (mind you don't forget them), and a new hat? I shall give out that I am ill, and stay in bed to dispense, as Duvicquet says, with responding to the attentions of my fellow-citizens. My fellow-citizens, by the bye, have given me a charming serenade. I am beginning to ask myself how many fools go to the composition of those three words 'my fellow-citizens,' now that I know the enthusiasm of Angoulême was set a-going by some of my schoolmates.

If you could manage to insert among your items a few lines about my reception here you would make me taller by several boot-heels. Moreover, it would teach the Cuttle-fish that I have, if not friends, at least some power over the Parisian press. As I have lost none of my hopes and expectations I will return you this service in kind. If you want a fine article of some depth for any of your publications I have time now to think it up. My last word is, dear friend — I count on you as you may count on

Yours ever,

LUCIEN DE R.

P. S. Address the packages to me, by diligence, Coach Office, to be left till called for.

This letter, in which Lucien resumed the tone of superiority which his success had produced in his inner man, recalled Paris to him. Existing for the last week in the dead calm of provincial life, his thoughts went to the gay days of his misery, and he began to have vague regrets and longings for them. He gave himself up for the next week to thoughts of Madame du Châtelet. He attached so much importance to his reappearance in her society that as he ran down to l'Houmeau after dark, to inquire at the coach-office for the parcels he expected from Paris, he suffered as many agonies of

21

uncertainty as a woman who sets her last hope upon a
dress which she despairs of receiving.

" Ah, Lousteau! I forgive you all your treachery!"
he said to himself as he caught sight of the packages
and knew by their shapes that they contained all he had
asked for.

He found the following letter in the hat-box : —

FROM FLORINE'S SALON.

MY DEAR BOY, — The tailor behaved very well; but (as
your sagacious retrospective glance enabled you to surmise)
the cravats, the hat, the silk stockings brought trouble to
our souls — for there was nothing to trouble in our purses.
We all agree with Blondet that there is a fortune to be
made by setting up a shop where young men could get the
things which cost next to nothing. Besides, did not the
great Napoleon when stopped on his way to India by the
want of a pair of boots, remark that " easy things are never
done?" This means that all went well, except the footgear
and — the hat! I saw you dressed to perfection but minus
a hat, waistcoated without shoes, and I thought of sending
you a pair of moccasins which an American gave to Florine
as a curiosity. Florine gave us a capital-stock of forty
francs with which to, play for your minor things. Nathan,
Blondet and I had such luck (just because we were not playing for ourselves) that we were able to take La Torpille, des
Lupeaulx's former ballet-girl, to supper. Frascati owed us
that, at any rate.

Florine took charge of the purchases, and she has added
three fine linen shirts on her own account. Nathan sends
you a cane ; Blondet (who won three hundred francs), a gold
chain ; and La Torpille, a gold watch, big as a forty-franc
piece, which some fool gave her, and which does'nt go.
Bixiou, who joined us at the Rocher de Cancale, insisted on
adding a bottle of *eau de Portugal* to these various gifts

which all Paris sends you. Our first comedian remarked, with that deep bass voice and bourgeois pomposity he takes off so well, "If such be his happiness let him be happy." All this, my dear fellow, ought to prove to you that we love our friends in misfortune. Florine, whom I have been weak enough to forgive, begs you to send us an article on Nathan's last book.

Adieu, my son. I can't help pitying you for being forced to return to the region you had just escaped when you made a comrade of

Your friend,

ÉTIENNE LOUSTEAU.

"Poor fellows! they played for me!" thought Lucien, quite affected.

There come sometimes from poisonous localities, or from places where men have greatly suffered, wafts of an odor that seems of Paradise.

Eve was amazed when her brother came down in his new clothes. She did not recognize him.

"Now I can go and walk in Beaulieu," he cried. "Nobody can say of me, 'He came back in rags.' See, here is a watch I'll give you, for it is really mine, — besides, it is like me; it is all out of order and does n't go."

"What a child you are!" said Eve; "one can't be angry with you."

"Do you believe, my dear girl, that I have got all these fine things for the silly purpose of dazzling the eyes of Angoulême, for which I don't care *that?*" he said, striking the air with his cane, which had a chased gold knob. "I want to repair the harm I have done, and I have put myself under arms; you'll know why soon."

Lucien's success as a fop was the (
he obtained ; but that was immense.
many tongues as admiration freeze
raved about him, the men sneered
exclaim, in the words of the song:
thank thee ! ' He left two cards at th
paid a visit to Petit-Claud, who was n
next day, which was the day of the b
journals all contained, under the head
lême," the following remarks : —

ANGOULÊME : The return of a young
has been most brilliant — the author, we me
of Charles IX.," the sole historic novel
which is not an imitation of Walter Sco
to which is a literary event — has been i
tion as flattering to the town itself as
Lucien de Rubempré. The new prefect
installed, has joined in this public manife
attentions to the author of " The Daisies,
so warmly encouraged from the first by M
du Châtelet."

In France, when an impulse of t
given there is no stopping it. Th
regiment in garrison offered his bar
of the Cloche hotel, whose exporta
turkey go as far as China, sent hi:
magnificent porcelain dishes ; the f
of l'Houmeau, in whose establishment
served, decorated his large hall with
crowns of laurel interspersed with i
fine effect. By five o'clock forty i
sembled, all in evening dress. A hu

the inhabitants, attracted principally by the band which was stationed in the courtyard, represented the fellow-citizens.

" All Angoulême is here ! " said Petit-Claud, stationing himself at a window.

" I can't understand a bit about it," said Postel to his wife, who had come to hear the music. " Goodness ! here's the prefect, the receiver-general, the colonel, the director of the powder-magazine ! and there's our deputy, and the mayor, the judge, the headmaster, and Monsieur Milaud the *procureur du roi* — why, all the authorities have come ! "

As the company sat down to table, the military band began, with variations on the air: " Vive le roi, vive la France ! " which by the bye, never became popular. This was at five o'clock. At eight, a dessert of sixty-five dishes, remarkable for an Olympus in sugar-candy surmounted by a France in chocolate, was the signal for the toasts.

" Gentlemen," said the prefect, rising. " The King! the Legitimacy ! Do we not owe to the peace which the Bourbons have restored to us the generation of poets and thinkers who maintain in the hands of France the sceptre of our literature? "

" Vive le roi ! " cried the guests, among whom the ministerials were in full force.

The venerable head of the college rose. " Let us drink," he said, " to the young poet, the hero of the day ; who has known how to add to the grace and poesy of Petrarch the talent of a prose-writer, — and that in a style which Boileau declared so difficult."

" Bravo ! bravo ! "

The colonel rose.

" Gentlemen, to the Royalist! for the hero of this festival has had the courage to defend right principles."

" Bravo !" said the prefect, giving a tone to the applause.

Petit-Claud rose.

" In the name of all Lucien's comrades, I call upon you to drink to the health of the glory of the College of Angoulême — our venerable Head-Master ; who is so dear to all of us, and to whom we owe whatever success in life we may obtain."

The old head-master, who did not expect the toast, wiped his eyes.

Lucien rose ; the deepest silence prevailed ; the poet turned white. At that moment the old head-master laid a crown of laurel on his head. Everybody clapped their hands. Lucien had tears in his eyes and in his voice.

" He is drunk," whispered Petit-Claud's neighbor.

" Yes, but not with wine," replied the lawyer.

" My dear townsmen, my dear comrades," said Lucien at last, " I would that all France were witness of this scene. It is thus that men are lifted into greatness — thus that noble works and splendid actions are obtained in this land of ours. But, seeing the little that I have done and the great honors that I receive, I cannot be otherwise than confused ; I look to the future to justify the greeting you bestow upon me to-day. The memory of this hour will give me courage to meet new difficulties. Permit me to offer to your homage the name of the lady who was my first inspiration and my patroness, and also to drink the health of

my native town. I give you, therefore, the beautiful
Comtesse Sixte du Châtelet, and the noble town of
Angoulême !"

" He did that pretty well," said the *procureur du roi,*
nodding his head in token of approval ; " for our toasts
were prepared, but his was improvised."

At ten o'clock the guests departed in groups. David
Séchard, hearing the unusual sounds of music, said to
Basine : " What is going on in l'Houmeau ? "

" A banquet to your brother-in-law," she replied.

" I know he must be sorry not to have me there,"
said David.

By midnight Petit-Claud and Lucien had returned together to the place du Mûrier. There, Lucien said to
the lawyer, as they parted; " My dear fellow, between
ourselves, I will admit to you that this is a matter of
life or death."

" To-morrow," said the lawyer, " my marriage contract is to be signed at Madame de Sénonches' house ;
I am to marry her goddaughter, Mademoiselle Françoise de la Haye. Do me the pleasure of being present. Madame de Sénonches asked me to bring you,
and you will there see Madame du Châtelet, who will
no doubt be extremely flattered by your toast, for they
will certainly tell her of it."

" I have my own ideas," said Lucien.

" Oh, you 'll save David ! " said the lawyer, smiling.

" I 'm sure of it," replied the poet.

At this instant David suddenly appeared as if by
magic ; and this is how it happened.

He had been placed in a very difficult position ; his
wife forbade him absolutely to see Lucien or even to

let her brother know where he was. Lucien, on the other hand, was writing him the most affectionate letters, assuring him that in a few days he should have undone all the harm he had done him. Mademoiselle Clerget had given David the following letters, when she told him the cause of the music, the sound of which had reached his ears : —

My dear Husband, — Continue to act as if Lucien were not here. Do not be uneasy at anything; and get into your dear head this one assurance : our safety depends entirely on the impossibility of your enemies finding out where you are. It is my misfortune that I have more confidence in Kolb, in Marion, in Basine, than in my brother. Alas ! my poor Lucien is no longer the open hearted, tender poet that he once was. It is precisely because he wants to meddle in your affairs and professes (out of vanity, dear David) to be able to pay our debts, that I fear him. He has received some handsome clothes from Paris, and five gold louis in a pretty purse. He gave me the money, and that is what we are now living on.

We have now one enemy the less, for your father has left us ; we owe that to Petit-Claud, who discovered his intentions and cut them short at once by telling him you would take no steps without first consulting him, Petit-Claud, and that he would not allow you to part with any share in your invention unless for an indemnity, paid in advance, of thirty thousand francs, — fifteen thousand to clear yourself, and fifteen thousand more to be paid in any case, success or no success. Petit-Claud is inexplicable to me.

I kiss you, dear, as a wife kisses a troubled husband. Our little Lucien is well. What a sight it is to see that tender blossom opening and coloring in the midst of our storm ! My mother, as usual prays to God and sends you her tender love.   Your Eve.

Petit-Claud and the Cointets, alarmed at old Séchard's peasant wiliness, had, as this letter tells us, got
rid of him, — all the more easily, however, because his
vintage required him in Marsac.

Lucien's letter, inclosed in that of Eve, was as follows : —

MY DEAR DAVID, — All goes well. I am armed from
head to foot; I enter upon the campaign to-day ; in a couple
more days I shall have made great strides. With what delight shall I put my arms around you when you are once
more at liberty and released from *my* debts ! But I am
wounded to the heart, and for life, by the distrust my sister
and my mother still show to me. As if I did not know that
you were at Basine's ! Every time Basine comes to the house
I am told news of you and I get your answers to my letters.
Besides, it is evident that my sister has no one else to trust
than that friend of hers. To-day I shall be close to you,
and cruelly distressed that you are not present at a banquet
they give me in l'Houmeau. I owe to the self-love of Angoulême a little triumph which will be forgotten in a few
days ; your joy, could you be present, would have been to
me the one true thing about it.

" Well, a few days more, and you will have reason to forgive him who counts it more than all the fame in the world
to be

Your brother,

LUCIEN.

David's heart was sharply tugged on both sides by
these two forces, although they were unequal ; for he
adored his wife and his affection for Lucien was diminished by the loss of some esteem. But in solitude
the power of feelings undergoes a change. A lonely
man, in the grasp of preoccupations such as now pos-

sessed David, yields to thoughts against which he would find support in the ordinary course of life. Reading Lucien's letter within sound of the music of his unexpected triumph, David was deeply moved to find expressed therein the regret at his absence on which his heart had counted. Tender souls are not proof against such touches of feeling, which they think as true in others as they would be in themselves. Surely they are the drops of water which fall from the overflowing cup? So, about midnight, all Basine's entreaties were powerless to keep David from going to see Lucien.

"No one," he said, "is in the streets at this hour; I shall not be seen; besides, they can't arrest me at night, and in case they do see me I can always use Kolb's method of getting away. It is too long a time since I have kissed my wife and child."

Basine yielded to these rather plausible reasons and let David out. He reached the place du Mûrier and cried out, "Lucien!" just as Lucien and Petit-Claud were bidding each other good night. The two brothers flung themselves into each other's arms, with tears in their eyes. There are not many such moments in life. Lucien felt the effusion of one of those attachments beyond peradventure with which we never reckon, and which we bitterly reproach ourselves for deceiving. David, on the other hand, felt the need of forgiving; the noble, generous inventor was above all things anxious to correct Lucien's error and brush away the clouds which obscured the affection of brother and sister. Before such considerations of feeling, the dangers caused by want of money vanished.

Petit-Claud said to his client, "Go in at once; profit,

at any rate, by your imprudence; embrace your wife and child, but let no one see you."

" What a misfortune ! " he added, when he was left alone on the place du Mûrier. "Ah ! if Cérizet were only here ! "

As the lawyer said these words half aloud to himself, he was walking along beside the boarding which concealed a building then in process of construction, and now called majestically the Palace of Justice. As he passed he heard a noise from within, like the tapping of a finger on a door.

" It is I," said Cérizet, whose voice came through a gap between two planks. " I saw David leaving l'Houmeau. I was beginning to suspect his hiding-place, and now I am sure of it; I can catch him any day. But before I can set my trap I must know something of Lucien's plans ; and here you have let them go into the house ! Do stay here on some pretence or other, and when David and Lucien come out get them to walk this way. They will think themselves alone and I shall hear their last words."

" You are a master-devil ! " said Petit-Claud, in a low voice.

" Heavens and earth ! " cried Cérizet. " What would n't a man be to get what you have promised me ? "

Petit-Claud left the boarding and walked about the place du Mûrier, looking at the windows of the room where the family were reunited, and thinking of his own future to give himself courage — for Cérizet's cleverness enabled him to play his last stroke. Petit-Claud was one of those profoundly artful and treacherously double-faced men, who, having observed the changes of the human heart and the strategy of self-interests, are never caught by the promises of the present or the mere baits of any alliance. Consequently, at the outset of this business he had relied very little upon Cointet. In case the project of his marriage fell through without his being able to accuse the tall Cointet of treachery, he had laid a plan to vex him; but since his reception by Madame de Sénonches as the suitor of her ward, Petit-Claud was playing fairly with him. His secret plot, now useless, would be dangerous in the political situation to which he aspired. The basis on which he had meant to build his future importance was as follows: Several of the leading merchants in l'Houmeau were about to form a Liberal committee, which attached itself, from business considerations, to the Opposition party. The accession of the Villèle ministry, accepted by Louis XVIII., then on his death-bed, was the signal for a change of conduct on the part of the Opposition, which, since the death of Napoleon, had renounced the perilous means of conspiracy. The Liberal party now organized in the provinces a system of legal resistance; it endeavored to make itself master of the electoral business so as to reach its ends by convincing the masses. Petit-Claud, being a frantic Liberal and son of l'Houmeau, was the promoter, soul, and secret counsellor of the Opposition of the Lower town oppressed by the aristocracy of the Upper. He was the first to see the danger of leaving to the Cointets the sole disposal of the press in the department of the Charente, where the Opposition ought certainly to have an organ, so as not to be behind the other towns.

"If we all contribute five hundred francs," Petit-

Claud had said, " we should have over twenty thousand francs, enough to buy the Séchard printing-house."

The lawyer worked secretly for the adoption of this idea, which seems to explain in a way his double position towards the Cointets and David Séchard ; and his eyes naturally turned to a rascal of Cérizet's make as a man who could be bought for the party.

" If you can unearth your old master and give him into my hands," he said to the former gamin, " some one will lend you twenty thousand francs with which to buy his printing-office, and you will probably be placed at the head of a newspaper. Therefore, go to work."

Far more sure of a man like Cérizet than he was of all the Doublons in the world, Petit-Claud confidently assured Cointet that David would be arrested. But, since Petit-Claud had reason to hug the hope of entering the magistracy, he foresaw the necessity of turning his back on the Liberals. By this time, however. he had stirred up the minds of l'Houmeau so successfully that the money for the purchase of the printing-house was all subscribed. Under these circumstances, Petit-Claud resolved to let matters follow their natural course.

" Pooh ! " he said to himself, " Cérizet will soon commit some press misdemeanor, and I shall profit by that to show my talents."

He now went to the door of the printing-room, where Kolb was standing sentry, and said to him, " Go up and tell David he had better take advantage of the hour to get away, and to be very cautious ; I can't wait any longer ; it is one o'clock."

When Kolb left his station Marion took his place. Lucien and David soon came down ; Kolb preceded them by a hundred feet, Marion brought up the rear at the same distance. When the two brothers reached the boarding Lucien was speaking eagerly.

" My dear friend," he was saying, " my plan is simplicity itself; but I could n't speak of it before Eve, who can't understand such means. I am certain that Louise has a feeling for me at the bottom of her heart, which I know how to awaken. I simply want to avenge myself on that imbecile of a prefect. If I succeed I shall get her to ask the ministry to give you a subsidy of twenty thousand francs for your invention. I am to see that woman to-morrow in the very boudoir where our love for each other first began. Petit-Claud tells me it is quite unchanged. I mean to play a comedy! So the day after to-morrow morning I 'll send you a little note by Basine to tell you whether or no *I have been hissed.* Who knows? perhaps you will be free at once. Now don't you understand why I wanted those clothes from Paris? You can't play the part of the leading gentleman in rags."

At six in the morning Cérizet went to see Petit-Claud.

" To-morrow at twelve o'clock Doublon must be ready to make the arrest; he can capture him, I 'll answer for it. I control one of Mademoiselle Clerget's work-girls — you understand."

After listening to Cérizet's plan Petit-Claud went off to find Cointet.

" If you make Monsieur du Hautoy decide this very evening to give Françoise the reversion of his property you shall, within the next two days, sign a deed of partnership with Séchard. I shall not be married for eight days after the contract; therefore, we shall still keep to the terms of our little agreement, — give and take, you know. We must both watch to-night what takes place at Madame de Sénonches' house between Lucien and Madame du Châtelet, for it is all there. If Lucien succeeds in persuading the countess, I hold David."

"You will certainly be Keeper of the Seals," said Cointet.

"Why not? Monsieur de Peyronnet is," replied Petit-Claud, who had not quite pulled off his Liberal skin.

IX.

LUCIEN'S REPRISALS AT THE HÔTEL DE BARGETON.

THE anomalous position of Mademoiselle de la Haye was the reason why almost all the nobles of Angoulême were present at the signing of her marriage contract. The poverty of the future household, starting without the benefits of a "corbeille," excited the sort of interest that society enjoys bestowing; for benevolence is like ovations, we love the forms of charity which gratify our self-love. Consequently the Marquise de Pimentel, the Comtesse du Châtelet, Monsieur de Sénonches and several of the habitués of the house made Françoise some handsome wedding-presents, which were talked of throughout the town. These pretty trinkets, added to the trousseau which Zéphirine had been preparing for over a year, the jewels given by the godfather, and the customary formal wedding-presents, reconciled Françoise to the marriage, and piqued the curiosity of several mothers who brought their daughters on this occasion.

Petit-Claud and Cointet had already had occasion to remark that the nobles of Angoulême only tolerated them in their Olympus as a necessity; one was the manager and legal guardian of Françoise's fortune; the other was as indispensable to the signing of the contract as the condemned man is to an execution. But if, on the morrow of her marriage, Madame Petit-Claud

claimed the right to return to her godmother's house
the husband felt it would be difficult to make good his
footing there, and he promised himself to make these
proud people fear him. Blushing for his humble par-
entage he had made his mother stay in Mansle, where
she had gone to live ; he requested her to say she was
ill, and to send him her consent in writing. Humiliated
to feel himself without friends or protectors or family,
in short with no one to sign the contract on his behalf,
Petit-Claud was only too happy to present himself with
the poet, the celebrated man, whom the Comtesse du
Châtelet desired to see again. He called for Lucien in
a carriage. The great man had dressed for this memor-
able evening in a way that was certain to give him an
indisputable superiority over the other men. Madame
de Sénonches had taken care to announce the presence
of the hero of the moment, and the meeting of the estranged lovers was one of those scenes which are particularly toothsome to provincial palates. Moreover,
Lucien had passed into the condition of a Lion ; it was
said he was so handsome, so changed, such an exquisite, that all the women of the Angoulême aristocracy
had a desire to see him.

In accordance with the fashion of that period, which
marked the transition from the ancient ball breeches
to the ignoble trousers of the present day, Lucien had
put on a pair of close-fitting pantaloons. Men still
exhibited their shapes, to the great despair of ill-made,
skinny beings ; but Lucien's proportions were Apollo-
nian. His open-worked gray silk stockings, his low
shoes, his black satin waistcoat, his cravat, all were
carefully put on ; in fact, one might say they were glued

22

upon him. His abundant fair hair set off the white forehead, around which the light wavy curls were arranged with studied grace. His eyes, full of pride, were sparkling. His feminine little hands, handsome in gloves, ought never to have been seen gloveless. He copied his demeanor from that of de Marsay, the famous Parisian dandy, holding his cane and hat (which he never laid aside) in one hand, and using the other for the few gestures with which he emphasized his words. Lucien would much have preferred to have glided elegantly into the salon, like those celebrated men who, it is recorded, bent their heads out of modesty as they passed beneath the Porte Saint-Denis. But Petit-Claud, who had but this one friend, used and abused the privilege. He led him almost pompously to Madame de Sénonches, who was standing in the centre of the room. As they passed along the poet heard murmurs that would formerly have turned his head, but to which he now listened coldly, for he felt that he could meet on equal terms the whole Olympus of Angoulême.

"Madame," he said to Madame de Sénonches, "I have already congratulated my friend Petit-Claud, who is of the stuff that Keepers of the Seals are made of; I rejoice in his great good-fortune in being allied to you — though the tie between a godmother and a god-daughter is but a slight one." (This was said with an epigrammatic air well understood by the women present, who were listening, though they affected not to be.) "For my part, I am grateful for an event which enables me to offer you my homage."

All this was said without embarrassment, and in the attitude and manner of a "grand seigneur" who was paying a visit among lesser folk. Lucien listened to Zéphirine's involved answer, casting looks all the while round the salon to get his bearings and prepare effects. Consequently he was presently able to bow with grace, graduating his smiles, to Francis du Hautoy and the prefect, who bowed to him; then he moved nearer to Madame du Châtelet, feigning to notice her for the first time. This meeting was so clearly the event of the evening, that the signing of the contract in the adjoining room, to which the notary was endeavoring to pilot the principal personages, was forgotten. Lucien made a few steps towards Louise de Nègrepelisse, and then he said with Parisian grace to the woman whose mind, since his entrance, had been filled with recollections : —

"Is it to you, madame, that I owe the invitation which procures me the pleasure of dining at the Prefecture? "

"You owe it only to your fame, monsieur," replied Louise, curtly, shocked at the turn of a sentence intended by Lucien to wound the pride of his former patroness.

"Ah! madame la comtesse," he said with an air that was subtle and foppish both, "I shall be unable to bring that guest to you if he has incurred your disapproval." Then, without waiting for an answer, he turned aside and, seeing the bishop, bowed to him in a stately manner. "Your Eminence was almost a prophet," he said in a charming tone of voice, "and I shall do my best to make you wholly one. I think myself very happy to have come here this evening, since it gives me the opportunity to offer you my respects."

Lucien then led the prelate into a conversation which

lasted ten minutes. All the women looked upon Lucien as a phenomenon. His unexpected impertinence had literally left Madame du Châtelet voiceless. Seeing her former lover admired by all the women present, perceiving how from group to group the tale went round of the speech in which he had, as it were, laid her flat with an air of disdain, Louise was gripped to the heart with a spasm of vanity.

" If he does not come to dinner to-morrow after that speech, what a scandal it will make," she thought. " What is the meaning of such pride? Can Mademoiselle des Touches have fallen in love with him? He is so handsome! They say she went to his house the very day that actress died ! "

A myriad of such thoughts rushed into her mind, and, unfortunately for her, she was looking all the while at Lucien, who stood talking to the bishop as though he were king of the salon. He bowed to no one, but simply waited until others came up and bowed to him, looking about him with a variety of expressions, and an ease that was worthy of de Marsay, his model. He did not even leave the bishop to bow to Monsieur de Sénonches who appeared at a little distance.

At the end of ten minutes Louise could bear it no longer. She rose, went up to the bishop, and said, " May I know, monseigneur, what it is that makes you smile so often? "

Lucien discreetly drew back a few steps to leave Madame du Châtelet with the prelate.

" Ah! madame la comtesse, this young man has great intelligence ; he has been telling me that he owes all his real strength to you."

"And *I* am not ungrateful, madame," said Lucien, with a reproachful glance at the countess which delighted her.

"Let us have an understanding," she said, beckoning Lucien to her with a motion of her fan ; " come into this room with monseigneur, and he shall judge between us." She pointed to the boudoir, and took the bishop's arm to lead the way.

"A curious business for Monseigneur!" said a woman from the camp of the Chandours, loud enough to be overheard.

"Our judge!" said Lucien, looking first at Madame du Châtelet and then at the bishop. "Is either of us in fault?"

Louise de Nègrepelisse seated herself on the sofa of her former boudoir. Having made Lucien sit on one side of her and the bishop on the other, she began to speak. Lucien did his former love the honor, the surprise, and the happiness of not listening to her. He assumed the attitude and gestures of Pasta in Tancredi when she is about to say *O patria!* He produced on his face the famous cavatina *del Rizzo.* He even found means to force a few tears to his eyes.

"Ah, Louise, how I loved you!" he whispered, without regard to the bishop or to what she was saying, as soon as he saw that the countess had seen his tears.

"Dry your eyes, or you will ruin me again," she said, in an aside which displeased the bishop.

"And once was enough, you think!" cried Lucien. "What a remark ! it would dry up the tears of a Madeline ! Good God ! I had returned for an instant to my hopes, my illusions, my twenty years, and you—"

Here Monseigneur retreated hastily to the salon, perceiving that his dignity might be compromised by these former lovers. Everybody affected to leave Lucien and Madame du Châtelet to themselves. But a quarter of an hour later Sixte, to whom the smiles and nods and promenades to the door of the boudoir were far from pleasing, went in with an air that was more than uneasy, and found Lucien and Louise in very animated conversation.

" Madame," said Sixte, in his wife's ear, " you who know Angoulême even better than I do ought to think of your position as wife of the prefect."

" My dear," replied Louise, looking at her responsible editor with a haughty air which made him tremble, " I am talking with Monsieur de Rubempré on matters that are very important to you. It is a question of saving a great inventor who is on the point of becoming a victim to the basest machinations, and you can prevent it. As to what those ladies think of me, you shall see how I conduct myself to ice the venom on their tongues."

So saying she left the boudoir, leaning on Lucien's arm, and took him to sign the contract, parading her act with all the audacity of a great lady.

" Let us sign together," she said, offering him a pen.

Lucien made her show him the place where she had just written her name, so that their two signatures should be side by side.

" Monsieur de Sénonches, would you ever have recognized Monsieur de Rubempré?" said the countess, thus compelling the insolent huntsman to bow to Lucien.

She carried Lucien back to the salon and placed him between herself and Zéphirine on the formidable sofa in the middle of the room. Then, as if she were a queen on her throne, she began, at first in a low voice, a conversation that was evidently epigrammatic, in which a number of her old friends and several women who wished to court her joined. Lucien, who was the hero of the circle, was prompted by the countess to talk of Parisian life, which he did with a ready satire and vim, interspersing the whole with anecdotes of celebrated persons, veritable tid-bits of conversation for which all provincial societies are greedy. The company now admired the wit as much as they had previously admired the beauty of the man. Madame la Comtesse Sixte was so complacent at Lucien's triumph, she played so well the part of a woman delighted with her instrument, she helped him so cleverly with appropriate remarks, and solicited applause with so compromising a look that several women began to suspect collusion in the simultaneous return of the pair.

"Well!" said , Louise, about one in the morning, speaking to Lucien in a low voice before rising from her seat, " day after to-morrow, remember, and do me the favor to be punctual."

She then left him with a little motion of the head that was only too amicable, and went to say a few words to Comte Sixte, who immediately looked for his hat.

" If what Madame du Châtelet tells me is so, my dear Lucien, you may count on me," said the prefect, starting in pursuit of his wife, who was going away without him, as they do in Paris. " Your brother-in-law may feel perfectly secure."

" Monsieur le comte owes me that much," replied Lucien, with a smile.

" Well! here we are, knocked in the head," said Cointet to Petit-Claud, who had witnessed the parting.

Petit-Claud, thunderstruck at Lucien's success, and dazzled by the sparkle of his wit and the easy display of his graces, looked at Françoise de la Haye, whose face, full of admiration for Lucien, seemed to say to her suitor : " Why are not you like your friend? "

A gleam of joy passed over Petit-Claud's features.

" The prefect's dinner is not till day after to-morrow," he replied to Cointet's remark. " We have another day before us. I answer for our success."

" Well, my dear fellow," said Lucien to Petit-Claud at two in the morning as they went home on foot. " I came, I saw, I conquered! David will be happy in a few hours."

" That's all I want to know," said Petit-Claud to himself. " I thought you only a poet," he said aloud, " but you are also a Lauzun, — in other words, twice a poet," he added, giving his friend a shake of the hand which was destined to be the last.

" My dear Eve," said Lucien, waking up his sister when he got home. " Good news! In less than a month David can pay his debts."

" How? "

" Well, under Madame du Châtelet's petticoat I have found my former Louise. She is fonder of me than ever, and she is going to make her husband send a report to the minister of the interior in favor of our discovery. Therefore you have only one month more to suffer." (Eve thought she was still dreaming as she listened to her brother.) " When I entered the little gray salon where I used to tremble like a child two years ago, and looked at the furniture, the pictures, and the faces, the scales fell from my eyes! How Paris does change one's ideas!"

"Is that a good?" asked Eve, who now understood her brother.

"Come, go to sleep again, and to-morrow after breakfast we'll talk it over," said Lucien.

Cérizet's plan was extremely simple. Though it belonged to the category of wiles which provincial sheriffs employ to trap their victims, the success of which is often problematical, it was fated to succeed, for it rested on an accurate knowledge of the characters of Lucien and David, as well as on these new hopes. Among the little workwomen of whom Cérizet was the Don Juan, and whom he governed by cleverly pitting one against the other, was an ironer in Basine Clerget's laundry, a girl almost as handsome as Madame Séchard, named Henriette Signol, whose parents were small vineyard owners living on their little property about six miles from Angoulême on the road to Saintes. The Signols, like all country-folk of their condition, were not rich enough to keep their only child at home, and they intended her to "enter a house," which means in other words to become a lady's maid. In the provinces, a lady's maid must know how to wash and get-up fine linen. The reputation of Madame Prieur, whom Basine succeeded, was such that the Signols apprenticed their daughter to her, paying a certain sum for the girl's board and lodging. Madame Prieur belonged to the race of employers who, in the provinces, consider themselves in the place of parents. She lived with her apprentices, took them to church, and looked after them conscientiously. Henriette Signol, a handsome brunette with a fine figure, bold eye, and strong, dark hair, had a dead-white skin, like a true daughter of the South, a complexion of the whiteness of a magnolia flower. She was one of the first grisettes on whom Cérizet cast his eye; but as she belonged to " honest vine-growers " she did not yield until vanquished by jealousy, by evil example, and by Cérizet's promise, " I will marry you." Learning that the Signols owned a little vineyard worth about twelve thousand francs, and a house that was quite inhabitable, Cérizet hastened to make it impossible that Henriette should marry any one else. Matters were in this state when Petit-Claud first talked of making him the owner of the Séchard printing-house and the publisher of the Liberal paper. Such a prospect dazzled the foreman, his head was turned ; Mademoiselle Signol seemed to him an obstacle to his ambition, and he neglected the poor girl. Henriette in despair clung to him all the more because he was evidently deserting her. But when Cérizet suspected that David was in hiding at Mademoiselle Clerget's, his ideas as to Henriette changed, though not his conduct ; he resolved to use to his own advantage the sort of madness which takes possession of a poor girl who hopes to hide her shame by marrying her seducer. During the morning of the day when Lucien re-appeared at the Hôtel de Bargeton, Cérizet imparted to Henriette Basine's secret, and told her that their fortune and their marriage depended on the discovery of the exact place where David was hiding. Once informed of this, Henriette had no difficulty in making sure that the printer was living in

Mademoiselle Clerget's dressing-room. She saw no harm in that amount of spying. But Cérizet used it as a first step toward other treachery.

Lucien was asleep when Cérizet, who came to Petit-Claud's office to know the result of the evening, listened to the lawyer's recital of the great little events which were rousing all Angoulême.

"Has Lucien written you anything since his return?" asked Cérizet, nodding his head in sign of satisfaction at what Petit-Claud told him.

"Nothing more than that," replied the lawyer, holdout a letter of a few lines which Lucien had written on his sister's note-paper.

"Very good," said Cerizet. "Tell Doublon to hide himself and his gendarmes behind the Porte-Palet ten minutes before sunset, and you shall have your man."

"Are you sure of your plan?" said Petit-Claud, eyeing Cérizet doubtfully.

"I trust to luck — the hussy!" said the ex-gamin, "she's always against honest folk."

"You must succeed," said the lawyer, sharply.

"I shall succeed," replied Cérizet. "You who have shoved me into this mudhole had better give me a few bank-bills to wipe off the slime. Monsieur," he added, detecting a look which displeased him on the lawyer's face, "if you are deceiving me, if you don't buy me that printing-office within a week — well! you shall leave a young widow to mourn your loss;" and the late gamin cast a deadly glance at Petit-Claud.

"If David is under lock and key at six o'clock this evening, come to Monsieur Gannerac's at nine, and your affair shall be concluded," replied the lawyer.

"So be it: you shall be satisfied, master," said Cérizet.

Cérizet was an adept at the trick of washing paper, which in these days threatens such loss to the Treasury. He washed out the four lines written by Lucien above his signature and substituted the following, imitating the handwriting with a perfection fraught with danger for his social future : —

MY DEAR DAVID, — You can come without fear to see the prefect. Your affair is settled. Besides, at this hour there is no danger; I will meet you outside to explain what you ought to say to the prefect.

Your brother,

LUCIEN.

When Lucien waked, about mid-day, he wrote to David telling him of the success of the evening, and assuring him of the prefect's assistance ; Monsieur du Châtelet, he said, was to write a report to the minister that very day on David's invention, about which he was very enthusiastic.

Marion took the letter to Mademoiselle Basine on pretext of carrying Lucien's shirts to the wash. Meantime Cérizet, informed by Petit-Claud that this letter would be sent, contrived to see Henriette. No doubt there was a struggle in the girl's mind, in which her conscience acted ; but not only were the interests of her child at stake, but her whole future, her happiness, her fortune ; and, after all, what Cérizet asked was a mere nothing, for he had taken good care not to tell her the consequences. Nevertheless the price he offered for that " mere nothing " did startle Henriette. However, Cérizet ended by persuading the girl to carry out his stratagem. At five o'clock Henriette was to tell Mademoiselle Clerget that Madame Séchard wanted her immediately. Then, a quarter of an hour after Basine had gone she was to knock at the door of the dressing-room and give the false letter to David. After that, Cérizet, as he had said, trusted to luck.

For the first time within a year Eve felt the iron bands in which her direful necessities had held her re-laxing. Hope returned to her at last. She, too — she wanted to enjoy her brother; to be seen on the arm of the man acclaimed by his townsmen, adored by women, admired by the haughty Comtesse du Châtelet. Eve dressed herself charmingly and proposed, after dinner, to walk to Beaulieu on her brother's arm. At that hour in September all Angoulême appears on the Promenade.

"There's the beautiful Madame Séchard," said several voices when Eve appeared.

"I never should have believed it of her," said one woman.

"The husband hides, but the wife exhibits herself," said Madame Postel, loud enough for the poor woman to hear.

"Oh! let us go home; I have done wrong," said Eve to her brother.

It was just before sunset, and the noise of a crowd coming up the steps which lead from l'Houmeau was heard. Lucien and his sister, feeling some curiosity, turned in that direction, for they heard several persons who had come up from l'Houmeau talking among them-selves as if a crime had been committed.

"It is probably some thief they have arrested — the man is as pale as death," said a passer to the brother and sister, seeing them follow the increasing crowd.

Neither Lucien nor his sister felt the slightest apprehension. They looked at the thirty or more children and the old women and workmen returning from their work who preceded the gendarmes, the silver lace of whose hats shone brightly in the principal group. That group, which was followed by a crowd of about a hundred persons, advanced rapidly like a thunder-cloud.

"Ah!" cried Eve, "it is my husband!"

"David!" exclaimed Lucien.

"That's his wife!" said the crowd, making way for her.

"What induced you to come out?" asked Lucien.

"Your letter," replied David, white and livid.

"I was sure of it!" said Eve, fainting dead away.

Lucien raised his sister, and two persons helped him to carry her home, where Marion put her to bed. Kolb rushed for the doctor. When the latter came Eve was still unconscious. Lucien was forced to admit to his mother that he was the cause of David's arrest — although he did not know of the substitution of the false letter. Annihilated by his mother's look, which was almost a curse, he went up to his room and locked himself in.

X.

A SUPREME FAREWELL, FOLLOWED BY A LECTURE ON HISTORY AND ANOTHER ON MORALITY.

THE following letter, written in the middle of the night, interrupted by many pauses, will show by its sentences, flung out as it were one by one, the agitation of Lucien's mind : —

MY BELOVED SISTER, — We have seen each other for the last time. My resolution is beyond recall. This is why : In many families there is a fatal being who is to his family *a disease.* I am that being to you. This assertion is not mine, it is that of a man who has seen much of the world. He and I were supping one night with friends at the Rocher de Cancale. Among other jests and tales that we all exchanged, this diplomatist told us that a certain young girl, whom society was surprised to see unmarried, was *ill of her father.* On that he developed his theory of family diseases. He explained how, without such a mother, such a family would have prospered; how such a son had ruined his father ; how such a father had ruined the future and the respectability of his children. Though he propounded all this with a laugh, he supported his social theory by so many facts that I was greatly struck by it. This truth was worth all the foolish paradoxes cleverly maintained with which journalists amuse themselves when there is no one by to impose upon. Well, I am that fatal being in our family. With a heart full of tenderness I act as your enemy. I return your devotion by injuries. This last blow, though involuntary, is the cruelest of all. While I was leading in Paris an unworthy life, full of pleasures, and of misery, mistaking comrades for friends, letting true friends go for the sake of men whose object was to use me, neglecting you, and only thinking of my family when the time came to injure it — while this was *my* life you were following the humble path of toil, painfully but surely leading to that fortune which I was trying to snatch. While you were growing better I was growing worse; I was putting into my life a fatal element. Yes, my ambitions are boundless; they will forever hinder me from accepting a humble life. I have tastes, I have had pleasures, the recollection of which will always poison the enjoyments now within my reach, which would formerly have satisfied me.

Oh! my dear Eve, I judge myself more severely than any one can judge me, no matter who; for I condemn myself absolutely and without self-pity. The struggle of life in Paris exacts incessant strength, and my will works only spasmodically; my brain is intermittent. The future terrifies me so much that I will not have a future, and the present is unbearable. I came here wishing to see you again, but I had better have left my country forever. And yet, expatriation without the means of living would be folly; no, I will not add that folly to all the rest. Death is preferable to an aborted life; for in any situation in which I might find myself I know that my excessive vanity will force me to commit mistakes. Some beings are like naughts; they need a figure to precede them, and then their nothingness becomes of tenfold value. I cannot acquire value except by marriage with a strong, unyielding will. Madame de Bargeton might have been my wife; I lost my future by not abandoning Coralie for her. David and you might have been my pilots; but neither of you was strong enough to master my weakness, which evades, as it were, all rule. I love an easy life, without annoyance; and to escape opposition I can be guilty of meannesses which have terrible results. I was born a prince. I have more dexterity of mind than I need for success, but it only comes to me by fits and starts; and the prizes of a career thronged by ambitious rivals are won by him only who husbands his powers and so has strength to reach an end.

It is my fate to do evil, as I have done it here, with the best intentions in the world. There are men of oak; I am, perhaps, but a graceful shrub, and I have tried to be a cedar. There you have my summary written down. This discrepancy between my means and my desires, this lack of equilibrium will forever neutralize all my efforts. There are many such natures among men of letters, the result of a perpetual disproportion between the intellect and the character, the will and the desire. What would be my fate? I can foresee it by remembering many men who once were famous and are now submerged and forgotten in Paris. If I reached the threshold of old age I should be older than my years, without fortune, without dignity. My whole being repels the thought of such an end. I will not be a social ruin.

Dear sister, adored for your late severity as much as for your former tenderness, though we have all paid dear for the happiness I have had in seeing you and David once again, later, perhaps, you will think that no price was too high for the last greetings of a poor heart that loved you. Make no search, either for me or to know my fate; my will will at least be strong enough to execute my desire. Resignation, dear angel, is a daily suicide. I have only resignation enough for one day, and I shall profit by it.

Two o'clock.

Yes, I am resolved. Farewell forever, my dear Eve. I find some comfort in thinking that henceforth I shall live only in your hearts. There is my grave. I ask no other. Farewell, again!

Your brother,

LUCIEN.

23

Having written this letter Lucien went downstairs without making any noise and laid it on his nephew's cradle ; he looked at his sleeping sister with tears in his eyes and left the room. The dawn was breaking ; he put out his candle, and gazed about him at the old house for the last time. Then he opened the door leading to the alley very softly ; but in spite of his precautions he woke Kolb, who slept on a mattress on the floor of the press-room.

"Who is there?" cried Kolb.

"I," said Lucien. "I am going away, Kolb."

"You had better never have come," growled Kolb to himself, but loud enough for Lucien to hear.

"I had better never have come into the world," said Lucien. "Good-bye, Kolb, I don't blame you for thinking what I think myself. Tell David that my last regret is that I could not press his hand once more."

By the time Kolb was up and dressed Lucien was on his way to the river by the Beaulieu promenade, dressed as if for a ball ; he had chosen for his shroud his Parisian clothes and his foppish trappings. Struck with the tone of Lucien's last words Kolb thought he would go and ask his mistress if she knew her brother had gone, and whether he had said good-bye to her ; but finding the house all quiet he concluded this departure was agreed on the night before, and he lay down again.

Very little has been written about suicide, if we consider the gravity of the subject ; it has not been studied. Perhaps this disease cannot be sufficiently observed. Suicide results from a sentiment which we will call, if you please, the *esteem of self,* in order that we may not confound it with the word *honor.* The day when a man despises himself, when he sees himself despised by others. when the reality of life is at variance with his hopes, he kills himself, and does homage in that way to society, in presence of which he will not remain when stripped of his virtues or of his splendor. No matter what may be said, among atheists (for exception must be made of the Christian's suicide) none but cowards will accept a dishonored life. Suicide is of three kinds : first, the suicide which is only the climax of a long illness and belongs, therefore, to pathology ; next, the suicide of despair ; lastly, the suicide of reason. Lucien wished to kill himself from despair and reason both — the two forms of suicide from which there can be a return ; for the only irrevocable suicide is the pathological ; often the three causes are combined, as in the case of Jean-Jacques Rousseau.

Lucien had no sooner taken his resolution than he began to consider the means ; for the poet wished to end poetically. He first thought of simply throwing himself into the Charente ; but as he went down the steps to l'Houmeau for the last time, he imagined the bustle his suicide would create, he saw the hideous spectacle of his body dragged from the water, bloated, and subjected to an inquest, and he felt. like many suicides, a posthumous vanity. During the day he had spent at Marsac. while the abbé announced his return to his family, he had walked along the river-bank and had noticed, not far from a mill, one of those round pools such as are often found in small water-courses, the great depth of which is shown by their tranquil surface. The water of such pools is neither green, nor blue, nor yellow, nor transparent ; it is like a polished steel mirror. On the shores of this mere were neither iris, nor reeds, nor even the broad leaves of the water-lily ; the grass on its banks was short and close, the willows wept as they grouped picturesquely around it. It was a little gulf brimming with water. Whoever had the courage to fill his pockets with stones and spring into that pool would find an inevitable death and never return to the surface. " There 's a spot," thought the poet, as he admired the peaceful scene, " which might make one in love with drowning."

The recollection of the place came to him as he reached l'Houmeau. He walked on therefore to Marsac, his mind full of his last funereal thoughts, with the firm intention of concealing thus the secret of his death and escaping an inquest and a funeral, but, above all, an exhibition of his body in the horrible state of drowned persons when they come to the surface of the water. He soon reached the foot of a hill, of which there are many between Angoulême and Poitiers. The diligence from Bordeaux to Paris was overtaking him rapidly, and the passengers would no doubt get out of the coach to mount the long hill on foot. Lucien, who did not wish to be seen, stepped aside into a little path below the road and began to gather flowers in a vineyard. When he returned he had a large bunch of sedum in his hand (a yellow flower, found on the stony soil of vineyards), and as he issued upon the high-road he found himself exactly behind a traveller dressed in black, with powdered hair, wearing shoes of Orleans leather with silver buckles, — brown of face and scarred as though he had fallen into the fire in his childhood. This traveller, whose appearance was evidently ecclesiastical, was walking slowly and smoking a cigar. Hearing Lucien as the latter jumped from the vineyard to the road he turned round, was apparently struck by the melancholy beauty of the poet, his symbolic bouquet, and the extraordinary elegance of his attire. At that moment the traveller resembled a huntsman who sees the game he has long and fruitlessly stalked. He allowed Lucien to overtake him and watched his step, though he seemed to be looking at something at the foot of the hill. Lucien turned and looked there, too, and then observed a little travelling-carriage drawn by two horses, the postilion walking beside them.

" You have allowed the diligence to outstrip you, monsieur; you will lose your place — unless indeed you will accept a seat in my carriage to overtake it; for post-horses go faster than those of a public conveyance," said the traveller, speaking with a strongly marked Spanish accent, and giving to his offer a tone of exquisite politeness.

Without waiting for Lucien's reply the Spaniard drew a case of cigars from his pocket, and offered it open to the young man that he might take one.

" I am not a traveller," said Lucien, " and I am too near the end of my way to allow myself to smoke."

" You are very rigid with yourself," said the Spaniard. " Though I am the honorary canon of the cathedral of Toledo, I allow myself, now and then, a bit of a cigar. God gave us tobacco to soothe our passions and our sorrows. You seem to be in trouble; at any rate you have the emblem of it in your hand, like the sad god Hymen. Come, take a cigar; all your griefs will end in smoke."

The priest again offered his straw case in a seductive manner, looking at Lucien with benevolent eyes.

" Pardon me, father," replied Lucien, shortly, " no cigars can relieve my grief."

So saying, his eyes filled with tears.

" Ah! young man ; was it Divine providence which made me wish to mount this hill on foot that I might, by consoling you, obey my mission here below? What great griefs can you have at your age? "

" Your consolations, father, will be useless ; you are Spanish, I am a Frenchman ; you believe in the commandments of the Church, I am an atheist — "

" *Santa Virgen del Pilar!* you are an atheist!" cried the priest, passing his arm through that of Lucien with an almost maternal tenderness. " Ah! here is one of the curiosities I am going to Paris to study. In Spain we do not believe there is such a thing as an atheist. It is only in France, and at nineteen years of age, that a man can hold such opinions."

" I am an utter atheist. I believe neither in God nor in society, nor in happiness. Look at me well, father, for in a few hours I shall cease to exist. This is my last sun! " said Lucien, with a sort of solemnity, pointing to the sky.

" Ah, ha! and what have you done that requires death? who has condemned you to die? "

" A sovereign judge — myself."

" Child! " cried the priest, " have you killed a man — is the scaffold before you? Let us argue this matter. If you wish to return, as you say you do, to nothingness, all is indifferent to you here below." Lucien bowed his head in token of assent. " Well, then, if you are indifferent you can tell me what the trouble is. Love affairs, perhaps, which have gone amiss?" Lucien made a very significant gesture with his shoulders. " You want to kill yourself to escape dishonor, or because you despair of life? Well, you can kill yourself just as well at Poitiers as you can at Angoulême, at Tours as well as at Poitiers — the quicksands of the Loire don't give up their prey — "

"No, father," replied Lucien, " I have made my plan. Three weeks ago I saw a charming raft on which a man disgusted with this world can ferry himself to another."

" Another world? then you are not an atheist?"

"Oh! what I mean by another world is my future transformation into an animal or a plant."

" Have you any incurable disease?"

" Yes, father."

" Ah; now we come to it ! " said the priest. " What is your disease?"

" Poverty."

The priest looked at Lucien and said, with infinite grace and a smile that was almost ironical, "The diamond is ignorant of its value."

"None but a priest could flatter a poor man who is about to die ! " cried Lucien.

" You will not die," said the priest, with authority.

" I have often heard of men being robbed on the high-road," returned Lucien, " but I never knew of their being enriched."

" You will know of it," said the priest, looking back to see if the carriage was still at such a distance that they might walk a little farther alone. " Listen to me," he said, biting off the end of a cigar, " your poverty is not a reason for dying. I want a secretary. Mine has lately died at Barcelona. I am in the position of Baron Goërtz, the famous minister of Charles XII. who arrived without a secretary at a little town on his way to Sweden, just as I have come here on my way to Paris. The baron met the son of a jeweller, remarkable for a beauty that was certainly not greater than yours. Goërtz saw intellect on the young man's face, just as I see poesy in yours ; he took him into his carriage, as I shall presently take you into mine, and out of that youth, condemned to burnish silver and manufacture trinkets, he made a favorite follower, as I shall make you mine. When they reached Stockholm he inducted his secretary into office and overwhelmed him with work. The young man spent his nights in writing, and, like all great workers, he contracted a habit, a trick — he chewed paper. The late Monsieur de Malesherbes himself puffed smoke into the eyes of those he talked with, and he did it, I may add, to one whose support he depended on. Well, our handsome young man began by chewing clean paper ; but he soon grew accustomed to that and took to written sheets, which he found more toothsome. They did n't smoke in those days as they do now. The little secretary finally passed from one savory morsel to another until he chewed parchments and swallowed them. There was a question at that time between Russia and Sweden of a treaty of peace which the Parliament was desirous of imposing on Charles XII. just as in 1814 they tried to force Napoleon to make peace. The basis of the negotiations was an agreement made between the two powers on the subject of Finland. Goërtz confided the original document of this agreement to the care of his secretary; but when it was necessary to submit it to Parliament a trifling difficulty arose — the document was nowhere to be found. Parliament imagined that the minister, to pander to the passions of the king had caused the disappearance of the paper; Baron Goërtz was accused, and his secretary was compelled to acknowledge having eaten the treaty. A trial was had, the fact was proved, and the secretary condemned to death. But, as you have not got as far as that, take a cigar while we wait for the carriage to overtake us."

Lucien took a cigar and lighted it, as they do in Spain, by that of the priest, thinking to himself: " He is right; I have time enough to kill myself."

" It often happens, said the Spaniard, " that the very moment when young men despair the most of their future is the one when their prosperity begins. That is what I want to show you, and I prefer to show it by an example. That handsome young secretary, condemned to death, was in a desperate condition; all the more because the King of Sweden could not pardon him, for the sentence had been pronounced by the Swedish Parliament; but the king shut his eyes to an escape. The little secretary did escape in a boat, with a few thalers in his pocket, and reached the Court of Courlande, furnished with a letter of introduction from Baron Goërtz to the duke, to whom the Swedish minister explained the mishap and also the mania of his protégé. The duke made the youth secretary to his steward. The duke was a spendthrift, he had a pretty wife, and he kept a steward, — three distinct causes of ruin. If you

suppose that the young man thus condemned to death
for eating up the Treaty of Finland corrected his depraved taste you know nothing of the power of vice
over a man ; a sentence of death won't stop him from
any enjoyment which he creates for himself. What is
the secret of this power? whence comes it? is it a force
inherent in vice, or is it the outcome of human weakness? Are there tastes which must be considered on
the verge of madness? I cannot help laughing at
moralists who try to fight such diseases with fine
phrases ! There came a time when the duke, alarmed
at a refusal given by his steward to a demand for
money, asked to see the accounts — absurdity ! There is
nothing easier than to write out an account ; the difficulty is never there ! The steward gave his secretary
the items and instructed him to make out the schedule
of the civil list of Courlande. In the middle of the
night, as the secretary was about to finish his work, he
perceived that he was munching up a receipt from the
duke for a considerable sum ; fear seized upon him ;
he ran to fling himself at the feet of the duchess, explained his mania, implored the protection of his
sovereign lady, — imploring it too, in the dead of
night. The beauty of the young clerk made such an
impression on her that she married him soon after on
becoming a widow. Thus, in the middle of the,
eighteenth century, in a land where heraldry is king,
the son of a jeweller became a sovereign prince. He became something better still ! He was made regent on
the death of the first Catherine, he governed the Empress Anne, and he tried to be the Richelieu of Russia.
Now, young man, let me tell you one thing : you are

handsomer than Biron, and I, a simple canon, am worth more than Baron Goërtz. Therefore, jump into the carriage and we'll find you a Duchy of Courlande in Paris — if there is no duchy there is certain to be a duchess."

The Spaniard slipped his hand under Lucien's arm and literally forced him to get into the vehicle; the postilion closed the door.

" Now speak ; I will listen to you," said the canon of Toledo to the bewildered Lucien. " I am an old priest to whom you can say anything without the slightest danger. You have no doubt squandered your patrimony or mamma's money? We have had our little escapades, but our honor is intact down to the soles of those pretty little boots? Come, confess boldly ; it will be absolutely as though you were speaking to yourself."

Lucien found himself in the position of the fisherman in the Arabian tale (I forget which) who, wishing to drown himself in the broad ocean, fell into a submarine country and there became a king. The Spanish priest seemed so truly interested that the poet opened his heart to him. He told him his whole life as they drove from Angoulême to Ruffec, omitting none of his misdeeds, and concluding with the last catastrophe of which he was the cause. As he ended his tale, which was all the more poetically told because Lucien had already narrated it three times in the course of the last fortnight, the carriage reached a part of the road near Ruffec which bordered the estate of the Rastignacs.

" There ! " he said, " Eugène de Rastignac, who is certainly not my equal, came from there; and he has had more luck than I have."

" Ah ! " said the Spaniard, with a start.

" Yes, that queer little building is his father's house. He became the lover of Madame de Nucingen, wife of the famous banker. I gave myself up to poesy ; he, shrewder than I, took to the practical."

The priest stopped the carriage ; he wished, out of curiosity, he said, to walk up the little avenue which led to the house ; and he looked at everything with more interest than Lucien expected in a Spanish ecclesiastic.

" Then you know the Rastignacs ? " said Lucien.

" I know all Paris," said the Spaniard, getting into the carriage. "And so for the want of ten or twelve thousand francs you were going to kill yourself ! You are a child ; you know neither men nor things. A man's destiny is what he rates it, and you value your future at twelve thousand francs ; well, I 'll buy it of you for more than that. As to the imprisonment of your brother-in-law, that 's a mere trifle. If your dear Monsieur Séchard has really invented something he 'll be a rich man. Rich men are never put in prison for debt. You don't seem to me very strong in history. There are two kinds of history : official history, lying history, that which they teach in colleges, — history *ad usum delphini;* and secret history, in which are the true causes of events, — shameful history. Allow me to tell you in three words another little story which you do not know. An ambitious man, a priest and a young one, made himself the spaniel of a favorite, the favorite of a queen. The favorite took an interest in the priest and made him a minister with a place in the council. On a certain evening one of those officious men who think they are doing a service (remember never to do a service unless it is asked of you) wrote to the ambitious young priest to tell him that the life of his benefactor was in danger. The king was angry at being superseded, and the next day the favorite was to be stabbed as he went to the palace. Well, young man, what would you have done on receiving that letter?"

" I should have warned my benefactor instantly," cried Lucien, eagerly.

" You are even more of a child than your account of your life told me," said the priest. " No, he said to himself, 'If the king has resolved on crime nothing will stop him ; my benefactor is a lost man. I had better not receive that letter till too late ;' and he turned over and went to sleep until the favorite was killed."

" Then he was a monster," said Lucien, who suspected the priest of wishing to test him.

" All great men are monsters ; that particular one was called Cardinal Richelieu," replied the canon; "his benefactor was Marshal d'Ancre. You see that you really do not know your French history. Was I not right in saying that HISTORY, as taught in schools and colleges, is a collection of dates and facts, doubtful in any case, and without the slightest signification as to actual conditions. What is the good of merely knowing that Joan of Arc existed? Did it ever lead you to think that if France had then accepted the Angevine dynasty of the Plantagenets the two peoples thus united would to-day be masters of the world ; and that the two islands where the political troubles of the continent of Europe are brewed would be French provinces? Did you never study the means by which the Medici, simple merchants, came to be grand dukes of Tuscany?"

"In France a poet is not expected to be as learned as a Benedictine," said Lucien.

"Then I will tell you, young man; they became grand dukes precisely as Richelieu became minister. If you had searched into the history of events instead of merely reading the headings, you would have found precepts by which to guide your conduct. From these, which I have taken at random from my collection of true facts, you may deduce this axiom: Regard men, above all regard women, as instruments only; but never let them see that you do so. Adore as a god the man who, being higher in station than yourself, may be useful to you; and do not leave him till he has paid a full price for your servility. In your dealings with the world be as grasping as a Jew, and as base; do for power that which the Jew does for pelf. Pay no more heed to a fallen man than if he did not exist. Do you know why you should guide your conduct in this way? You wish to master the world, don't you? Very good; then begin by obeying it and studying it. Learned men study books; statesmen study men, their interests, the generating causes of their actions. Now the world, society, men taken as a whole, are fatalists; they await what happens. Do you know why I have given you a lecture on history? Because I think your ambition is unbounded."

"Yes, it is, father."

"I see it is," resumed the canon. "But just at this moment you are saying to yourself, 'This Spanish priest invents these anecdotes and twists history to prove to me that I have too much virtue.'" (Lucien smiled at seeing his thoughts so well translated.) "Well, young man ; let us take certain facts that are the tritest ones of history. Once upon a time France was almost conquered by England ; the king had only one province left. From the heart of the people arose two beings ; one a poor young girl, that Joan of Arc of whom I have spoken ; the other a burgher named Jacques Cœur. One gave her arm and the spell of her virginity, the other gave his gold. The kingdom was saved. But the maid was captured. The king, who could have ransomed her, allowed her to be burned alive. As to the generous burgher, the king permitted his courtiers to accuse him of capital crimes ; they divided his property among them. The spoils of that innocent man, hunted, hemmed in, hounded down by justice, enriched five noble houses — and the father of the archbishop of Bourges left the kingdom, never to return, without one penny of all his property in France, and no money but a little that he had lent to the Arabs. Perhaps you will say that that is ancient history, and that all this ingratitude has been duly taught in the public schools for three hundred years, and besides, that the skeletons of that period are doubtful. Well then, young man, do you believe in the last demigod of France, Napoleon ? He regarded one of his generals with displeasure ; he only made him marshal against his will ; and he never voluntarily employed him. That was Marshal Kellerman. Do you know why this was ? Kellerman saved France and the First Consul at Marengo by a daring charge which won applause in the midst of the fire and carnage. That heroic deed was never even mentioned in the bulletin. The cause of Napoleon's coldness to Kellerman was also the cause of Fouché's disgrace and that of Prince

Talleyrand, — ingratitude, the ingratitude of Charles VII., of Richelieu!"

" But, father, supposing it possible that you should preserve my life and secure my fortune," said Lucien, "do you not make the burden of gratitude a very light one?"

"Little scamp!" said the abbé, smiling, and twisting Lucien's ear with a familiarity that was almost royal. " If you are ungrateful to me you will prove yourself a strong man, and I will bow down to you. But you have not got so far as that! though, schoolboy that you are, you have attempted to be a master before your time. That's the defect of the Frenchmen of your day. They have all been spoilt by the example of Napoleon. You are sending in your resignation because you have n't got the epaulet that you want. But have you as yet concentrated your will and all your actions on one idea?"

" Alas, no," said Lucien.

" You have been what the English call 'inconsistent,' " said the abbé, smiling.

" What matters it what I have been if I am to be nothing more?" answered Lucien.

" If there be a force behind your fine qualities of person and mind that is *semper virens*," said the priest, apparently desirous of airing his Latin, " nothing can resist you. I like you already — " (Lucien smiled incredulously.) " Yes," continued the priest, replying to Lucien's smile, " you excite my interest as though you were my son, and I am sufficiently powerful to speak to you frankly, as you have just spoken to me. Do you know what it is that I like in you? You have made yourself a blank page, and you can now listen to a lecture on morality such as you cannot hear elsewhere; for men, when assembled together, are even more hypocritical than when their interests force them to play a part. We pass the latter part of our lives in mowing down what we grew in our hearts when young. We call that operation ' acquiring experience.' "

Lucien, as he listened, was thinking to himself: "He is an old politician who is glad to find amusement on his journey. He thinks it entertaining to change the opinions of a poor fellow he finds on the brink of suicide; he 'll drop me when he has had his fun out. But he certainly is a master of paradox; as clever at it as Blondet or Lousteau."

In spite of this sage reflection, the corruption now poured into Lucien's ears entered deeply into a soul that was only too ready to receive it; making its ravages with the greater certainty because it was enforced by great examples. Caught by the charm of this cynical conversation, Lucien once more attached himself to life, and all the more willingly because he felt that the arm which was dragging him from suicide was a powerful one.

As for that, the priest had evidently triumphed ; and, from time to time he accompanied his historical sarcasms with a sly smile.

" If your method of treating morality is like your manner of considering history," said Lucien, " I should really like to know what is, at this moment, the motive of your apparent charity ? "

" That, young man, is the last point of my discourse, and you must permit me to reserve it for a time — for

24

we shall not part to-day," he replied, with the shrewdness of a priest who sees his wiles succeeding.

" Well, then, propound to me morality," said Lucien, thinking to himself: " That will make him pose."

"Morality, young man," said the priest, " begins at the law. If it were merely a question of religion laws would be useless; religious nations have few laws. Above civil law is political law. Well, then, do you wish to know what, to the eye of a politician, is written on the forehead of your nineteenth century? Frenchmen invented in 1793 a popular sovereignty which has ended in a despotic empire. So much for your national history. As to morals: Madame Tallien and Madame de Beauharnais were precisely the same in conduct. Napoleon married one and made her your empress, and he never received the other at his court, although she was a princess. A sans-culotte in 1793, Napoleon donned the iron crown in 1804. The ferocious lovers of ' Equality or Death,' in 1792 became in 1806 the accomplices of an aristocracy which Louis XVIII. legitimatized. In foreign lands the aristocracy which now lords it in the faubourg Saint-Germain did even worse; it drove the trade of usurers, shopkeepers, made pies, cooked, farmed, and kept sheep. In France, therefore, political law as well as moral law, each and all, have forsworn their promise by their results, their opinions by their conduct, or their conduct by opinions. There has been no logic either in governments or in private life. Consequently, France now has no morality. Success is the sole motive of all your actions, no matter what they be. An act is no longer anything in itself, it is wholly in the idea that others may form of it. Hence,

young man, another precept: Present a fine exterior;
hide the inside of your life, and make a brilliant show
of your externals. Discretion, that motto of ambitious
minds, is that of my cloth — make it yours. Great men
commit almost as many vile acts as poor men, but they
commit them in the dark, they parade their virtues in
the sunshine, and remain great men. Small men display their virtue in the dark and expose their baseness
to the light of day, and are despised. You have hidden
your greatness, and exhibited your sores. You took an
actress for your mistress and lived with her, in her
house publicly. That was not reprehensible, for you
were, both of you, absolutely free; but you ran a tilt
against the ideas of the world, and you lost the respect
which the world gives only to those who obey its laws.
If you had left Coralie with that old man, if you had
hidden your relations to her, you could have married
Madame de Bargeton, and you would now be prefect
of Angoulême and Marquis de Rubempré. Alter your
conduct; exhibit only your beauty, your grace, your
wit, your poesy. If you allow yourself a few little
ignominies keep them within four walls. Follow this
precept and you will never again be guilty of soiling
the decorations of that great theatre which we name
the world. Napoleon called that ' washing our dirty
linen at home.' From this, my second precept, issues
a corollary: All depends on form. Understand what
I mean by form. There are uneducated persons who,
being pressed by want, take something by violence
which belongs to another. These are called criminals,
and they are forced to reckon with the law. But a poor
man of genius discovers a secret, the application of

which is equivalent to enormous wealth ; he owes you
three thousand francs (just the sum the Cointets hold of
yours and which enables them to despoil your brother-
in-law) ; you torment that poor man with the law until
you make him give you the whole or part of his secret ;
there is nothing to hinder you but your conscience, and
your conscience doesn't accuse you of anything. The
enemies of social order make use of such inconsis-
tencies to yelp at justice and rail in the name of the
People because the law sends the man who steals
chickens at night to the galleys, while other men who
ruin families escape (if punished at all) with a few
weeks in prison. But these hypocrites know very well
that in condemning the thief the judges maintained the
barrier between the poor and the rich, the overturning
of which would put an end to social order ; whereas the
bankrupt, the adroit purloiner of inheritances, the
banker who throttles another man's enterprise to his
own profit, are only making money change hands.
Society, my son, is forced to distinguish, on its own
account that which I am telling you to distinguish on
yours. The great point is to put one's self on the level
of the society we live in. Napoleon, Richelieu, the
Medici, were all on the level of their age ; and you, you
rate yourself at twelve thousand francs ! Remember
that your world no longer worships the true God, but
the Golden Calf. That is the religion of your Charter,
which takes account in its policy of nothing but property. Isn't that as good as saying to all its subjects :
' Strive to get rich '? When you have managed to
make a fortune legally, and are Marquis de Rubempré,
you can allow yourself the luxury of honor. You will

then exhibit such delicacy in that respect that no one
will dare to accuse you of having ever failed in it; if
indeed you ever do fail in it while making your fortune
— which I should never advise you to do," said the
priest. taking Lucien's hand and tapping it. "Now
what is it you ought to get into that handsome head of
yours? Solely this : Set before you a splendid object ;
hide your means of reaching it, and also your steps.
You have been behaving like a child ; be a man, be a
huntsman, watch the game, lurk in Parisian society,
trust to chance, and seize your prey when it comes
along ; never spare either your person or what is
called your dignity, — for we all obey something, be it a
vice or a necessity, — but remember to observe the
supreme rule, secrecy."

"You frighten me, father !" cried Lucien ; "that
seems to me the theory of a highwayman."

"You are right," said the canon, "but it is not
mine. That is the reasoning of the moderns, the House
of Austria and the House of France. You have nothing ; you are in the situation of the Medici. of Richelieu,
and Napoleon at the dawn of their ambition. Those
men, my lad, estimated their future at the cost of ingratitude, treachery, and the most violent oppositions.
We must dare all to win all. Let us argue that. When
you sit down to play bouillotte, do you dispute the conditions? No, the rules are there, and you accept them."

"So !" thought Lucien, "he knows bouillotte !"

"How do you behave when you are playing bouillotte?" continued the priest. "Do you practise that
noblest of virtues, frankness? You not only hide your
own game, but you try to make others believe that you

are certain to lose it, when you know you are going to win. You dissimulate, don't you? You lie to win five louis. What would you say of a player who was generous enough to tell the others he had three cards of a suit? Well, the ambitious man who attempts the struggle of life on the principles of virtue which his antagonists have long laid aside is a child, to whom veterans would say, as the players would to the man who laid down his three cards, ' Monsieur, don't play bouillotte again.' Is it you who make the rules in the game of ambition? Why did I tell you that a man must put himself on the level of the world he lives in? Because, young man, society has insensibly arrogated to itself so many rights over individuals that an individual standing alone would have to fight it single-handed. There are no longer any laws, only what are called customs; that is to say conventions, pretences, form. form — always form." (Lucien made a gesture of amazement.) " Ah, my son,'' said the priest, fearing perhaps to have revolted Lucien's innocence, '' you must not expect to find the Angel Gabriel in an abbé who is charged with all the iniquities of the counter-diplomacy of two great kings (I am the intermediary between Ferdinand VII. and Louis XVIII., two great kings, who both owe their crowns to profound and far-reaching compromises) ! I believe in God, but I believe far more in our Order, and our Order believes in nothing but the temporal power. To make the temporal power strong, our Order maintains the Catholic, Apostolic. and Roman Church ; that is to say, the embodiment of the sentiments which compel the people to obedience. We are modern Templars ; we have but one doctrine. Our Order was overthrown

like theirs, and for the same reason — *it put itself on
the level of the times.* If you will be a soldier, I will be
your captain. Obey me as a wife obeys her husband,
as a child obeys its mother, and I will guarantee you
that in less than three years you shall be Marquis de
Rubempré, and the husband of one of the proudest
daughters of Saint-Germain, and you shall sit at some
future day on the bench of Peers. If I had not amused you
by my conversation what would you be at this moment?
A corpse sunk in a bed of slime. Come, make an effort
at poesy ; I 'll give you a theme (Lucien looked at his
deliverer with curiosity). Take the young man who is
seated here in this carriage beside the Abbé Don Carlos
Herrera, honorary canon of the Chapter of Toledo,
secret envoy from His Majesty Ferdinand VII. to His
Majesty the King of France, and bearer of a despatch
in which may be the words : ' When you have delivered
me, hang all those I flatter at this moment ; especially
my envoy who takes this letter, so that he may keep it
a dead secret.' This young man," continued the abbé,
" has nothing in common with the poet who has just
died. I fished you out ; I gave you life ; you belong to
me as a creature does to the Creator, as the Afrite to
the genii, as the page to the sultan, the body to the soul.
I will sustain you, — I, myself, with a powerful hand, —
in the path of power ; and I promise you besides a life
of pleasures, honors, and continual enjoyment. Never
shall you lack money. You shall shine, you shall display yourself before the eyes of the world, while I, toil-
ing in the mud of the foundations, will secure the
brilliant edifice of your fortune. I love power for
power's sake myself ; I shall always rejoice in your

enjoyments though to me they are forbidden. In short
1 shall be you. Well, if the day comes on which this
compact of man and devil, child and diplomatist, ceases
to please you, you shall be free to find a pretty spot like
that you spoke of, and drown yourself; you would then
be, a little more or a little less, what you are to-day —
unfortunate or dishonored."

" 'That is not the homily of an archbishop of Gran-
ada," cried Lucien, as the carriage stopped at a
post-house.

" 'I don't know what name you may choose to give to
that concise lesson, my son, — for I adopt you as my son
and will make you my heir, — but it is the Code of Ambition. The elect of God are few in number. There is
no choice ; we must either go to the depths of a cloister
(and there we shall find the world in little), or accept
this code."

" Perhaps it would be better not to be so learned,"
said Lucien, endeavoring to fathom the soul of this
terrible priest.

" What ! " exclaimed the canon ; " after playing your
cards without any knowledge of the rules of the game,
do you throw them down when you are becoming skilled
and find a strong backer behind you? Are you without
so much as a desire for revenge? Don't you long to
leap upon the backs of those who drove you from
Paris ? "

Lucien shuddered as if some iron instrument, some
Chinese gong, had clanged its terrible sounds in his ears
and rasped his nerves.

" I am but a humble priest," continued the man, per-
mitting a horrible expression to cross his face, bronzed

by the sun of Spain ; " but if I had been humiliated, vexed, tortured, betrayed, sold, as you have been by those scoundrels you spoke of, I would be like the Bedouin of the desert — yes, I would devote myself soul and body to revenge. Would I care if I ended my days by swinging from a gibbet, or impaled, or guillotined, as in France? No! but they should not take my head till I had crushed my enemies underfoot."

Lucien was silent ; he no longer thought of making the priest pose.

" Some men are the descendants of Abel, some of Cain," said the canon, in conclusion. " I myself am of mixed blood, — Abel to my friends, and sorrow to him who awakens Cain. After all, you are a Frenchman, I am a Spaniard, and, what is more, a canon — "

" A Bedouin indeed ! " thought Lucien, examining the protector whom heaven had sent him.

The Abbé Carlos Herrera bore no signs in himself which revealed the Jesuit, nor, indeed, a priest of any order. Stout and short, with large hands, a broad chest herculean in strength, a terrible glance, softened at will into gentleness, a bronzed skin which suffered nothing to pass from the inner to the outer, he inspired at once far more repulsion than attraction. Very fine long hair, powdered after the fashion of that of Talleyrand, gave the look of a prelate to this singular diplomatist, and the blue ribbon edged with white by which hung a cross of gold pointed him out, unmistakably, as an ecclesiastical dignitary. His black silk stockings defined the legs of an athlete. His clothes, of an exquisite nicety, revealed that minute care of the person which ordinary priests, especially in Spain, are not prone to take. A

three-cornered hat was lying on the front seat of the
carriage, the panels of which bore the arms of Spain.
In spite of certain causes for repulsion, the manners
of the man, which were brusque and yet insinuating, les-
sened the unpleasant effect of his physiognomy, and in
speaking to Lucien the priest had made himself caress-
ing, winning, almost feline.

Lucien watched and considered everything with an
anxious air. He felt his decision was at that moment
a matter of life or death, for they had now reached the
second relay after Ruffec. The last words of the Spanish
priest stirred many of the chords of his heart; and, let
us say it to Lucien's shame and that of the priest, who
watched with a discerning eye the handsome features
of the poet, these chords were among the worst that
vibrate in the human soul. Again Lucien beheld Paris,
once more he seized the reins of a power his unskilled
hands had dropped, and he avenged himself! The comparison of provincial life with Parisian life which his
stay at Angoulême had afforded him and which was
perhaps the most active cause of his suicide, disap-
peared from his mind; he was about to find himself
once more in his natural element, but protected, this
time, by a powerful backer, the villany of whose principles equalled that of Cromwell.

" I was one, we shall be two," Lucien said to himself. The more he had revealed the disgrace of his
former life, the more the priest had shown his interest.
The charity of the man had increased in proportion
to his unhappiness; he seemed surprised by nothing.
Nevertheless, Lucien asked himself what could be the
motive of this manager of court intrigues. At first he

was contented with a commonplace reason ; the Spanish were a generous people ! A Spaniard is generous,
we may remark, just as an Italian is jealous and a
poisoner, a Frenchman frivolous, a German frank, an
Englishman noble, a Jew ignoble. Reverse those prop-
ositions and you get at the truth. Jews accumulate
money, they compose " Robert le Diable," they act
" Phèdre," they sing " Guillaume Tell," they buy pictures, they build palaces, they write the " Reisebilder"
and other admirable poetry, they are now more powerful than ever, their religion is conceded to them, they
even do business with the Pope. Germans will say in
the smallest matter : " We must have a contract, there
is so much trickery." In France we have applauded for
the last fifty years the dullest national plays, we continue to wear inexplicable hats, and we change the government from time to time on condition that it shall
be always the same ! England displays to the eyes of
the world a treachery equalled only by her greed. The
Spaniard after possessing all the gold of the two Indies
has nothing left. There is not a country in the world
where there is less poisoning than in Italy, and where
the manners and customs are easier and more courteous.
Spaniards have really existed on the reputation of the
Moors. So much for proverbial sayings !

When the Spanish priest returned to the carriage he
whispered to the postilion : " A large fee for your best
speed."

Lucien hesitated ; the priest said : " Come," and he
got in, under pretext in his own mind of pursuing the
argument *ad hominem.*

" Father," he said, " a man who has just unfolded

with the utmost coolness doctrines which ordinary minds would call profoundly immoral — "

" And which are so," said the priest.   " That is why Jesus Christ said that offences must be made known. And it is also why the world manifests such horror at the making known of scandals."

" A man of your stamp cannot be surprised at the question I wish to put to you."

" Go on, my son," said Carlos Herrera.   " You do not know me. Do you suppose I should take a secretary without discovering whether his principles are such that he would not rob me? I am satisfied with what I see of you. You still have all the innocence of a man who kills himself at the age of twenty. Go on ; your question ? "

" Why do you take an interest in me? What price do you demand for my obedience? Why do you give me all? What are your motives? "

The Spaniard looked at Lucien and smiled.

" Let us wait for the next hill, and walk up," he said ; " then we can talk in the open air ; a travelling-carriage is sometimes indiscreet."

Silence reigned for some time between the two companions ; the rapidity with which the carriage was driven aided what we must call Lucien's moral intoxication.

" Father, here is a hill," he said after a time, as if waking from a dream.

" Then let us walk," said the priest, calling out to the postilion in a strong voice to pull up.

The two men sprang out upon the road.

" Child," said the Spaniard, taking Lucien by the arm, " have you ever meditated over Otway's ' Venice

Preserved'? Do you understand the profound friendship of man to man, which binds Pierre to Jaffier, makes woman of no account, and changes all social terms? Well, that is what the poet tells us."

"He knows the stage, too!" thought Lucien. "Have you read Voltaire?" he asked aloud.

"I have done better still," replied the canon; "I have put him in practice."

"You don't believe in God?"

"Ha! now it is I who am the atheist!" said the priest, laughing. "But let us get to the practical, my young friend," he continued. "I am forty-six years old,— the natural son of a great seigneur, consequently without family; and I have a heart. Now, learn this; carve it on that soft brain of yours: man has a horror of solitude. And of all solitudes, moral solitude is that which terrifies him most. The first hermits lived with God; they inhabited the most populous of worlds,— the spiritual world. Misers inhabit a world of fancy and possession; a miser has all, even his sex, in his brain. The first desire of man, be he a leper or a galley-slave, infamous or diseased, is to have a sharer in his fate. To satisfy that desire, which is existence itself to him, he employs his whole strength, his every faculty, the very sap of his life. Without that sovereign need would Satan have found companions? A whole poem might be made on that theme, a prelude to Paradise Lost, which is only an apology for the revolt —"

"And the other would be the Iliad of corruption," said Lucien.

"Well, I am alone,— I live alone. Though I wear the robe, I have not the heart of a priest. I love to devote myself; that is my vice. I live by devotion. I do not fear ingratitude, and I am grateful. The Church can be nothing to my heart; it is only an idea. I am devoted to the King of Spain, but one cannot love a king ; he protects me, he towers above me. I wish to love my own creation ; to fashion him, mould him to my needs, in short to love him as a father loves his child. Yes, my son, I shall roll in your tilbury, I shall rejoice in your success among women, I shall say to myself : ' That splendid youth is I ! that Marquis de Rubempré, I created him, I placed him among his peers ; his greatness is my work, he speaks or is silent according to my voice ; he consults me in everything.' That is what the Abbé de Vermont was to Marie-Antoinette."

" And he led her to the scaffold ! "

" He did not love the queen," replied the priest, " he loved only the Abbé de Vermont."

" But I have left desolation behind me," said Lucien. " I have wealth ; you shall share it."

" Certainly I would do much at this moment to rescue Séchard," replied Lucien, in a voice that plainly said he gave up suicide.

" Say the word, my son, and to-morrow he shall receive the money necessary to liberate him."

" What! would you give me twelve thousand francs? "

" Child! we are driving at twelve miles an hour, we shall dine at Poitiers. There, if you will sign our compact, the diligence to Bordeaux shall carry fifteen thousand francs to your sister."

" Where are they? "

The priest made no reply, and Lucien said to himself, " I have caught him ; he is only laughing at me."

An instant later the priest and the poet got back into the carriage silently. Silently, too, the priest put his hand into the pocket of the carriage and drew forth a leathern pouch made like a game bag, in three compartments, of a kind that was well-known to travellers at that period. From it he took a hundred *portugaises*, plunging his hand in two or three times and withdrawing it filled with gold.

" Father, I am yours," said Lucien, dazzled by the flood of gold.

" Child ! " said the priest, kissing Lucien on the forehead tenderly, " that is but a fraction of the gold in that bag, which contains thirty thousand francs, beside the money for this journey."

" And you dare to travel alone? " exclaimed Lucien.

" Oh ! that is nothing," said the Spaniard ; " I have bills of exchange for more than three hundred thousand francs on Paris. A diplomatist without money is what you were just now,— a poet without will."

XI.

A DAY TOO LATE.

AT the moment when Lucien was first getting into the carriage of the pretended Spanish diplomat, Eve was rising to feed her child. She saw the fatal letter and read it. A cold sweat chilled the warm moisture produced by her morning sleep; she turned giddy and called to Kolb and Marion.

To her question : " Has my brother gone out? " Kolb answered. " Yes, madame, before daylight."

" Keep secret what I tell you," said Eve to the two servants ; " my brother has probably gone to end his life. Go both of you and make inquiries with the greatest caution. Search along the banks of the river."

Eve remained alone in a state of stupor that was piteous to see. It was in the midst of this new trouble that, as early as seven o'clock in the morning, Petit-Claud came to her on business. At such moments we are ready to give ear to any one.

" Madame," said the lawyer, " our poor dear David is in prison, and he is now in the situation I foresaw from the very first of this affair. I advised him then to take his competitors, the Cointets, into partnership for

the practical working out of his invention. They have
in their hands all the means of executing that which so
far is only a conception in your husband's mind. So
last night, as soon as the news of his arrest reached me,
what did I do? I went to see the Messrs. Cointet in
the hope of getting out of them concessions which
might satisfy you. If David continues to hold on to
this discovery your lives will remain what they now
are — harassed by legal chicanery in which you will
be worsted; worn-out by the struggle you will end,
probably to your detriment, with doing with some
moneyed man what I now propose to you to do, to your
advantage, with the Cointets. By taking the course I
suggest you will save yourselves all the privations and
also the distress of the inevitable struggle of an inventor against the greed of capitalists and the indifference of people at large. See! if the Cointets pay
your debts, and if (your debts being paid) they give
you a certain sum whatever be the merit, or the fate, or
the possibilities of David's invention, agreeing, moreover, to give you a specified share in the profits of the
enterprise, will not that content you? You are now,
yourself, madame, the owner of the material of the
printing-house, and you can certainly sell it; I will, in
fact, guarantee you a purchaser at twenty thousand
francs. If you realize fifteen thousand more by the
partnership with the Messrs. Cointet, that gives you a
little capital of thirty-five thousand francs; at the
present rate of interest you will have two thousand
francs a year to live on,— that 's enough to live com-
fortably in the country. And remember also that you
will have further profits if the Messrs. Cointet succeed in

25

the enterprise. I say ' succeed ' because there is always a chance of failure. Well, here is what I have every hope of obtaining for you : first, David's immediate liberation ; then, fifteen thousand francs paid for his discovery by the Messrs. Cointet in any case, whether the discovery is productive or not; next, a partnership formed between David and the Messrs. Cointet for the working of the patent (which they will take out) and for the fabrication of the paper, on the following basis : Messieurs Cointet to pay all costs ; David's capital to be the patent; he to have one fourth of the profits. You are a woman of good judgment with whom one can reason — which is not always the case with a very beautiful woman ; reflect on these proposals, and I am sure you will think them acceptable."

" Ah, monsieur," said the poor woman, bursting into tears, " why did you not make me this proposal yesterday ? We might have escaped dishonor then ; and, oh, worse, worse ! "

" My discussion with the Cointets, who, as you have probably known all along, are behind Métivier, did not end till midnight. But what can have happened worse than poor David's arrest ? " asked Petit-Claud.

" This, which I found when I woke," replied Eve, giving him Lucien's letter. " You prove to me now that you are really interested for us, and a true friend to David and Lucien. I ask you to keep this secret."

" Don't be uneasy," said Petit-Claud, returning the letter after reading it; " Lucien will not kill himself. After being the cause of his brother-in-law's arrest he had to find a reason for leaving you. That is only a bit of stage business."

The Cointets had attained their object. After torturing the inventor and his family they seized the moment when the torture left the victims wearied out and
glad of rest on any terms. All inventors are not bulldogs who will die with their prize in their jaws, and the
Cointets had sagaciously studied the character of their
prey. To the tall Cointet David's arrest was but the
last scene of the first act of the drama. The second act
began with the proposal Petit-Claud had just made. To
the little lawyer's masterly eye Lucien's folly was one of
those unexpected bits of luck which decide a game. He
saw Eve so completely crushed by this event that he
resolved to profit by it to win her confidence ; for he
had long suspected the influence of the wife over the
husband. So, instead of plunging her deeper into
despair, he tried to reassure her and lead her mind to
David in prison, believing that she would soon see the
necessity of the compromise with the Cointets.

" David has always told me, madame, that he desired
wealth solely for you and for your brother. Now as
for your brother, you must see by this time that it would
be folly to give him money ; he would squander three
fortunes."

Eve's attitude showed only too plainly that her last
illusion as to Lucien had taken to itself wings ; the
lawyer therefore made a pause to convert his client's
silence into a sort of consent.

" So, in this matter of the invention, it becomes only
a question of yourself and your child. It is for you to
know whether two thousand francs a year will be enough
for your comfort ; not considering, of course, your future
inheritance from old Séchard. He has laid by in the

course of his long life enough to give him now an income of seven or eight thousand francs, without counting the interest he gets on his other property. You have, in any case, a good future before you. Why be harassed now?"

Petit-Claud left Madame Séchard to reflect on this perspective, rather cleverly suggested to him by the tall Cointet.

" Go and show them the possibility of getting some kind of a sum in hand," the lynx of Angoulême had said, when the lawyer came to tell him of the arrest. " When they get accustomed to the idea of actually having money we can do what we like with them ; we can bargain then, and little by little we can get them down to a price we are willing to pay."

That sentence contained what may be called the argument of the second act of this financial drama.

When Madame Séchard, with a heart wrung by apprehensions as to her brother's fate, was dressed and ready to go to the prison and see her husband, she was overcome with dread at the idea of walking through the streets alone. At this moment Petit-Claud, with no thought of his client's anxiety, returned to offer her his arm, moved thereto by a reflection that was sufficiently Machiavelian ; and he had the merit of a delicacy of which Eve was not aware, for he allowed her to thank him without correcting her mistake. This little attention in a man so hard and unbending, and at such a moment, softened, as Petit-Claud meant it should, the opinion that Madame Séchard had hitherto held of him.

" I shall take you by the longest way," he said, " so that you may meet no one."

" This is the first time, monsieur, that I have not the right to carry my head high ! they taught me a hard lesson yesterday."

" The first and the last," replied Petit-Claud.

" Oh ! I will never stay in this town."

" If your husband consents to the proposals which are as good as made by the Cointets to me," said Petit-Claud, as they reached the gates of the prison, " send me word, and I will come at once with an order from Cachan, on which David will be released, and apparently there will be no reason for his return to prison."

This proposal, made in front of the jail, was what the Italians call a " combinazione." The word with them means an indefinable act in which a little trickery is mingled with legal right, the opportunity for permissible fraud, a knavery that is half legitimate and well schemed.

For reasons lately explained, imprisonment for debt is so rare an occurrence in the provinces that in most of the towns of France there is no house of detention. When that is the case the debtor is locked up in the same prison where they incarcerate accused persons, prisoners before trial, and convicts ; such are the divers names applied legally and successively to those who are generically called *criminals*. David was therefore put provisionally in one of the lower rooms of the prison of Angoulême, from which some convict had probably just been let out after serving his time. When he was locked in, with the sum decreed by law to provide his food for the period of one month, David found himself in presence of a stout man who was to the captives a power greater than the king himself; namely, the jailer. There is no such thing in the provinces as a thin jailer. First, because the place is almost a sinecure; next, because a jailer is something like an innkeeper without any rent to pay; he feeds himself very well and his prisoners very ill, lodging them moreover (like the innkeeper) according to their means. He knew David by name through his father, and he felt confidence enough in that relationship to lodge the son for one night well, though he knew that David had not a penny of his own.

The prison of Angoulême dates from the middle ages and has been left as unchanged as the cathedral. It is still called the House of Justice, and is backed by the old law courts. The entrance is classic; the door, which is studded with enormous iron nails, solid but worn, is low in height, and seems all the more Cyclopean because of a peep-hole in its centre (through which the jailer looks before he opens it), which has the effect of a single eye. A corridor runs the whole length of the front of the building on the ground-floor, and on this corridor open several rooms, the tall windows of which look out upon the yard. The jailer occupied an apartment separated from these rooms by a vaulted space which divided the ground-floor into two divisions, at the farther end of which could be seen from the entrance an iron gate opening into the yard. David was conducted by the jailer into one of the rooms which was nearest to this vaulted space; the man was evidently not unwilling to have for his neighbor a prisoner with whom he could talk.

"This is the best room," he said, seeing that David seemed stupefied at the aspect of the abode.

The walls of the room were of stone and quite damp. The windows, which were very high up, were barred

with iron. The stone pavement was icy. The regular
step of the sentry resounded as he paced the corridor.
That monotonous sound, like that of the tide. keeps the
one thought before your mind : "You are not free ! you
are not free ! you are guarded !" These details and
the general impression thus produced, act powerfully
on the mental condition of honest men.

David saw before him an execrable bed : but persons
just incarcerated are so violently agitated during the
first night that they do not find out the miseries of their
couch till the second. The jailer was gracious; he
proposed to his prisoner to walk in the yard till bed-
time. He was forbidden to let the prisoners have
lights ; and it would require an application to the *procureur du roi* to exempt a prisoner for debt from a
regulation which evidently concerned only those who
were in the hands of justice. The jailer even admitted
David to his own room, but was forced to lock him up
when bed-time came. Eve's poor husband then knew
the horrors of a prison and the coarseness of its customs, which sickened him. But, by one of those reac-
tions familiar enough to thinkers, he isolated himself
in this solitude, taking refuge in a dream such as poets
have the power to dream awake. The poor soul's
mind at last reverted to reflection on his present situation. A prison has an extraordinary power to drive a
man to examine his conscience. David asked himself
whether he had done his duty as head of a family.
What must now be the desolation of his wife? Why
had he not, as Marion said, earned enough money to
support his family and worked at his invention later?

"And now," he said to himself, "how can we stay

in Angoulême after this disgrace? If I get out of prison, what will become of us? where can we go?"

It was an agony of mind such as none can understand but inventors themselves. Going from doubt to doubt, David came at last to see his situation clearly, and he said to himself, what the Cointets had said to his father, what Petit-Claud had just said to Eve: "Even supposing all goes well with the discovery, how can I work it? I must have a patent, and that means money! I must have a manufactory to test my invention on a larger scale, and that will give my secret to everybody! Yes, Petit-Claud was right. Ah!" said David, turning over to go to sleep on the camp bedstead, with the horrible mattress covered with coarse brown cloth, "I shall certainly see Petit-Claud to-morrow morning."

David was therefore prepared by his own mind to listen to the proposals which his wife brought him from his enemies. After kissing her husband and sitting down on the foot of his bed (for there was only one wooden chair of the vilest kind) her wifely eyes fell on the horrible pail standing in a corner of the cell, and the names and epigrams written on the walls by his predecessors. Then the tears began again to flow from her reddened eyes; after the many that she had shed a fresh flood came when she saw her husband in the condition of a criminal.

"This is what comes in this world of a desire for fame!" she cried. "Oh! my angel, abandon it! Let us tread together the beaten path, and cease to seek a rapid fortune. I need so little to make me happy — especially now that I have suffered so much. Oh, if you knew all! this dishonoring arrest is not our greatest misfortune! — read that."

She gave him Lucien's letter, but to lessen the shock she repeated Petit-Claud's scoffing speech.

" If Lucien is to kill himself it is done by this time," said David; "and if it is not already done, he will never do it. He has not, as he says himself, courage enough for more than one morning."

"But to keep us in such anxiety!" cried the sister, who had been ready to forgive all in the presence of death.

She repeated to her husband the proposals which Petit-Claud professed to have made to the Cointets. David agreed to them with evident pleasure.

" We shall have enough to live on in the village beyond l'Houmeau where the Cointets' factory is, and all I want now is tranquillity," said the inventor. " If Lucien has punished himself by death, we shall be able to support ourselves while my father lives; if the poor lad is still alive he must learn to conform himself to our poverty. The Cointets will of course profit by my discovery; but, after all, what am I in comparison to the good that will be done to the country! — only one man. If my invention is a benefit to all, well, I am satisfied! Dear Eve, we were neither of us born to be merchants. We have not that love of gain, nor that hatred of parting with money which are, perhaps, the virtues of the mercantile mind — for they call those two forms of avarice, Prudence and Commercial Genius!"

Delighted with this conformity of opinion (one of the sweetest flowers of love, for minds and self-interests are only in harmony where two beings love each other)

Eve begged the jailer to send a note to Petit-Claud, in
which she asked him to come and release David, and
assured him of their mutual consent to the basis of his
proposed settlement. Ten minutes later the lawyer appeared in the horrible room and said to Eve: "Go
home, madame, and we will follow you."

"My dear friend," said Petit-Claud, when they were
alone, "how came you to be taken? How could you
be so unwise as to leave your hiding-place?"

"I could not help coming out; here is what Lucien
wrote me."

David gave Petit-Claud Lucien's note. The lawyer
took it, read it, looked at it, felt the paper and folded
the letter, as if abstractedly; then, as the conversation
went on, he slipped it unperceived into his pocket.
Presently he put his arm within David's and went out
with him; for the jailer had brought the discharge
during their conversation.

When David reached home he felt in heaven. He
cried like a child as he kissed his little Lucien and found
himself again in that blue and white bedroom after
twenty days' detention, the last of which was, according
to provincial ideas, degrading. Kolb and Marion had
returned. Marion heard in l'Houmeau that Lucien had
been seen walking along the road to Paris beyond Marsac. His dandified dress was noticed by the country-
men who were bringing their produce to market. Kolb,
who had made his search on horseback, was told at
Mansle that Lucien had been recognized in a travelling
carriage with post-horses on the road to Poitiers.

"What did I tell you?" cried Petit-Claud. "He is
not a poet, that fellow, he's a perpetual romance."

" Post-horses ! " said Eve, " where can he be going this time? "

" Now," said Petit-Claud to David, " come and see the Messrs. Cointet; they are expecting you."

" Ah, monsieur," said Madame Séchard, " protect our interests, I implore you ; you have our future in your hands."

" Should you like the conference to take place here, madame? " said the lawyer. " If so, I will leave David now. The Messrs. Cointet can come here this evening, and you shall see for yourself how I defend your interests."

" You will greatly oblige me," said Eve.

" Very good, then," said Petit-Claud. " To-night, here, about seven o'clock."

" Thank you," said Eve, with a look and accent which proved to Petit-Claud what strides he had made in his client's confidence.

" Fear nothing now," he added. " As for your brother, he is fifty miles away from suicide by this time. To-night you will be the possessors of a small fortune. I have already had a proposal for the printing-office."

" If we can sell that," said Eve, " why not wait before committing ourselves to the Cointets? "

" You forget, madame," said Petit-Claud, who saw his blunder, " that you will be free to sell the establishment only after you have paid Monsieur Métivier, for all the utensils are attached."

As soon as he got back to his office Petit-Claud sent for Cérizet. When the ex-gamin arrived he took him into the embrasure of a window.

" You shall, to-morrow, be the proprietor of the

Séchard printing-house and sufficiently backed to obtain a license," he whispered to him ; " but you don't want to end at the galleys, do you? "

" What ! what ! — the galleys? " exclaimed Cérizet.

" Your letter to David is a forgery, and I have got it. If anyone inquires of Henriette Signol, what will she reply? I don't want to ruin you," went on Petit-Claud, as Cérizet turned pale.

" You want something more of me," cried Cérizet, recovering himself.

" I want this," resumed Petit-Claud, " and pay attention to what I say. You will be a printer in Angoulême, *but* you will owe for your printing-house and you cannot pay it off in ten years ! You will have to work long and hard for your capitalists, and, moreover, you will be made the cat's-paw of the Liberals. I shall draw up your deed of agreement with Gannerac ; and I shall do it in a way to secure the printing-house to you eventually. But, if they start a newspaper, if you are the publisher of it, if I am the first assistant-procureur of Angoulême as I shall be, you are to arrange with the tall Cointet privately to put such articles of a political nature into your paper that it will be seized and suppressed. The Cointets will pay you handsomely for that service ; I admit that you will be condemned and sent to prison, but that will make you important,— you will be called persecuted, and end in becoming a great personage in the Liberal party,— a Sergeant Mercier, a Paul-Louis Courrier, a Manuel on a small scale. The day that newspaper is suppressed I 'll burn that forged letter before your eyes. Your fortune won't cost you dear."

People of the lower ranks have very mistaken ideas about the legal distinctions as to forgery, and Cérizet, who fancied himself already in a police-court, breathed easier.

" Three years from now I shall be *procureur du roi* in Angoulême," continued Petit-Claud, "and you may have need of me,— remember that."

" That 's understood," said Cérizet. " But you don't know me ; burn that letter before me now and trust to my gratitude."

Petit-Claud looked at him. It was one of those duels of eye to eye when the glance of him who observes is like a scalpel with which he attempts to search the soul through the eyes of the man who struggles to bring his virtues to the front ; it was indeed a dramatic spectacle.

Petit-Claud made no answer ; he lighted a candle and burned the letter, saying to himself, " He has his fortune to make."

" You have a slave through thick and thin," said the ex-gamin.

David awaited in vague uneasiness his conference with the Cointets ; it was neither the discussion of his interests nor the nature of the compact to be made which troubled him, but the opinion the manufacturers might form on his discovery. He was in the position of a dramatic author before his judges. The self-love of the inventor and his anxiety on the verge of attaining his end paled all other feelings. At last, about seven o'clock in the evening, just as Madame la Comtesse du Châtelet was going to bed under pretence of a headache, but really to let her husband do the honors of the dinner, so disturbed was she at the various contradictory stories about Lucien's disappearance which were flying through the town, the two Cointets, tall and stout, accompanied by Petit-Claud, entered the house of their competitor, who was now delivered over to them bound hand and foot.

A preliminary difficulty presented itself at once. How could a deed of partnership be drawn up unless David's process was known? and if he made known his process he was at the mercy of the Cointets. Petit-Claud, however, obtained the concession that the deed should be drawn before the secret was divulged. The tall Cointet then asked David to show his products, and the inventor produced samples of the last paper he had made, guaranteeing the net cost of it.

"Why, there!" said Petit-Claud, "there's basis enough for the deed; why not take that sum and introduce a clause of dissolution of partnership in case the conditions of the patent are not carried out when it comes to the manufacture of the paper?"

"It is one thing, monsieur," said the tall Cointet, addressing David, "to produce in one's own room over a small furnace a few samples of paper, and quite another to manufacture a satisfactory paper on a large scale. You can judge of that by one fact. We make colored papers; and we buy, in order to color them, blocks of color which are supposed to be identically the same. The indigo we use for the bluing of our post-demy paper is taken from a case in which all the cakes come from the same manufactory, and yet we have never been able to make two batches of the same shade. There is something in the preparation of our materials which we have never yet been able to get hold of. The quantity and quality change instantly on the slightest provocation. When you hold in a pan a portion of the ingredients (I do not ask what they are) you are master of them; you can act upon all the parts uniformly; you can mix them, knead them, work them up as you please, amalgamate them thoroughly. But who can guarantee that in a vat of five hundred reams the same thing can be done? and, if not certain, your process may be a failure."

David, Eve, and Petit-Claud looked at each other, saying many things by their eyes.

"Take an example which offers some analogy," said the tall Cointet, after a pause. "You cut two bales of hay in your field, and you put them very closely together in your loft, not allowing the grass to strike fire, as the peasants say. Fermentation takes place, but it does no harm. You rely on that experience to put two thousand bales in a wooden granary; the hay ignites, and the barn burns like a match. You are a man of intelligence," said Cointet to David; "draw your own inference. You have at this moment cut your two bales of hay, but we are afraid of destroying our paper-works by putting in two thousand bales. In other words, we are liable to lose whole vats full, make heavy losses, and find ourselves with nothing in hand after spending a great deal of money."

David was struck dumb. The practical man was talking practice to theory, whose own language is always of the future.

"The devil take me if I sign any such deed of partnership," cried the stout Cointet, roughly. "You can lose your money if you like, Boniface, I shall keep mine ; I offer to pay the debts of Monsieur Séchard and six thousand francs — no, three thousand in notes," he said, catching himself up, " payable in twelve and fifteen months. That's risk enough to run. We shall have fully twelve thousand francs to pay to Métivier — in all, fifteen thousand francs ; and that's as much as I shall agree to pay for this secret. So this is the discovery you have been talking about, Boniface? Well, I gave you credit for more sense. No, that's not what I call a good business affair."

" The question for you," said Petit-Claud, not alarmed by this outburst, " reduces itself to this : Will you risk twenty thousand francs to buy a secret which may enrich you? Why, gentlemen, risks are always in proportion to profits. This is a stake of twenty thousand francs against fortune. A player puts down a louis to win thirty-six at roulette ; why not do the same thing? "

" I want time to reflect," said the stout Cointet ; " for my part, I am not so long-headed as my brother. I'm only a poor chap who knows but one thing — how to make a prayer-book for twenty sous, and sell it at forty. I consider an invention which hasn't been tried a road to ruin. You may succeed in the first vat and fail in the second, and so on, and so on ; you get drawn in ; and when your arm is once caught in that sort of machinery the body follows."

The stout Cointet clinched his remarks by citing the example of a merchant in Bordeaux who was ruined because he would cultivate waste lands on the advice of a man of science ; he produced six other examples, all of the same nature, in the department of the Charente and the Dordogne ; then he got angry and would listen to nothing ; Petit-Claud's corrections seemed only to increase his irritation instead of calming it.

"I would much rather pay dearer for a sure thing and get smaller profits," he cried, looking at his brother. "In my opinion, nothing is advanced enough to go upon."

"But you came here with some intention or other," said Petit-Claud. "What do you propose?"

"To free Monsieur Séchard and to guarantee him, in case of success, thirty per cent on the profits," said the tall Cointet, quickly.

"But monsieur," said Eve, "what should we have to live on until the profits come in? My husband has had the shame of going to prison ; he can return there without incurring more, and we will pay our debts by —"

Petit-Claud put his finger on his lips and looked at Eve.

"You are not reasonable," he said to the two brothers : "You have seen the samples, and old Monsieur Séchard told you that his son, who was locked in by him, did make in a single night with ingredients that cost him next to nothing, a most excellent paper. You are here to bring this negotiation to a crisis. Will you buy the invention, yes or no?"

"Yes," said the tall Cointet. "Whether my brother agrees or not, I am willing to risk, on my own account, the payment of Monsieur Séchard's debts, and six thousand francs cash down, and thirty per cent profits to Monsieur Séchard ; provided — listen to this — that if,

in the course of one year, he has not realized the conditions which he will himself put into the deed he is
to return the six thousand francs, and the patent is to
belong to us, to make any use we can of it."

" Are you quite sure of yourself? " said Petit-Claud,
taking David aside.

"Yes," replied the inventor who was completely
caught by the tactics of the two brothers, and who
dreaded lest the stout Cointet should again interfere
and frustrate an agreement on which the future of his
family depended.

" Very good, then I will at once go and draw up the
deed," said Petit-Claud turning to the Cointets and
Eve. " You shall each have a copy to-night, you can
think it over to-morrow morning ; and at four in the
afternoon, as soon as the court rises we will meet here
and sign the papers. You, gentlemen, must at once
settle the matter with Métivier ; and I will write to stop
the suit in the Royal Court."

Here follows the clause of the deed containing
David Séchard's obligations : —

" BETWEEN THE UNDERSIGNED, ETC.

" Monsieur David Séchard, printer at Angoulême affirming
that he has discovered the means of sizing paper in the vat,
and also the means of reducing the cost of manufacturing
paper of all kinds at least fifty per cent by the introduction
of vegetable matters into the pulp, either by mixing them
with the rags already employed, or by using them without
the admixture of rags, a partnership for the taking out of a
patent and working the same, is hereby formed between
Monsieur David Séchard, jr., and the Messrs. Cointet
Brothers, on the following clauses and conditions : — "

One of the articles of the deed deprived David completely of all his rights in case he did not fulfil the promises made in this document, which was carefully dictated by the tall Cointet and agreed to by David. When Petit-Claud brought the deed at half-past seven the next morning he informed David and his wife that Cérizet offered twenty-two thousand francs in ready money for the printing-house. The deed of sale could be signed that evening.

" But," he said, " if the Cointets hear of this purchase they are capable of not signing the other deed ; they might try to harass you — "

" Are you sure that the purchase money will be paid? " said Eve, astonished at the settlement of a matter she had long despaired of ; a settlement which, had it been made three months earlier would have saved everything.

" I have the money now in my hands," said Petit-Claud, plainly.

" It is magic ! " said David, as if to ask Petit-Claud for an explanation of this good luck.

" No, it is a very simple thing ; the merchants of l'Houmeau want to found a newspaper," said the lawyer.

" But I have signed a paper not to do so," cried David.

" You have ; but your successor has n't. Besides, don't worry yourself about anything ; sell the place, pocket the money, and leave Cérizet to wriggle out of any difficulty that may arise — he knows very well how to do that."

" Yes, yes," said Eve.

" If you are restrained from printing a newspaper in Angoulême the merchants of l'Houmeau will have it issued there, that's all."

Eve, dazzled by the perspective of having thirty thousand francs and being thus placed above want, regarded the deed of partnership as a secondary consideration; consequently Monsieur and Madame Séchard yielded a point in that deed which gave rise to a last discussion. The tall Cointet demanded the right to have the patent made out in his name. He succeeded in showing that as David's rights were clearly defined in the deed the patent could be held indifferently by either of them. His brother clinched the matter by saying : " It is Boniface who pays for the patent and the costs of the journey,— and they'll amount to at least two thousand francs. Let him have it in his own name, or give the thing up altogether." The lynx triumphed; he triumphed at all points. The deed of partnership was signed about half-past four. The tall Cointet gallantly presented to Madame Séchard a dozen forks and spoons in silver filagree and a handsome Tornaux shawl, by way of pin-money, to induce her, he said, to forget the asperities of the discussion.

The copies of the deed were scarcely exchanged, Cachan had just handed over to Petit-Claud the legal releases and receipts and the fatal notes forged by Lucien, when the rumbling cart of the Messageries stopped before the door, and Kolb's voice echoed up the stairway : —

" Madame ! madame ! Fifteen thousand francs ! " he cried, " sent from Poitiers in real money, by Monsieur Lucien ! "

" Fifteen thousand francs ! " cried Eve, throwing up her arms.

" Yes, madame," said the carrier, following Kolb, " fifteen thousand francs brought by the Bordeaux diligence, and a pretty load it was. I have two men below to bring up the bags. They are sent by Monsieur Lucien Chardon de Rubempré. I have brought up a small leather bag containing five hundred francs for you, and this letter : —

Eve thought she was dreaming as she read what follows : —

My DEAR SISTER, — Here are fifteen thousand francs.

Instead of taking my life I have sold myself. I am no longer my own master ; I am the secretary, the creature of a Spanish diplomatist.

I begin once more my terrible existence. Perhaps I had better have drowned myself.

Farewell. David will be free, and with the other four thousand francs he can buy himself a little paper-mill and make his fortune.

Forget — I demand this of you — forget

Your unhappy brother,

LUCIEN.

" It is written," cried Madame Chardon, " that my poor son is fated to do evil, as he said he was, even in doing good."

" That was a narrow escape ! " cried the tall Cointet, as soon as he was safely out of the house. " An hour later the possession of that money would have changed the face of everything ; our man would never have signed the deed. Three months hence we shall see how he keeps that promise, and know where we stand."

XII.

AN ILLUSION RESIGNED.

At seven o'clock that evening Cérizet bought the printing-house and paid for it, keeping back the rent of the last three months. The next day Eve remitted forty thousand francs to the Receiver-General to purchase funds in her husband's name, yielding two thousand five hundred francs a year. Then she wrote to her father-in-law asking him to find her a little estate near Marsac worth about ten thousand francs, in which to invest her personal property.

The scheme of the tall Cointet was formidably simple. At the start, he believed David's idea of sizing the pulp in the vat to be impracticable. The mixture of vegetable matters of little cost with the pulp of rags seemed to him the true and only merit of the invention. He therefore intended to make very little of the cheapness of the pulp and enormously much of the sizing in the vat. Let us explain why. The manufacturers of Angoulême (paper being the chief product of the town) were then making, almost exclusively, those writing-papers which go by the names of crown or copy, note, school, and demy-post paper, all of which are glazed. These had long been the glory of the Angoulême paper-mills. Therefore, this specialty, monopolized by

the Angoulême manufacturers for very many years, was
reason enough for the view Cointet took of the matter;
glazed, that is, sized paper, did not, as we shall see,
enter into his calculations. The demand for writing-
paper is limited, whereas that for printing-paper is
almost unlimited. During the journey which he made
to Paris to take out the patent, Boniface Cointet arranged certain business matters which enabled him to
make great changes in his modes of manufacture. He
stayed at Métivier's; and to him Cointet gave directions to get away the custom of the newspapers from his
rival paper-makers in the course of the coming year,
by putting the price of the ream so low that no manufactory could compete with it; and to promise each
journal a paper superior in quality and whiteness to the
finest sorts hitherto used. As contracts with journals
are always made for periods of time, it would take some
months of subterraneous toil to obtain this monopoly;
but Cointet calculated that he would gain time to get
rid of Séchard altogether, while Métivier was making
arrangements with the Parisian newspapers, who were
at that time consuming some two hundred reams a day.
Cointet naturally allowed Métivier a certain percentage
on these contracts, so as to have an able representative
in the Paris market and not lose his own time and
money in going there. Métivier's subsequent fortune,
which was one of the largest ever made in the paper
business, had its origin in this affair. For ten years he
controlled, without a possible rival, the paper supply of
the Parisian journals.

Easy as to his future market, Cointet returned to
Angoulême in time to be present at Petit-Claud's mar-

riage. The lawyer had sold his practice and was now awaiting the transference of Monsieur Miland to Angers to step into his place, which had been promised to Petit-Claud through the influence of the Comtesse du Châtelet. The second assistant *procureur du roi* at Angoulême was appointed first assistant at Limoges, and the Keeper of the Seals sent a protégé of his own to the court of Angoulême, where the post of first assistant remained vacant for two months. This was the period of Petit-Claud's honeymoon.

While the tall Cointet was in Paris, ostensibly to secure the patent, David made, as a preliminary, a first vat-ful of unglazed pulp, which produced a printing-paper far superior to any that the newspapers were using. Next he made a second paper called " vellum," of the finest quality, intended for engravings, and this was used by the Cointets themselves for an edition of the diocesan prayer-book. The materials had been prepared by David in secret, with no other assistants than Kolb and Marion.

On the return of Boniface Cointet a total change came over the face of things. He looked at the papers just made and was none too well satisfied.

" My dear friend," he said to David, " the true business of Angoulême is in writing-paper; the very first thing to be done is to make the finest possible demy-post for fifty per cent below the present net cost."

David then tried to make a vat full of sized pulp, and obtained a paper as rough as a brush, in which the sizing granulated in lumps. The day of this experiment, when David held the paper in his hand, he went apart by himself to swallow his grief; but the tall Cointet

sought him out and was charmingly amiable and consoling.

" Don't be discouraged," he said. " Go on ! I 'm a
good fellow ; I understand the matter, and I 'll stand by
you to the end."

"After all," said David to his wife, when he went
home to dinner, " we are in the hands of good people,
though I never should have supposed the tall Cointet
could be so generous." And he related his conversation
with his wily partner.

Three months went by in experiments. David slept
at the manufactory ; he observed the results of the
various compositions of his pulp. Sometimes he attributed his want of success to the mixture of rags with his
other ingredients, and then he tried a vat full of those
ingredients alone. Sometimes he tried to size a pulp
made of nothing but rags. While pursuing his work
with wonderful perseverance, and under the very eyes
of Boniface Cointet (whom he no longer, poor soul !
distrusted), he went from material to material until, at
last, the whole series of ingredients was exhausted, and
he had mixed them in turn with every variety of size.
During the first six months of the year 1823 David
Séchard lived in the factory with Kolb, — if it can be
called living to neglect his food and clothing and person. He fought so desperately with his difficulties that
to any man but Cointet the spectacle would have seemed
sublime ; for no thought of self-interest entered the
mind of the brave fighter. There came a time when he
desired success for its own sake only. He watched with
marvellous sagacity the capricious effects of substances
transformed by man into products to suit his purposes,

where nature is, as it were, quelled in its secret resistance; from this he deduced great laws for industry, observing that such creations cannot be obtained except by conforming to the ulterior relations of things, and to what he called the second nature of substances.

At last, in the month of August, he obtained a paper, sized in the vat, precisely like that which all paper-mills are making at the present day for use as " proof paper " in printing-houses, but in which there is no certain uniformity, for the sizing can never be relied on. This result (a fine thing in 1823, when we consider the then condition of paper-making) had cost ten thousand francs, and David now hoped to solve the last difficulties of his problem. But about this time a singular rumor began to be current in Angoulême and l'Houmeau: it was said that David Séchard was ruining the Cointets. After wasting thirty thousand francs in experiments he had obtained, so it was said, a worthless paper. The other manufacturers and those who were jealous of the Cointets talked of the possible failure of that ambitious house. The tall Cointet set up new machinery and let it be supposed that this was necessary for David's experiments. But the Jesuit used it to make a paper with David's ingredients without sizing, all the while urging the latter to give his whole mind to the one thing required, namely, sizing the pulp. Meantime he was despatching to Métivier thousands of reams of printing-paper for the journals.

In September Boniface Cointet took David aside, and after hearing from him that he was on the point of making a triumphant experiment, he dissuaded him from continuing the struggle.

"My dear David, go to Marsac and see your wife and take a rest from all this toil; we don't want to ruin ourselves," he said, in a friendly way. "What you regard as a great triumph is only a point of departure. We will wait now before attempting further experiments. Be reasonable; look at results. We are not only paper-makers, we are also printers and bankers; the public thinks you are ruining us (David made a beautifully ingenuous gesture, protesting his loyalty). I don't mean that fifty thousand francs thrown away could ruin us," continued Cointet: "but we are afraid of being obliged in consequence of this rumor to pay our obligations in ready money, and that would embarrass us. It is better to pause now. We are near the limit agreed on in the deed; and we ought each to think the matter over."

"He is right," thought David, who, completely absorbed in his experiments, had paid no heed to what had been taking place in the manufactory.

He returned to Marsac, where, for the last six months he had gone every Saturday evening to see Eve, returning to the factory Tuesday morning. Well-advised by old Séchard, Eve had bought, exactly in front of her father-in-law's vineyard, a house called La Verberie, with three acres of garden and a vineyard, surrounded on three sides by that of the old man. She lived there with her mother and Marion very economically, for she still owed five thousand francs on the purchase of this charming little property, the prettiest in Marsac. The house, standing between a courtyard and the garden, was built of white sand-stone, roofed with slate, and ornamented with carvings, which are not very costly, owing to the ease with which the soft stone can be cut. The pretty furniture from Angoulême seemed prettier still in the country, where no one as yet displayed any luxury. In front of the house on the garden side were rows of pomegranates, oranges, and other rare plants which the former proprietor, an old general now dead, cultivated himself. It was under an orange tree where David was playing with his wife and boy that the sheriff of Mansle brought a summons from the Brothers Cointet to their partner to select referees, before whom, according to the terms of the deed of partnership, the settlement of their mutual claims was to be brought. Old Séchard was present. The Brothers Cointet demanded the restitution of the six thousand francs formerly advanced, also the sole right to the patent, and the future profits that might accrue therefrom, as indemnity for the exorbitant expenses incurred by them without result.

" People say you 've ruined them," said old Séchard, to his son. " That 's the only thing you have ever done that pleases me."

The next day at nine o'clock Eve and David were in the antechamber of Monsieur Petit-Claud, now promoted to be the defender of wives and the guardian of orphans, whose advice seemed to them the only one to follow. The new magistrate received them warmly and insisted that Monsieur and Madame Séchard should give him the pleasure of breakfasting with him.

" The Cointets claim that six thousand francs ! " he exclaimed. " How much do you still owe for La Verberie?"

" Five thousand," said Eve, " but I have laid by two thousand of it."

" Keep your two thousand," replied Petit Claud.
" Let me see, five thousand ! Then you want ten thousand more to make you perfectly comfortable down there. Well, in two hours the Cointets shall give you fifteen thousand francs — "

Eve made a gesture of surprise.

" — against your renunciation of all the profits from that deed of partnership, which you will agree to dissolve amicably," said the magistrate. " Will that suit you ? "

" Will the money be legally ours ? " said Eve.

" Yes, legally," replied the magistrate, smiling. " The Cointets have caused you sorrow enough, and I am going to put an end to their claims. Listen : I am now a magistrate, and I owe you the truth. Well, the Cointets are even now deceiving you ; but you are completely in their hands. You might possibly win the suit they would bring against you if you declare war. But do you want ten years of litigation ? They will multiply experts and arbitrations, and you will be at the mercy of contradictory judgments. And," he added, smiling, " I don't see any lawyer here to defend you ; my successor is of no account. Come, don't you think a bad settlement now is better than a good cause won ten years hence ? "

" Any settlement that gives us peace of mind will be good," said David.

" Paul ! " cried Petit-Claud, to his valet. " go and fetch Monsieur Ségaud, my successor. While we breakfast Ségaud will see the Cointets," he said to his old clients, " and in a few hours you shall go back to Marsac ruined, but in peace. With ten thousand francs

you can buy another five hundred francs a year, and on
that pretty little estate of yours at La Verberie you will
live happily."

At the end of two hours Maître Ségaud returned,
bringing, as Petit-Claud said he would, all the necessary papers signed in proper form by the Brothers
Cointet, and fifteen banknotes of a thousand francs
each.

" We owe a great deal to you," said David to Petit-
Claud.

" But I have just ruined you," replied Petit-Claud to
his astonished clients. " I have ruined you ; I repeat
it, and you will see it in time. But I know you ; you
would prefer your present ruin to the possession of a
fortune which might come too late."

" We are not seeking money, monsieur ; and we
thank you for giving us the means of happiness," said
Madame Eve. " You will find us forever grateful."

"Good God! don't bless me!" cried Petit-Claud,
" you fill me with remorse — but I do think I have to-
day repaired all. If I am now a magistrate it is thanks
to you ; if any one should be grateful, it is I. Adieu."

In March, 1829, old Séchard died, leaving about two
hundred thousand francs' worth of landed property,
which, joined to La Verberie, made a fine estate. For
two years before the old man's death Kolb had managed it for him very well. In course of time the
Alsacian had changed his opinion of the old bear, who
on his side took Kolb to his heart, finding that, like
himself, he could neither read nor write and was easily
made drunk. He taught him to manage a vineyard
and sell the products ; he formed him with the idea, so

he said, of leaving a man with some head to look after
his children; for in his last days his fears were great
and puerile as to the fate of his worldly goods. He
took Courtois, the miller, into his confidence. "You 'll
see," he said, "how things will go with my children
when I 'm underground. Their future makes me
tremble."

David and his wife found nearly three hundred thousand francs in gold in their father's house. Public
rumor, as usual, so magnified the old man's wealth that
he was believed throughout the department to have left
a million. Eve and David had an income of about
thirty thousand francs, counting their own little fortune;
for they waited some time before investing the gold,
so that they were able to place it to advantage in government funds after the Revolution of July.

Then, and not till then, did David Séchard and the
community know the truth about the prosperity of the
tall Cointet. Rich by many millions, elected deputy,
Boniface Cointet is now a peer of France, and will be,
they say, Minister of Commerce in the approaching
coalition. In 1842 he married the daughter of one of the
most influential statesmen of the Orléans dynasty, Mademoiselle Popinot, daughter of Monsieur Anselme Popinot, deputy of Paris and mayor of an arrondissement.

David Séchard's discovery has passed into French
manufactures as food into a body. Thanks to the introduction of other material than rags, France manufactures paper cheaper than any other European nation.
Holland paper, as David foresaw, no longer exists.
Sooner or later it will be necessary, no doubt, to estab-
lish a royal manufactory of paper, like those of the

Gobelins, Sèvres, la Savonnerie, and the Imprimerie Royale, which have so far withstood the attacks of the bourgeois vandals.

David Séchard, loved by his wife, the father of two children, has had the good taste never to speak of his experiments. Eve has been able to make him renounce forever the terrible vocation of an inventor — that Moses drunken with the drink of Horeb. He cultivates letters for amusement and leads the happy and lazily busy life of a landowner improving his property. After bidding a long and irrevocable farewell to the hope of fame, he has bravely entered the class of dreamers and collectors; he is devoted to entomology, and studies the transformations of insects; which are still so secret that science knows them only in their final state.

Everybody has heard of the successes of Petit-Claud as *procureur-général;* he is the rival of the famous Vinet of Provins, and his ambition is to become chief-justice of the Royal Court of Poitiers.

Cérizet, who has often been condemned for political misdemeanors, has made himself much talked about. Having been forced by Petit-Claud's successor to sell the printing-house in Angoulême, he suddenly took to the stage, and began a new life on the provincial boards, which his native talent for acting made a brilliant one. Circumstances having taken him to Paris he has curried favor with the Liberal party; being among the boldest of the scapegraces of that party he is known by the name of the Brave Cérizet.

THE END.

PIERRETTE

AND

THE VICAR OF TOURS.

BY HONORÉ DE BALZAC.

Translated by Katharine Prescott Wormeley.

In *Pierrette*, which Miss Wormeley has added to her series of felicitous translations from the French master-fictionists, Balzac has made within brief compass a marvellously sympathetic study of the martyrdom of a young girl. Pierrette, a flower of Brittany, beautiful, pale, and fair and sweet, is taken as an undesired charge by sordid-minded cousins in Provins, and like an exotic transplanted into a harsh and sour soil she withers and fades under the cruel conditions of her new environment. Incidentally Balzac depicts in vivid colors the struggles of two shop-keepers — a brother and sister, who have amassed a little fortune in Paris — to gain a foothold among the bourgeoisie of their native town. These two become the prey of conspirators for political advancement, and the rivalries thus engendered shake the small provincial society to its centre. But the charm of the tale is in the portrayal of the character of Pierrette, who understands only how to love, and who cannot live in an atmosphere of suspicion and ill-treatment. The story is of course sad, but its fidelity to life and the pathos of it are elements of unfailing interest. Balzac brings a score or more of people upon the stage, shows each one as he or she really is both in outward appearance and inward nature, and then allows motives and circumstances to work out an inevitable result. To watch this process is like being present at some wonderful chemical experiment where the ingredients are mixed with a deft and careful hand, and combine to produce effects of astonishing significance. The social genesis of the old maid in her most abhorrent form occupies much of Balzac's attention in *Pierrette,* and this theme also has a place in the story of *The Vicar of Tours,* bound up in this same volume. The vicar is a simple-minded priest who is happy enough till he takes up his quarters with an old maid landlady, who pesters and annoys him in many ways, and finally sends him forth despoiled of his worldly goods and a laughing-stock for the country-side. There is a great deal of humor in the tale, but one must confess that the humor is of a rather heavy sort, it being weighed down by a dominant satirical purpose. — *The Beacon.*

One handsome 12mo volume, uniform with "Père Goriot," "The Duchesse de Langeais," "César Birotteau," "Eugénie Grandet," "Cousin Pons," "The Country Doctor," "The Two Brothers," and "The Alkahest." Half morocco, French style. Price, $1.50.

ROBERTS BROTHERS, PUBLISHERS, BOSTON.

Balzac in English.

Albert Savarus, with Paz (La Fausse Maitresse) and Madame Firmiani. By
HONORÉ DE BALZAC. Translated by Katharine Prescott Wormeley.

There is much in this, one of the most remarkable of his books, which is synonymous with Balzac's own life. It is the story of a man's first love for woman, his inspirer, the source from whom he derives his power of action. It also contains many details on his habits of life and work.

THE three short stories in this volume,—'Albert Savarus,' 'Paz' and 'Madame Firmiani'—are chips from that astounding workshop which never ceased its Hephœstian labors and products until Balzac was no more Short stories of this character flew from his glowing forge like sparks from an anvil, the playthings of an idle hour, the interludes of a more vivid drama. Three of them gathered here illustrate as usual Parisian and provincial life, two in a very noble fashion, Balzacian to the core. The third—'Albert Savarus'—has many elements of tragedy and grandeur in it, spoiled only by an abruptness in the conclusion and an accumulation of unnecessary horrors that chill the reader. It is a block of tragic marble hewn, not to a finish, but to a fine prophetic suggestion of what is to follow if —— ! The *if* never emerges from conditionality to fulfilment. The beautiful lines and sinuous curves of the nascent statue are there, not fully born of the encasing stone ; what sculptors call the 'tenons' show in all their visibility—the supports and scaffoldings reveal their presence ; the forefront is finished as in a Greek metope or Olympian tympanum, where broken Lapiths and Centaurs disport themselves ; but the background is rude and primitive

In 'Madame Firmiani' a few brilliant pages suffice to a perfect picture,—one of the few spotless pictures of this superb yet sinning magician so rich in pictures. It is French nature that Balzac depicts, warm with all the physical impulses, undisguised in its assaults on the soul, ingeniously sensual, odiously loose in its views of marriage and the marriage relation, but splendidly picturesque. In this brief romance noble words are wedded to noble music. In ' Paz ' an almost equal nobility of thought — the nobility of self-renunciation — is attained. Balzac endows his men and women with happy millions and unhappy natures : the red ruby — the broken heart — blazes in a setting of gold. ' Paz,' the sublime Pole who loves the wife of his best friend, a Slav Crœsus, is no exception to the rule. The richest rhetoric, the sunniest colors, fail to counteract the Acherontian gloom of these lives and sorrows snatched from the cauldron of urban and rural France,—a cauldron that burns hotter than any other with its strange Roman and Celtic ardors. Balzac was perpetually dipping into it and drawing from it the wonderful and extraordinary incidents of his novels, incidents often monstrous in their untruth if looked at from any other than a French point of view. Thus, the devilish ingenuity of the jealous woman in ' Albert Savarus ' would seem unnatural anywhere else than in the sombre French provinces of 1836,—a toadstool sprung up in the rank moonlight of the religious conventual system of education for women ; but the here, and then, and as one result of this system of repression, it seems perfectly natural. And so does the beautiful self-abnegation of Albert himself, that high strung soul that could have been born only in nervous and passionate France.

As usual, Miss Wormeley's charming translation floats the reader over these pages in the swiftest and airiest manner. — *The Critic.*

One handsome 12mo volume, uniform with " Père Goriot," " The Duchesse de Langeais," " César Birotteau," " Eugénie Grandet," " Cousin Pons," " The Country Doctor," " The Two Brothers," and " The Alkahest." Half morocco, French style. Price, $1.50.

ROBERTS BROTHERS, PUBLISHERS, BOSTON.

A MEMOIR OF HONORÉ DE BALZAC.

Compiled and written by KATHARINE PRESCOTT WORMELEY, translator of Balzac's works. With portrait of Balzac, taken one hour after death, by Eugène Giraud, and a Sketch of the Prison of the Collège de Vendôme. One volume, 12mo. Half Russia, uniform with our edition of Balzac's works. Price, $1.50.

A complete life of Balzac can probably never be written. The sole object of the present volume is to present Balzac to American readers. This memoir is meant to be a presentation of the man, — and not of his work, except as it was a part of himself, — derived from authentic sources of information, and presented in their own words, with such simple elucidations as a close intercourse with Balzac's mind, necessitated by conscientious translation, naturally gives. The portrait in this volume was considered by Madame de Balzac the best likeness of her husband.

Miss Wormeley's discussion of the subject is of value in many ways, and it has long been needed as a help to comprehension of his life and character. Personally, he lived up to his theory. His life was in fact austere. Any detailed account of the conditions under which he worked, such as are given in this volume, will show that this must have been the case; and the fact strongly reinforces the doctrine. Miss Wormeley, in arranging her account of his career, has, almost of necessity, made free use of the letters and memoir published by Balzac's sister, Madame Surville. She has also, whenever it would serve the purpose of illustration better, quoted from the sketches of him by his contemporaries, wisely rejecting the trivialities and frivolities by the exaggeration of which many of his first chroniclers seemed bent upon giving the great author a kind of opera-bouffe aspect. To judge from some of these accounts, he was flighty, irresponsible, possibly a little mad, prone to lose touch of actualities by the dominance of his imagination, fond of wild and impracticable schemes, and altogether an eccentric and unstable person. But it is not difficult to prove that Balzac was quite a different character; that he possessed a marvellous power of intellectual organization; that he was the most methodical and indefatigable of workers; that he was a man of a most delicate sense of honor; that his life was not simply devoted to literary ambition, but was a martyrdom to obligations which were his misfortune, but not his fault.

All this Miss Wormley has well set forth; and in doing so she has certainly relieved Balzac of much unmerited odium, and has enabled those who have not made a study of his character and work to understand how high the place is in any estimate of the helpers of modern progress and enlightenment to which his genius and the loftiness of his aims entitle him. This memoir is a very modest biography, though a very good one. The author has effaced herself as much as possible, and has relied upon " documents " whenever they were trustworthy. — *N. Y. Tribune.*

Sold by all booksellers. Mailed, postpaid, on receipt of price, by the publishers,

ROBERTS BROTHERS, BOSTON.

BALZAC IN ENGLISH.

An Historical Mystery.

Translated by KATHARINE PRESCOTT WORMELEY.

12mo. Half Russia. Uniform with Balzac's Works. Price, $1.50.

An Historical Mystery is the title given to "Une Ténébreuse Affaire," which has just appeared in the series of translations of Honoré de Balzac's novels, by Katharine Prescott Wormeley This exciting romance is full of stirring interest, and is distinguished by that minute analysis of character in which its eminent author excelled. The characters stand boldly out from the surrounding incidents, and with a fidelity as wonderful as it is truthful. Plot and counterplot follow each other with marvellous rapidity; and around the exciting days when Napoleon was First Consul, and afterward when he was Emperor, a mystery is woven in which some royalists are concerned that is concealed with masterly ingenuity until the novelist sees fit to take his reader into his confidence. The heroine, Laurence, is a remarkably strong character; and the love-story in which she figures is refreshing in its departure from the beaten path of the ordinary writer of fiction. Michu, her devoted servant, has also a marked individuality, which leaves a lasting impression. Napoleon, Talleyrand, Fouché, and other historical personages, appear in the tale in a manner that is at once natural and impressive. As an addition to a remarkable series, the book is one that no admirer of Balzac can afford to neglect. Miss Wormeley's translation reproduces the peculiarities of the author's style with the faithfulness for which she has hitherto been celebrated. — *Saturday Evening Gazette.*

It makes very interesting reading at this distance of time, however; and Balzac has given to the legendary account much of the solidity of history by his adroit manipulation. For the main story it must be said that the action is swifter and more varied than in many of the author's books, and that there are not wanting many of those cameo-like portraits necessary to warn the reader against slovenly perusal of this carefully written story; for the complications are such, and the relations between the several plots involved so intricate, that the thread might easily be lost and much of the interest be thus destroyed The usual Balzac compactness is of course present throughout, to give body and significance to the work, and the stage is crowded with impressive figures. It would be impossible to find a book which gives a better or more faithful illustration of one of the strangest periods in French history, in short; and its attraction as a story is at least equalled by its value as a true picture of the time it is concerned with. The translation is as spirited and close as Miss Wormeley has taught us to expect in this admirable series. — *New York Tribune.*

One of the most intensely interesting novels that Balzac ever wrote is *An Historical Mystery*, whose translation has just been added to the preceding novels that compose the "Comédie Humaine" so admirably translated by Miss Katharine Prescott Wormeley. The story opens in the autumn of 1803, in the time of the Empire, and the motive is in deep-laid political plots, which are revealed with the subtle and ingenious skill that marks the art of Balzac. . . The story is a deep-laid political conspiracy of the secret service of the ministry of the police. Talleyrand, M'lle de Cinq-Cygne, the Princess de Cadigan, Louis XVIII, as well as Napoleon, figure as characters of this thrilling historic romance. An absorbing love-story is also told, in which State intrigue plays an important part. The character-drawing is faithful to history, and the story illuminates French life in the early years of the century as if a calcium light were thrown on the scene.

It is a romance of remarkable power, and one of the most deeply fascinating of all the novels of the "Comédie Humaine."

Sold by all booksellers. Mailed, post-paid, on receipt of price by the Publishers,

ROBERTS BROTHERS, BOSTON.

BALZAC IN ENGLISH.

FAME AND SORROW,

And Other Stories.

TRANSLATED BY KATHARINE PRESCOTT WORMELEY.

12mo. Half Russia. Uniform with our edition of Balzac's Works. Price, $1.50. In addition to this remarkable story, the volume contains the following, namely : "Colonel Chabert," "The Atheist's Mass," "La Grande Bretèche," "The Purse," and "La Grenadière."

The force and passion of the stories of Balzac are unapproachable. He had the art of putting into half a dozen pages all the fire and stress which many writers, who are still great, cannot compass in a volume. The present volume is an admirable collection, and presents well his power of handling the short story. That the translation is excellent need hardly be said — *Boston Courier.*

The six stories, admirably translated by Miss Wormeley, afford good examples of Balzac's work in what not a few critics have thought his chief specialty. It is certain that no writer of many novels wrote so many short stories as he ; and it is equally as certain that his short stories are, almost without an exception, models of what such compositions ought to be. . . No modern author, however, of any school whatever, has succeeded in producing short stories half so good as Balzac's best. Balzac did not, indeed, attempt to display his subtility and deftness by writing short stories about nothing. Every one of his tales contains an episode, not necessarily, but usually, a dramatic episode The first in the present collection, better known as "La Maison du Chat-qui-pelote," is really a short novel. It has all the machinery, all the interest, all the detail of a regular story. The difference is that it is compressed as Balzac only could compress ; that here and there important events, changes, etc., are indicated in a few powerful lines instead of being elaborated : that the vital points are thrown into strong relief. Take the pathetic story of "Colonel Chabert" It begins with an elaboration of detail. The description of the lawyer's office might seem to some too minute. But it is the stage upon which the Colonel is to appear, and when he enters we see the value of the preliminaries, for a picture is presented which the memory seizes and holds. As the action progresses, detail is used more parsimoniously, because the *mise-en-scene* has already been completed, and because. also, the characters once clearly described, the development of character and the working of passion can be indicated with a few pregnant strokes. Notwithstanding this increasing economy of space, the action takes on a swifter intensity, and the culmination or the tragedy leaves the reader breathless.

In "The Atheist s Mass" we have quite a new kind of story This is rather a psychological study than a narrative of action. Two widely distinguished characters are thrown on the canvas here, — that of the great surgeon and that of the humble patron ; and one knows not which most to admire, the vigor of the drawing, or the subtle and lucid psychical analysis. In both there is rare beauty of soul, and perhaps, after all, the poor Auvergnat surpasses the eminent surgeon, though this is a delicate and difficult question. But how complete the little story is : how much it tells ; with what skill, and in how delightful a manner I Then there is that tremendous haunting legend of "La Grande Bretèche," a story which has always been turned into more languages and twisted into more new forms than almost any other of its kind extant. What author has equalled the continuing horror of that unfaithful wife's agony, compelled to look on and assist at the slow murder of her entrapped lover? . . Then the death of the husband and wife, — the one by quick and fiercer dissipation, the other by simple refusal to live longer, — and the abandonment of the accursed dwelling to solitude and decay, complete a picture, which for vividness, emotional force, imaginative power, and comprehensiveness of effects, can be said to have few equals in its own class of fiction. — *Kansas City Journal.*

Sold by all booksellers. Mailed, postpaid, on receipt of price, by the publishers,

ROBERTS BROTHERS, BOSTON.

BALZAC'S PHILOSOPHICAL NOVELS.

— ❖ —

THE MAGIC SKIN.—LOUIS LAMBERT.
——SERAPHITA.——

TRANSLATED BY
KATHARINE PRESCOTT WORMELEY.

WITH AN INTRODUCTION TO EACH NOVEL BY
GEORGE FREDERIC PARSONS.

[From *Le Livre, Revue du Monde Littéraire*, Paris, March, 1889.]

There are men so great that humanity passes generations of existences in measuring them. . . . Certain it is that to-day the French Academy makes Balzac's work the theme for its prize of eloquence, that the great writer is translated and commented upon in foreign countries, and that in Paris and even at Tours, his native place, statues are in process of being erected to him. . . . But the marble of M. Chapus, the bronze of M. Fournier, — Balzac sad or Balzac seated, — are of little consequence to the glory of the writer standing before the world, who bore a world in his brain and brought it forth, who was at once the Diderot and the Rabelais of this century, and who, above and beyond their fire, their imagination, their superabounding life, their hilarious spirit, paradoxical and marvellously sagacious as it was, had in the highest degree the mystical gift of intuition, and is able, beyond all others, to open to us illimitable vistas of the Unseen.

It is this side of Balzac's genius which at the present time attracts and preoccupies foreign critics. Mlle Katharine Prescott Wormeley has undertaken to translate the "Comédie Humaine" into English. She has already published several volumes which show a most intelligent sympathy and a talent that is both simple and vigorous. Lately she translated "La Peau de Chagrin" ("The Magic Skin"), and now, taking another step into the esoteric work of the Master, she gives to the Anglo-Saxon public "Louis Lambert." But she does not venture upon this arduous task without support. Mr. George Frederic Parsons has undertaken in a long introduction to initiate the reader into the meaning hidden, or, we should rather say, encased, in the psychologic study of a lofty soul which ends by inspiring mundane minds with respect for its seeming madness and a deep sense of the Beyond. . . . Many critics, and several noted ones, have so little understood the real meaning of "Louis Lambert" and "Seraphita" that they have wondered why the author gave them a place in the "Comédie Humaine," which, nevertheless, without them would be a temple without a pediment, as M. Taine very clearly saw and said. Mr. Parsons takes advantage of Miss Wormeley's translation to state and prove and elucidate this truth. The commentary may be thought a little long, a little replete, or too full of comparisons and erudite reference; but all serious readers who follow it throughout will never regret that they have thus prepared themselves to understand Balzac's work. We call the attention of the philosophical and theosophical journals to this powerful study. [Translated.]

——◆——

Handsome 12mo volumes; bound in half Russia, French style. Price, $1.50 per volume.

ROBERTS BROTHERS, *Publishers*, BOSTON.

BALZAC IN ENGLISH.

LOUIS LAMBERT.

"As for Balzac," writes Oscar Wilde, "he was a most remarkable combination of the artistic temperament with the scientific spirit." It is his artistic temperament which reveals itself the most clearly in the novel before us. As we read "Louis Lambert," we feel convinced that it is largely autobiographical. It is a psychical study as delicate as Amiel's Journal, and nearly as spiritual. We follow the life of the sensitive, poetical schoolboy, feeling that it is a true picture of Balzac's own youth. When the literary work on which the hero had written for years in all his spare moments is destroyed, we do not need to be told by Mr. Parsons that this is an episode in Balzac's own experience ; we are sure of this fact already ; and no writer could describe so sympathetically the deep spiritual experiences of an aspiring soul who had not at heart felt them keenly. No materialist could have written " Louis Lambert." — *Boston Transcript.*

Of all of Balzac's works thus far translated by Miss Katharine Prescott Wormeley, the last in the series, " Louis Lambert," is the most difficult of comprehension. It is the second of the author's Philosophical Studies, "The Magic Skin" being the first, and " Seraphita," shortly to be published, being the third and last. In " Louis Lambert" Balzac has presented a study of a noble soul — a spirit of exalted and lofty aspirations which chafes under the fetters of earthly existence, and has no sympathy with the world of materialism. This pure-souled genius is made the medium, moreover, for the enunciation of the outlines of a system of philosophy which goes to the very roots of Oriental occultism and mysticism as its source, and which thus reveals the marvellous scope of Balzac's learning. The scholarly introduction to the book by George Frederic Parsons, in addition to throwing a great deal of valuable light upon other phases of the work, shows how many of the most recent scientific theories are directly in line with the doctrines broadly set forth by Balzac nearly sixty years ago. The book is one to be studied rather than read ; and it is made intelligible by the extremely able introduction and by Miss Wormeley's excellent translation. — *The Book-Buyer.*

" Louis Lambert," with the two other members of the Trilogy, " La Peau de Chagrin " and " Seraphita," is a book which presents many difficulties to the student. It deals with profound and unfamiliar subjects, and the meaning of the author by no means lies on the surface. It is the study of a great, aspiring soul enshrined in a feeble body, the sword wearing out the scabbard, the spirit soaring away from its prison-house of flesh to its more congenial home. It is in marked contrast to the study of the destructive and debasing process which we see in the " Peau de Chagrin." It stands midway between this study of the mean and base and that noble presentation of the final evolution of a soul on the very borders of Divinity which Balzac gives us in " Seraphita."

The reader not accustomed to such high ponderings needs a guide to place him *en rapport* with the Seer. Such a guide and friend he finds in Mr. Parsons, whose introduction of one hundred and fifty pages is by no means the least valuable part of this volume. It is impossible to do more than sketch the analysis of Balzac's philosophy and the demonstration so successfully attempted by Mr. Parsons of the exact correlation between many of Balzac's speculations and the newest scientific theories. The introduction is so closely written that it defies much condensation. It is so intrinsically valuable that it will thoroughly repay careful and minute study. — *From " Light," a London Journal of Psychical and Occult Research, March 9, 1889.*

One handsome 12mo volume, uniform with " Père Goriot," " The Duchesse de Langeais," " César Birotteau," " Eugénie Grandet," " Cousin Pons," " The Country Doctor," " The Two Brothers," " The Alkahest," " Modeste Mignon," " The Magic Skin," " Cousin Bette." Bound in half morocco, French Style. Price, $1.50.

ROBERTS BROTHERS, Publishers,
BOSTON.